Judicial Activism

IUS GENTIUM

COMPARATIVE PERSPECTIVES ON LAW AND JUSTICE

VOLUME 44

More information about this series at http://www.springer.com/series/7888

Luís Pereira Coutinho · Massimo La Torre
Steven D. Smith
Editors

Judicial Activism

An Interdisciplinary Approach to the American and European Experiences

Springer

Editors
Luís Pereira Coutinho
Faculdade de Direito da Universidade de Lisboa
Lisboa
Portugal

Steven D. Smith
University of San Diego
San Diego, CA
USA

Massimo La Torre
Università "Magna Graecia" di Catanzaro
Catanzaro
Italy

ISSN 1534-6781 ISSN 2214-9902 (electronic)
IUS Gentium: Comparative Perspectives on Law and Justice
ISBN 978-3-319-18548-4 ISBN 978-3-319-18549-1 (eBook)
DOI 10.1007/978-3-319-18549-1

Library of Congress Control Number: 2015938315

Springer Cham Heidelberg New York Dordrecht London

Printed on acid-free paper

Springer International Publishing AG Switzerland is part of Springer Science+Business Media
(www.springer.com)

Preface

I. “Judicial activism” is an expression widely used in popular discourse since its introduction in 1947 in a lay magazine by Arthur Schlesinger Jr., who used the term pejoratively to describe a tendency within the US Supreme Court. Although the phrase acquired currency among public opinion both in America and Europe, its translation into a proper legal concept is no easy task, if at all possible or desirable. Several contributors to this book undertake that task and believe that the concept is intelligible and useful.

Notwithstanding the conceptual concerns that run through the volume, the phrase is mostly a pretext for reflection on judicial practice in the European and American contexts, both arguably characterized in these last decades by the introduction of novel normative claims and even policies by judges. That within supposed exercises of practical reason departing from conventional legal method—or legal method as conventionally understood. An understanding of judicial activism around these tenets can be gained from the contributions to this volume.

II. There is inevitably a central question deserving the attention of the different contributors, which concerns the degree in which judicial exercises in practical reasoning may amount to forms of judicial usurpation of the legislative function by courts. Moreover, different views as to the nature and scope of legal reasoning lead to different degrees of tolerance regarding what should be admissible to courts.

Massimo La Torre, on the one side, and Lawrence Alexander, on the other, find themselves on opposite sides of the spectrum. La Torre, rejecting the platonic noble dream (or nightmare, in his view) of judicial reasoning as a matter of mere acknowledgment or cognition, defends that the main rationale of judicial decisions must be understood as argumentative and interpretative, implying a thorough involvement of the judge in practical reasoning. Contrarily, Alexander looks unfavorably at the exercise of what he names as “first-order practical reason” by judges.

Indeed, Alexander utterly rejects any judicial practice—such as the application of legal standards (e.g., proportionality), or the appeal by judges to concepts or principles with a meaning or weight to be determined by themselves—, lacking in “truthmakers” of a cognitive nature. For him, such practices are forms of judicial usurpation, implying the use of judicial office to legislate under the guise of adjudicating. The virtuous middle point between judicial usurpation and its opposite vice—judicial abdication—is what one should seek when considering judicial adjudication at the theoretical and practical levels.

Sharing a suspicious view of a corresponding exercise of practical reasoning by courts, Steven Smith takes aim at the particular claim that judicial activism is to be endorsed as a form of "reason in governance." For Smith, a discourse that aspires to an ideal of reason to be carried out by courts degenerates into the opposite of reason, namely in the demonization of opponents. Given the "discursive situation" in which contemporary courts operate, one characterized by radical pluralism and by an inherent incommensurability between premises and conceptions of morality, Smith argues that there is no feasible ideal of practical rationality susceptible of offering an independent standpoint on which courts could base their activist judgments.

Gonçalo de Almeida Ribeiro's perspective distances itself from the latter and approximates La Torre's, since it embraces the possibility of practical reasoning by courts bounded by what he takes to be the ultimate criteria of legal justification: justice, certainty, legitimacy, equality, and prudence. Still, for Almeida Ribeiro, activism should be avoided. He uses this last term in a classic pejorative sense that encompasses degenerate forms of judicial practice, which should no longer be considered as forms of fidelity to law—the main purpose of the judicial function—but of judicial usurpation of the legislative function.

On a first approximation, one could say that there is a divide here between a Continental perspective, on the one side—shared by La Torre and Almeida Ribeiro to a degree—and an American perspective, on the other—shared by Alexander and Smith. Jorge Silva Sampaio's paper points precisely in that direction, claiming that judicial practice should be measured and assessed differently according to the cultural and legal context. In this light, the European context will accommodate practices that would be downright condemned as activist in the American legal culture. Maria Benedita Urbano, however, brings a moderating perspective, adopting a different view on what practices should be accommodated also in the European context, in light of basic principles endorsed by corresponding Constitutions: democracy, the rule of law and the separation of powers. In the same light, Urbano proposes some remedies to tame what she believes to be egregious judicial excesses.

III. One can conclude from the above that a discussion of judicial activism is necessarily a discussion with core implications within the theory of legal reasoning. Contemporary approaches—such as those approving the judicial application of legal standards, or those endorsing balancing or weighing as legitimate methodological tools—will necessarily be more favorable to practices condemned as activist by their adversaries.

It should not be assumed though that activism, understood as judicial policy-making, can only emerge within novel methodological approaches. On the contrary, Pierre Legrand clarifies that activism may emerge within that which appears to be the most conventional of legal methods, named as "grammatication." Taking into account the French judicial practice, Legrand concludes that "every judgment is the expression of both a legal and of a political intervention." even when it apparently is a strictly grammatical exercise.

Conceptions of judicial activism do not play out solely at the practical level. The debate carries important implications at the conceptual level too, which can be clearly inferred from La Torre's and Almeida Ribeiro's contributions. Both understand law, not as an object subject to cognition and vocalized by the judge, but as a reason-giving practice. This leads them to develop a conception of fidelity to law that is necessarily different from that which is implicitly endorsed by Alexander.

IV. A discussion on judicial activism would necessarily be incomplete if one did not take into consideration the impact of judicial decisions at the political level or, from a different perspective, the political element of judicial decisions.

Miguel Nogueira de Brito addresses the theme departing from the classical debate between Carl Schmitt and Hans Kelsen on who should be the guardian of the Constitution. The political element that is inevitably present in every judicial decision referred to a Constitution—which Kelsen acknowledged and on which Schmitt fundamentally based his rejection of courts as guardians of Constitutions—is a central part of that debate. For Nogueira de Brito, Kelsen's defense and Schmitt's critique of judicial review help us understand the real risks of judicialization of politics present in contemporary constitutional democracies, acutely felt during the ongoing Euro crisis.

This latter context is also considered by Almeida Ribeiro. However, for the latter, any criticism of that activist proclivity—admittedly leading to forms of judicial usurpation—should not lead us to view proper judicial adjudication as politically neutral. On the contrary, it is political, both in its premises, since it inevitably engages each judges' sense of justice in a context of pluralism, and in its performance, implying balancing judgments—first of all, on the relative weight of the said criteria—that are inevitably complex and controversial.

Almeida Ribeiro's assumption according to which a political element is a necessary and legitimate part of legal adjudication is not of course shared by all. Smith's contribution—particularly when pointing out the incommensurability between premises and conceptions involved in each judge's sense of justice—is relevant here, as is James Allan's. Allan approaches the theme from the standpoint of moral philosophy, in particular, in light of that branch known as utilitarianism. Accepting its premises—more specifically, the premises of rule utilitarianism—Allan claims they lead to the condemnation of judges who decide not to apply rules in light of their moral and political sensibilities, sense of fairness or otherwise.

The debate regarding the political nature of judicial decisions is not confined to general jurisprudence. It has been the subject of theories of judicial behavior articulated within the field of political science. Tiago Fidalgo de Freitas takes stock of those positive theories, exploring their weaknesses, even if conceding that they pose a standing challenge to normative theories to get fine-tuned.

The above-mentioned contributions, when considering the political element or political impact of judicial decisions, take these as decisions yielded by legal reasoning, even if sharing different perspectives as to the nature and scope of the latter.

Luís Pereira Coutinho explores other possibility: the deployment of political rationality by constitutional courts facing exceptional circumstances of the security, financial or economic type. If admitted, these latter kinds of decisions are unquestionably political, transcending legal reasoning. Correspondingly, according to Coutinho, their admissibility can only be considered within state theory.

V. The bulk of this volume addresses judicial activism at the domestic or state level. There are two other levels in which the charge of judicial activism has been widespread in these last decades—the European and international levels—which deserve specific attention.

In this volume, Lourenço Vilhena de Freitas focuses specifically on the practice of the European Court of Justice, contending that it has developed a weak form of activism—weak since it does not concern primarily material aspects—but still with great impact, since it concerns the formal structure of European Union Law. Complementarily, Francisco Pereira Coutinho focuses on the practice of Member States courts, exploring the reasons leading them to "internalize" European Union Law, even in the absence of enforcement mechanisms of central decisions erecting the European legal federalism.

In the last contribution to this volume, Maimon Schwarzschild addresses in particular the practice of international courts. He argues that judicial activism—taken to be the making or imposition of policies by judges—is all the more concerning as it develops within fragmentary body of law and all the more threatening as it empowers courts acting outside supervision of a responsible body of jurists and whose judges are often appointed following relatively opaque procedures. Schwarzschild considers above all the risks for judicial independence that may derive from extreme forms of judicial activism, named as "judicial hubris," occurring at the moment in which courts, international or otherwise, are transformed into near culture warriors, i.e., into partisan forces in the great political and cultural disputes of the era.

VI. The book is divided into three parts. The first comprises essays by La Torre, Alexander, Almeida Ribeiro, Smith, and Legrand that are contributions in the area of general jurisprudence. In the second part—which includes essays by Allan, Nogueira de Brito, Fidalgo de Freitas, and Luís Pereira Coutinho—judicial activism is considered from the standpoint of other theoretical fields such as moral philosophy, constitutional theory, and political science. Finally, the third part—encompassing the contributions of Sampaio, Urbano, Vilhena de Freitas, Francisco Pereira Coutinho, and Schwarzschild—considers judicial activism in a variety of landmark contexts.

As can be inferred from their essays, the editors do not share a common perspective. The aim of this book was not to endorse a particular perspective on the theme, but to present and evaluate the state of a contemporary debate of enormous significance.

Luís Pereira Coutinho
Massimo La Torre
Steven D. Smith

Contents

Editors and Contributors

About the Editors

Luís Pereira Coutinho is professor at the University of Lisbon School of Law and a senior researcher at CIDP—Lisbon Centre for Research in Public Law where he coordinates the area of political science. Beforehand, he lectured at the Universidade Nova de Lisboa's Faculty of Human and Social Sciences. His publications include, as author, *A Autoridade Moral da Constituição* (Coimbra Editora, 2009) and *Teoria dos Regimes Políticos* (AAFDL, 2013), and, as co-editor and author, *Eichmann in Jerusalem—50 Years After* (Duncker und Humblot, 2013) and *O Tribunal Constitucional e a Crise* (Almedina, 2014).

Massimo La Torre is professor at the Department of Law of the Università di Catanzaro (Italy) and at the Law School of the University of Hull (UK). Before that, he taught in Florence, Bologna, and Murcia. He held numerous visiting professorial fellowships at European and American universities, and he was fellow of the Alliance Française, the Consiglio Nazionale delle Ricerche, the British Council, and the Alexander von Humboldt Foundation. In 2009, La Torre was honored with the Research Award of the Alexander von Humboldt Foundation. His publications include *Norme, istituzioni, valori* [Norms, Institutions, Values] (Laterza [3]2008); *La lucha contra el derecho subjetivo* [The Fight against Subjective Rights] (Dykinson 2008); and *Constitutionalism and Legal Reasoning* (Kluwer 2007).

Steven D. Smith is Warren Distinguished Professor of Law at the University of San Diego since 2002. Before that, he taught at the University of Notre Dame Law School, the University of Colorado School of Law, and the University of Idaho. He was a visiting professor at the University of Michigan and the University of Virginia. Smith's publications include *The Disenchantment of Secular Discourse* (Harvard University Press, 2010); *Law's Quandary* (Harvard University Press, 2004); *The Constitution and the Pride of Reason* (Oxford University Press, 1998); *Foreordained Failure: The Quest for a Constitutional Principle of Religious*

Freedom (Oxford University Press, 1995); "Discourse in the Dusk: The Twilight of Religious Freedom" in 122 *Harvard Law Review* 1869 (2009); and "How to Remove a Federal Judge" in 116 *Yale Law Journal* 72 (with Prakash) (2006).

Contributors

Lawrence A. Alexander is *Warren Distinguished Professor of Law* at the University of San Diego School of Law since 1970. His publications include *Crime and Culpability: A Theory of Criminal Law* (with Ferzan) (Cambridge University Press, 2009); *Demystifying Legal Reasoning* (with Sherwin) (Cambridge University Press, 2008); *Is There a Right of Freedom of Expression?* (Cambridge University Press, 2005); *The Rule of Rules: Morality, Rules, and the Dilemmas of Law* (with Sherwin) (Duke University Press, 2001); "With Me It's All 'Er Nuthin: Formalism in Law and Morality" in 66 *University of Chicago Law Review* 530 (1999); "On Extrajudicial Constitutional Interpretation" in 110 *Harvard Law Review* 1539 (with Schauer) (1997); "Self-Defense, Justification, and Excuse" in 22 *Philosophy & Public Affairs* 53 (1993); and "What Makes Wrongful Discrimination Wrong?" in 141 *University of Pennsylvania Law Review* 149 (1992). Alexander serves on the editorial boards of the journals *Law & Philosophy*, *Ethics*, *Criminal Law and Philosophy*, and the *Ohio State Journal of Criminal Law*.

James Allan is Professor of Law at the University of Queensland School of Law where he holds the oldest named chair. His publications include *Democracy in Decline* (McGill-Queen's University Press, Canada 2013); *The Vantage of Law* (Ashgate Publishing Limited, Great Britain 2011); *Sympathy and Antipathy: Essays Legal and Philosophical* (Ashgate, Aldershot, UK 2002); *A Sceptical Theory of Morality and Law* (Peter Lang, New York 1998); and *The Speluncean Case: Making Jurisprudence Seriously Enjoyable* (Barry Rose, Little London, UK 1998).

Francisco Pereira Coutinho is assistant professor at the Universidade Nova de Lisboa's School of Law, where he obtained his Ph.D. (2009). He is a former lecturer at the Instituto Superior de Ciências Sociais e Políticas of the University of Lisbon and advisor at the Portuguese Diplomatic Institute. His most recent publication is *Os Tribunais Nacionais na Ordem Jurídica da União Europeia: O Caso Português* (Coimbra Editora, 2014).

Gonçalo de Almeida Ribeiro is Gulbenkian Professor at the Católica School of Law & Global School of Law in Lisbon. He earned his doctoral (S.J.D., 2012) and master (LL.M., 2007) degrees from Harvard Law School and a basic law degree (Licenciatura, 2006) from the School of Law of the Universidade Nova de Lisboa (with the highest distinction). His most recent publication is *O Tribunal Constitucional e a Crise* (with Pereira Coutinho et al. Almedina, 2014).

Miguel Nogueira de Brito is professor at the University of Lisbon School of Law and a senior researcher at CIDP—Lisbon Centre for Research in Public Law where he coordinates the area of Constitutional Law. He worked as a law clerk at the

Portuguese Constitutional Court. His publications include *A Justificação da Propriedade Privada numa Democracia Constitucional* (Coimbra, 2007) e *As Andanças de Cândido* (Lisboa, 2011).

Tiago Fidalgo de Freitas is a Ph.D. researcher at the European University Institute, a guest lecturer at the University of Lisbon School of Law, and an associate researcher at CIDP—Lisbon Centre for Research in Public Law. On the former capacity, he has been a Visiting Doctoral Researcher at the Rio de Janeiro Getúlio Vargas Foundation School of Law. Beforehand, he completed an LL.M. at New York University School of Law as a Hauser Global Scholar (2007) and has taught as a guest lecturer at the Portuguese Catholic University School of Law. He also holds the Diploma of the Academy of European Public Law (2005) and a law degree, *magna cum laude*, from the University of Lisbon School of Law (2004).

Lourenço Vilhena de Freitas is professor at the University of Lisbon School of Law and member of CIDP—Lisbon Centre for Research in Public Law. His publications include *Os Contratos de Direito Público da União Europeia no Quadro do Direito Europeu* (Coimbra Editora, 2012).

Pierre Legrand A graduate of the Sorbonne and Oxford, where he studied as a Rhodes Scholar, Pierre Legrand acts as Professor of Law at the Ecole de droit de la Sorbonne, Paris, whose postgraduate program in globalization and legal pluralism he has long been directing. In addition, Legrand offers a course in comparative law every autumn as Law Board of Visitors Distinguished Visiting Professor at the University of San Diego Law School and has been a visiting professor at Northwestern University Law School, Chicago. He also lectures every summer on the University of Cambridge's program in English Legal Methods. For many years, Legrand gave the seminar in comparative law on the University of Melbourne Law School's postgraduate program while teaching comparative law repeatedly for undergraduates in Romania and Brazil. He has recently held formal visiting professorships at the University of Toronto, the China University of Political Science and Law in Beijing, the University of Copenhagen, the Georgetown University Law Center, and the National University of Singapore. Legrand publishes in English and French, and his work being regularly translated in various languages. He is preparing *Negative Comparative Law* for Routledge, a critical conspectus on salient theoretical issues arising from research into foreign law and comparative interventions in a globalized world.

Jorge Silva Sampaio is a guest assistant lecturer in legal and political sciences at University of Lisbon School of Law where he is currently doing his Ph.D. He is also a guest assistant lecturer at the Ricardo Espírito Santo Foundation. His publications include *O Dever de Proteção Political de Direitos, Liberdades e Garantias* (Coimbra Editora, 2012) and *O Controlo Jurisdicional das Políticas Públicas de Direitos Sociais* (Coimbra Editora, 2015).

Maimon Schwarzschild is Professor of Law at the University of San Diego School of Law. He is affiliated professor at the University of Haifa. He obtained his JD at Columbia University in 1976 and was called to the English Bar at Lincoln's Inn in London. He is a regular visiting professor at the Sorbonne in Paris and has been a visiting professor at the Hebrew University in Jerusalem. Schwarzschild's publications include "The Role of the US Supreme Court in the Protection of Religious Liberty: How Much Autonomy Do You Want?" in The Culture of Judicial Independence (Shetreet, ed; Martinus Nijhof 2014); "A Class Act: Social Class Affirmative Action and Higher Education" in 50 San Diego Law Review 44 (2013); "Constitutional Law and Equality" in A Companion to Philosophy of Law and Legal Theory, 2nd Ed. (Patterson, ed.) (Wiley-Blackwell, 2010); "The Ethics and Economics of American Legal Education Today" in 17 Journal of Contemporary Legal Issues 3 (2008); "Keeping It Private" in 25 University of Queensland Law Journal 215 (2006) and 44 San Diego Law Review 677; "Civil Rights and Free Speech" in the Encyclopedia of American Civil Liberties (Findelman ed.; Routledge 2006); and "Value Pluralism and the Constitution: In Defence of the State Action Doctrine" in Constitutional Theory (Sadurski, ed.) (Ashgate, 2005).

Maria Benedita Urbano is professor of Constitutional Law at the University of Coimbra, Portugal, and a judge at the Portuguese Supreme Administrative Court. Her publications include *Representação Política e Parlamento* (Almedina, 2009); *Curso de Justiça Constitucional* (Almedina, 2014); "Estado de crise económico-financeira e o papel do Tribunal Constitucional" (*Until debt tear us apart*, ed. Pedro Gonçalves et al., ICJP, 2013); and *O Tribunal Constitucional e a Crise* (with Pereira Coutinho et al., Almedina, 2014).

Part I
Judicial Activism, Legal Reasoning and the Concept of Law

Chapter 1
Between Nightmare and Noble Dream: Judicial Activism and Legal Theory

Massimo La Torre

1.1 The Judge and the Authority

Judges, I was taught in law school, are passive actors in the scene of law. They do not take the initiative, they relate to other parties' actions and claims. This is their status' main difference with respect to other branches of government, namely the executive power or the State administration, to be permanently active in providing services and protections to citizens, planning in advance policies and defining the best way of implementing laws aimed at the public good. In the legal process, parties and their legal representatives, attorneys and advocates, take the initiative, raise claims, sue other parties while the judge remains passive, silent, more or less at least till the final verdict.

That being so, an active judge seems to be either an oximoron or a bad judge. Apparently, activism is his more serious vice or fault. But "activism" regarding judicial competences and actions could mean not so much that the judge is becoming an actor in law—anticipating the advocates' moves or the government's usual business—, but rather an officer exercising his own constitutional powers not merely as an executioner of laws, but as a law-maker, albeit in more or less limited dimensions. In this sense more than of an "active" judge we should speak of a law-making judge, or of a political actor, of an actor that fills in the gaps in the law with pieces of jurisprudence or case-law with an authority comparable to legislation, even capable of altering and changing it through some kind of addition. *Auctoritas*

M. La Torre (✉)
Edificio dell'area Giuridico-Economica e delle Scienze Sociali,
Universita Magna Graecia di Catanzaro, Viale Europa, Loc. Germaneto,
88100 Catanzaro, Italy
e-mail: mla_torre@hotmail.com

L.P. Coutinho et al. (eds.), *Judicial Activism*,
Ius Gentium: Comparative Perspectives on Law and Justice 44,
DOI 10.1007/978-3-319-18549-1_1

comes from *augere*—as Hannah Arendt reminds us (Arendt 2006, 91ff.)—and this, improving the legislation, adding further rules to it, seems to be precisely the way the contemporary judge often conceives his role.

1.2 Constitution, Weak and Strong

I assume that in order to discuss and understand the judicial role and corresponding acts we should take into account three dimensions or point of views. (i) The first is how we conceive the constitution of a polity. (ii) The second is what we mean by judicial reasoning, that is, how we believe judges could and should reason in arriving at their decisions. (iii) And the third one is the more philosophical view of what law‘s nature is. We will get different results, we will assess judges' "activity" and "activism" in a different way, according to the stance we take on each of these three points.

We need first, I believe, to have a look at the notion of constitution. Here we are usually confronted with two different set of ideas, actually with two different traditions, that I would propose to call,—referring to the classic book by Charles McIlwain—constitutionalism of the Ancients and constitutionalism of the Moderns (see McIlwain 2008). In the former a constitution is a pact, a compact, between two main parties, one of which is an already existing power, a King usually, a full sovereign, that however accepts an agreement, striking a compromise with other subjects (the barons, the people), thus defining and limiting his own competences. The outcome will be a distinction between two areas, one circumscribed by public law in which the King is subject to common rules and one other, restricted, in which the original supreme power keeps sovereign prerogatives not subordinated as such to common laws. In this model a judge usually is a civil servant, or an officer, performing an adjudicating role in the proper application of common laws. He will cover the area subjected to rules that are valid for both parties. He will not however have any competence on the restricted prerogative area. Nonetheless, out of this restricted area of competence, and as a mark of the special prerogative, an original judicial power may arise.

In the constitutionalism of Moderns a constitution is much more than a pact, or a bilateral agreement, since it has to play the role of shaping the entire political structure. There is here no constituted power before the constitution. There is no original power that could eschew or dodge the efficacy of constitutional rules. No prerogative seems to be left. In such a landscape the judicial power is first of all submitted to the constitution. It cannot claim any constitution-making competence. However, once the constitution is considered to be a supreme rule, a ground-norm that is generally binding, and not just a framework regulation to which legislation contributes by addition and derogation at a parity level, such architectural ground-norm will also bind the legislator, and the issue of a super partes arbitrator that is able to check the legislation, that is, that reviewes legislation's possible unconstitutional outcomes, will be more or less unavoidable.

If the constitution is a rule with prescriptive, not just programmatic force, if it is a legal rule then, though a very special, but stronger one because of its superior dignity in the hierarchy of sources of law, there must be some remedy for its violation, and the need will arise to design a special jurisdiction able to ascertain whether or not that supreme rule has been followed by the inferior law-making instances, especially at the level of ordinary law-making agencies. This—it's well-known—was Justice Marshall's topical argument for judicial review of legislation, and this was again in short the rationale the European Court of Justice offered to ground its own wide and supreme reviewing powers vis-à-vis EEC Member States' national legislation in the Costa ruling.

A strong concept of constitution seems then to imply a strong, active judge that could abrogate, or declare invalid ordinary legislation because of its being unconstitutional. Ordinary legislation, parliaments nonetheless remain the place where the constitutional moment that produced the constitution continues to operate in less dramatic circumstances. Legislation in a sense is the normality and the perpetuation of constitution-making, a collective instance of public deliberation, that is no longer exercised on the fundamentals of collective existence, but nevertheless on the needs it manifests and claims to be met and satisfied through the representative participation of citizens.

Could such instance, this institutionalization of the constituent power, citizens' participation, be preempted by judiciary decision? Is this not doomed to replace the collective decision of the people by the will of a few more or less expert lawyers, once again a few Law-Lords? Could we conceive a formula such as "we the judges" as opposed or even corrective of "we the people"?

1.3 Judges as Kings? On Rules and Algorithms

Here we'll step into the second dimension I have said to be basic in our discussion, I mean, the practice and justification of judicial reasoning. In this area we are confronted with two extreme views, a "nightmare" and a "noble dream". The judge —says Plato—does not play a royal function. He's not a statesman, especially not a king, in spite of the ancient Greek meaning of "basileus"—as it's certified in Hesiodos' "Days and Works"—signifying a judge. Judges—we are told—do not decide independently, but merely repeat rules layed down by other people, kings in this case. The problem here immediately arises: is that saying of the rule just a cognitive function, which does not add any new force or meaning to it, or is it rather a task that somehow involves a new prescription, something that transforms the still inoperative rule into an effective command, and that in order to do so should be itself a prescription, some kind of rule, an individual rule in Kelsen's wording?

Plato hopes the individual rule to be a matter of acknowledgment or of cognition, that is, that it could be deduced from the more general and royal rule through some sort of logical inference without any semantic addition. This hope enduringly inspired the history of legal thought and jurisprudence, from its beginnings until its great climax, the liberal codified State after the French revolution. This actually was —as we learn from Michelet's and Tocqueville's grand narratives—a revolution against judges, not only against the aristocracy and the King.

The law should recover its certainty and determinacy by being once again reserved to the sovereign, albeit this time a collective and turbulent entity, the people. Judicial abuses and strong powers were no longer to be tolerated in a legal system proclaimed as the triumph of the rule of law—of a law consecrated by the general will of citizens, not to be twisted by the particular discretion of a few lords in robe. In order to achieve this great aim the law had to be simplified, rationalised, made clear, so clear that interpretation had no special role to play. It also had to be complete, so complete that no gap remained to be filled in by doctrine or adjudication. Once these conditions were fulfilled, one could believe that the judge was nothing but an additional, operative "voice" given to statutes or just a "machine" for legal rulings.

However, this "noble dream" (or "nightmare"?) was immediately disclaimed by the way judges necessarily reason, which is far from being simply deductive. There may be a lot of deduction in a judicial decision, but, and this is the point, its main rationale is not deductive, but argumentative and interpretive. It is interpretive since the reasoning's premises are to be first understood and hermeneutically construed, and it is argumentative since some or several—perhaps all—arguments are to be assessed in terms of their weight or force. In other terms, an argument (or a reason) does not have an infinite weight; otherwise it would be an algorithm. And rules, standards and principles are not algorithms. Indeed, even rules are not algorithms, having a topical, semantycal and pragmatic dimension much more relevant than their syntactic structure. Rules are about something; algorithms are not about anything. The latter are symbols without meaning (cf. Searle 1991, 30–31).

Meanings have a history, algorithms have none. Meanings change in time, algorithms do not. Besides, through rules, you tell a story, through algorithms you tell none: two and two makes four is not a story. But to say that the one who intentionally kills a human being, shall be punished, is indeed a story, a fiction that anticipates reality. Meaning moreover is not to be made operational through computation and mathematics. The application of rules, since it is connected with their meaning, is a matter of understanding and deliberation, not of calculus, which is why—to repeat a formula layed down by Wittgenstein and then suggestively repeated by Hart—rules do not (fully) rule their application (Hart 1983, 106). Rules are defensible, algorithms are not.

1.4 Once Again: Natural Law Versus Legal Positivism

The third variable I have chosen to assess the force and necessity of judicial activism is the adopted concept of law. Here we are confronted, if not with a clash of civilizations, perhaps with a clash of worldviews. The fight is the long lasting one between legal positivism and natural law, or more accurately between (i) a view of practical rationality and law as domains with which arguments and reason don't have much to do and thus in which either will or emotion and decision prevail, and (ii) a view according to which practical rationality does stand beyond strategic interests and theoretical efforts, this being much more a matter of justified assertability and endorsement than of will and discretion.

We could reformulate this clash in two further different ways. (a) We could conceive of it as a confrontation regarding the role facts play in legal deliberation and normativity. For the positivist view, facts are what matters most, these facts corresponding to commands, or conventions, or posited rules. What lies between and beyond facts, namely their semantic purport and their reasonableness, is less relevant. This belief can have a decisionist twist, since, once it is stressed that facts are not related through logic, laws being treated as mere facts, "there is no reason to assume—in Andrei Marmor's words—that entailed law is law, just in virtue of such entailment relation" (Marmor 2002, 124). Something of the kind is Hans Kelsen's final destination in his posthumous work on the theory of rules (Kelsen 1978) where he firmly declares the inapplicability of logic (especially inference and contradiction) to the domain of legal rules. These are said to be imperatives, which are facts, and two facts can be only opposed or causally connected but they cannot be logically contradictory nor can they be logically inferred the one from the other. The opposite view is defended by natural law: here facts are determinations or instantiations of previous rules or of practically transcendental principles that are well inferentially related.

For the legal positivist, normativity is made law by facts and facts only; this is sometimes called the "source thesis". Directive reasons are fully entrenched in facts, their meaning and their contents are rooted in these only. On the contrary, for a natural lawyer facts only play a subsidiary role, though it may happen that facticity itself is interpreted as a providential and somewhat blind condition for the basic goods to be realized. Under this light facticity is seen as "authority", as both the capacity of enforcing rule or commands, and the deference due to that which is given in the world (this being sometimes read as the outcome of some providential design), then nearly acquiring the dignity of a good itself.

(b) A different shape of that fight is the well-known dispute on the relationship between law and morality. For one camp morality is neatly severed from law, so that law can be ascertained without any reference whatsoever to morality. Such camp can nonetheless concede that for law to be followed or to be abode by a moral attitude, a strong normative justification is required. Law thus can be known, but not enforced (at least on the part of its addressees) without being considered as somehow moral or as meeting moral standards or as deserving some sort of moral endorsement. On the other side, law is said to be blind, at least to some extent, without reference to moral criteria, i.e., not sufficiently informative and able to direct decisions and conducts. Here law can neither be known nor be enforced or operationalised without incorporating a moral discourse.

The first practical consequence of this fight is the two camps' at least prima facie opposite way of conceiving judicial reasoning—and also of allowing for judicial activism, I would add. Legal positivism, in its very successful continental version based on the fact of codifications, nurtured the hope, or rather the confidence, in being able to avoid any possible judicial discretion. Under codification, a judge could be assumed to be no more than a *Subsumptionsautomat*, and was even so declared by the German *Kronjurist* of late Nineteenth century, Paul Laband. The legal system, conceived as gapless, does not allow for any active or creative role of the judiciary. Something of the kind is still echoed by Kelsen, who however generally conceded for judicial discretion. When dealing in a thick treatise with the United Nations new law, Kelsen claims that international law is gapless and does not need to be applied with any further reference to legal principles; the international judge can solve any case through the positive law in force without looking for any other source.

A different view is the one presented by John Austin, the founding father of British legal theory. In his classical book *Province of Jurisprudence Determined* we find a phrase that is a sort of celebration of the activist judge: "I cannot understand how any person who has considered the subject can suppose that society could have possibly gone on if judges had not legislated, or that there is any danger whatever in allowing them that power which they have in fact exercised, to make up for the negligence or the incapacity of the avowed legislator" (Austin 1954, 191).

In Austin's view, a passive judge is no more than a childish fiction; adjudication is sovereignty delegated, but still sovereignty, law-making power, thus unavoidably discretional. We find then that legal positivists defend two apparently opposite claims about judicial initiative and reasoning. For the continental *Rechtswissenschaft*, the judge is a machine for legal deductions from the *Gesetz*, the statute; the judge's main virtue is a logical or even mathematical virtue, and not much more than a descriptive attitude towards the law is required. Once found and properly described the rule, its application will be more or less a matter of course, a matter of logic. No argumentation and no moral deliberation will be necessary. To the British analytical jurisprudent this picture does not render justice to real adjudication: a judge is rather a decider, though a subordinate one. Logic or knowledge are not sufficient for the decision; an exercise of will, strong discretion, is required. However, between such view and the one held by Continental positivists, there is something distinctive in common: once more no special argumentation is considered as the basis for legal decisions, morality being again out of the picture. The law that "ought to be" for the judge seems equivalent to the law that "is". Discretion, delegated sovereignty is a matter of the law that "is", not of a dreamy and fancy law that "ought to be".

The opposite camp, we know, is natural law. This has been defined in diverse ways and often, in modern times, used as a kind a recrimination, if not a true insult. According to Karl Bergbohm, probably the most typical Continental legal positivist, whoever claims to need more than statutes in force in a positive legal order for knowing what is valid law, is a natural lawyer, something—it's implicit in his argument—a lawyer should be very worried about. However, there is a misunderstanding to be set aside, when considering natural law doctrines. There isn't a single one, at least to my knowledge, that would deny the necessity of positive law.

Natural law does not claim to be able to regulate human conduct in and by itself; it needs to be enforced and to be concretised through posited ruling and effective authority. In this sense, it is less radical in its claims than positivist theories, since a positivist denies natural law's claim to existence, while a natural lawyer in the end bases its capacity of direction on the efficacy and force of positive law. This somehow explains why we find here again an ambiguous relation with judicial decision. Natural law theories do not conceive judges as machines for logical deduction: deliberation is required from them. However, such deliberation can be guided from more or less objective values or principles that are accessible through practical reason or moral intuition. One right answer is not always considered possible, depending on how basic goods are conceived and the role and justification given to authority. Room might be given to rational disagreement.

On the one side, we have views that believe in the incommensurability of values and their inevitable clash in Weberian terms, though a domain is singled out where a strong normative evidence dictates right legal rulings. Given incommensurability, and the openness of several values, and a pessimist political anthropology, authority plays a fundamental role in implementing basic values and offering them a chance of success in the social world. Authority itself is not here to be tested, or produced, but only to be justified. Its phenomenology, basically consisting of force, violence and discretion, is not pliable to a reformist, or a constructivist strategy; there is not in it too much to be reformed or reflected upon. And its justification is offered by its capacity or success. Strangely enough the natural lawyer nears those legal positivists who conceive law in an exclusivist way as founded just on the fact of authority. The difference between the two is only to be found is the additional normative source added to the fact of authority by the natural lawyer, at least when specific, most supreme basic goods are at stake.

On the other side, we have the defender of the one right answer, who is much less pessimistic about the unity of practical reason and political anthropology, so that one right answer is conceivable and moreover possible. This however does not pass by the fiction of a judge as a deductive machine, but by the reference to a scheme of normative coherence that is to be found in a reflective equilibrium between fit and justification, the facticity of past posited law, and the principles that can give a best moral account of it.

In this later view, the judge is *passive* by being *actively* involved in moral reasoning, while for the former type of natural lawyer passivity is an exception to be reserved to rulings on matters that impinge on the first moral principles and basic goods. In this second case a judge, beyond the threshold of a basic normative core, decides in a more or less discretionary way. For the one right answer believer, on the contrary, discretion as a ruling without decisive and conclusive reasons means to compromise the role of the judge and its constitutional capacity. His thesis is backed by the consideration of the phenomenolgy of the legal controversy, in which parties claiming their rights do also claim *to be right*, a fact that the "pluralist"—so to say—natural lawyer cannot easily explain from his half-positivist stance.

1.5 A Middle Course

I will try now to synthesize my argument. A fundamental virtue of a judge is passivity; his model is that of an arbitrator impartially giving everyone his due once it is claimed in a controversy between parties before him. He renders justice to parties, if asked to do so. A judge as a civil servant, who held some enforcement power and therefore couldn't or wouldn't remain passive, would be—as once said by Professor Cappelletti—more a policeman than a member of the judiciary. He is not to be active. Passivity is a merit to him. Nonetheless, he is not to remain so passive as to refuse justice once this is called or claimed for before him. The darkest nightmare of law would be, beside the crooked judge, a judge that decides not to decide. His passivity cannot overstep into silence, *non liquet*, judicial abdication. The prohibition of passivity becomes here the "state of necessity" that should first of all guide his official conduct (see Schmitt 1969). And yet we experience a contrary necessity that recommends filtering only those cases that are constitutionally relevant. Passivity here becomes a precondition for a better focussed activity.

I have said above that our issue, judicial activism, could be discussed by considering three fundamental variables: (i) the idea of a constitution, (ii) the theory of judicial reasoning, and (iii) the concept of law. I believe a most appropriate concept of law for legal practice is one able to combine the facticity of positive law and the normativity of claims for justice. A strong positivism, such as for instance the "exclusivist", should in the end give up the internal point of view, since this seems to imply a reference to moral standards. In the "exclusivist" perspective is the concept of law is a matter of a natural kind, it has an "essence" and as a consequence "practice", the way that "essence" is used or made manifest in social collective acts, is downplayed. Judicial or legal reasoning is separated from the nature of law, and the latter can be defined independently from the former. Now, such view would more likely than not make our issue trivial, undeserving of a theoretical or philosophical interest or beforehand solved once and for all. Either the judge's authority is more or less original (being positive law in his hands as holder of discretionary powers) or he doesn't have such central dignity, being called only to reformulate the dictates of a superior authority (in case positive law is equated with legislation, not with adjudication and past decisions).

A more appropriate concept of law would seem to be the one mentioned above as "inclusive" natural law. From this perspective law's moral invalidity is not yet a reason for declaring that the law is void, that it is not law (as it is stated by "exclusive" or strong natural law). It is rather a defective law. However, such defectiveness is not just an issue that could be ascertained through a contemplative consideration of the substantive properties of the law itself. We would need to consider and enter into its "practice". We would need to take an internal point of view. At stake is no "essence" without "existence", there being no "existence" without engaging in action, this implying a moment of public deliberation, where the moral point or the directive reasonableness that lays at the bottom of law is made explicit and elaborated in an intersubective and institutional form.

Stepping forward to the variable of judicial reasoning, we are as seen confronted with two main approaches, of which one tries to bind judicial deliberation to an objectivity external to the practice of reasoning itself, that through social or institutional arrangements. It's the noble dream of the judge as "bouche de la loi", or, somehow, of today's American originalists, or again of some French realist's sociological and political "constraints". The insurmountable problem, not to say the "tragedy", of such approach is however that laws as such are not "facts" that you can observe or that limit and constrain you by simple causality. Unfortunately, for laws to have an effect on you, you should first recognize them as being binding laws, and for that you have to understand them, i.e., to find and reconstruct their meaning. And the meaning of words and propositions won't have a practical consequence in the sense of a stone hitting you.

Moreover, words, propositions, and helas positive laws are much more, or much less, as you prefer, than intentional subjective preferences or assertions of will. What I mean by a word or a proposition, and a directive too, is first of all fixed by the independent (independent since social) meaning of words and sentences, as they are structured within a language, a linguistic and cultural context or "game", and within a form of life with its own values. "We must distinguish (Hart 1982, 154)—says Herbert Hart—between the meaning of what a man says and the way he intends what he says to be taken by those to whom he speaks". Humpty-Dumpty ("'When *I* use a word,' Humpty Dumpty said, in rather a scornful tone, 'it means just what I choose it to mean—neither more nor less'") would be a crazy and ineffective legislator, and much more so if he were put in charge of writing down a constitution for a community of citizens, drafted to be valid and last through generations. As a consequence the nobly dreamed bond to the law-giver's original intentions is not much more than wishful thinking doomed to be refuted by any interpretive practice. Meaning cannot be enacted. Humpty-Dumpty's "originalism" would only be possible—this is Hannah Arendt's argument—, once we "ceased to live in a common world where the words we have in common possess an unquestionable meaningfulness" (Arendt 2006, 95). Only then, could we take refuge and retreat in the armoured solitude of voluntaristic nominalism.

Mirroring somehow the "noble dream", at least in its imperativist philosophy of language, we face on the other side the nightmare of a solipsistic judge, the one for whom there is no normative reality beyond his discretion, the one for whom every and each ascription of meaning is a decision, the one that decides without any objective normative background through reasons that are such for himself alone, amounting then to more or less personal motives. If this were indeed the reality of adjudication, it would be idle for us to linger in law schools trying to teach students what is valid law and how to win a case trough good points of law. The case would be just as that which was made by one of the discussants in Cicero's *De natura deorum* on the job of priests and the nature of religion: their inconclusiveness is revealed—he says—in the look of complicity they exchange when they meet; they know they are all cheating. In this vein, lawyers would be nothing but accomplices of a huge show ultimately designed to ever delude citizens about their expectations of justice.

What we thus need is a middle course between noble dreams and nighmares, between the hope of strong objectivity and the despair of solipsistic self-complacency. Noble dreams are hopes of "fit", nightmares are desperations about "justification". Now, we need, I gather, to compromise and combine the two dimensions. However, the compromise I believe to be possible is not to be realized through the banal fact that judges "sometimes do the one and sometimes do the other" (Hart 1983, 144): this fact is as true as the fact that some people follow rules and some people don't, that not excluding the wrongness of the second alternative.

A more or less coherent and successful theory, and a plausible way out of too much hope and too much despair, could be found, I believe, in a sort of constructivist solution to what seems to be an insoluble issue. Paradoxically perhaps, "fit" needs "justification" to be objective, that is, an objective meaning given to positive rules has to refer to intersubjective reasons for actions. In the end hermeneutics must somehow be based on ethics, and "justification", to escape solipsism or self-complacency, needs a good dose of "fit", that is, we can have moral reasoning only once we have found a context of action defined by positive normative rules.

"Justification" would require that our lawyers were trained, educated, not only in hermeneutics or dialectics, but also in philosophy. Black-letter legal education tends to produce either clinical or moralist lawyers, or a strange combination of both. Legal theory must be backed by an appropriate legal pedagogy.

We reach finally the variable of constitution. I have said that the constitution of the Moderns is one that shapes the entire legal system and claims normative primacy. Could the judge through his activism preempt this superiority principle, replacing constitutional fundamental rules by his own decisions? If we share a strong sense and a rigid idea of what a constitution is, he could not. How is it then possible to have judicial review assessing the constitutional validity of statutes and official acts, if these flow from the valid constitution and indeed are an application of the constitution itself?

The constitution is a dramatic moment of public deliberation about the right and the good of the community of citizens and is shaped through basic overarching rules. This moment claims to be original and fundamental, a new beginning. However, the deliberative moment is not—so to say—consummated and exhausted once and for all by the laying down of constitutional norms. A constitution as foundational discourse and decision about the public sphere and its shape needs to be further feeded through a rehearsal and additional moments of public deliberation.

A constitution as a more or less dramatic act of self-government needs, to be maintained, to be reproduced through an on-going series of much less dramatic acts of self-government. In this perspective, a constitution does not preempt or, better said, does not make ordinary legislation less relevant. Ordinary law-giving is what gives a permanent new life to the constitution, simulating at each moment its deliberative drama, so to speak. The constitutional moment is reflected and continued in the parliamentary discussion and drafting of statutes. In this way a constitution is not first of all a limit to legislation, but a model to follow for the legislator by shaping its deliberative and discoursive scheme, and the spring, the engine that maintains democracy in motion, a sort of institutional and normative "prime mover".

But a constitution is a scheme of fundamental rights too and these consist of individual legal rights, not just of rhetorical proclamations without legal effect. This strong legal character of constitutional rights means that, although ordinary legislation is justified as an enduring reproduction of the constitutional scheme of public deliberation, it is still bound to guarantee and implement constitutional rights. A judge may then be required to fuel and monitor the legal force of those rights. The "activity" of the constitutional judge should in the end only protect and focus on the permanent active force of the constitutional moment both in its scheme of collective public deliberation as granted to the legislator and in its catalogue of rights directly ascribed to citizens who may consequently claim to have them reassessed before a court of justice.

Courts' fundamental function in any case is to discuss and solve *cases*, that is individual claims of rights, a controversy between parties that ask for justice to be done, through the constitution's eyes. They judge about a past that is brought before them. In this sense they cannot but remain passive, something that is precluded to legislators that do not institutionally operate *ad personam*. Clearly, it is not enough, for the judge to replace the legislator, that they share the same values.

References

Arendt, H. 2006. "What is Authority", in Id., *Between Past and Future*, Penguin, London.

Austin, J. 1954. *The Province of Jurisprudence Determined*, London: Weidenfeld & Nicolson.

Hart, H. L. A. 1982. "Legal Duty and Obligation", in Id., *Essays on Bentham: Jurisprudence and Political Theory*, Oxford: Clarendon Press.

Hart, H. L. A. 1983. "American Jurisprudence Through English Eyes: The Nightmare and the Noble Dream", in Id,, *Essays in Jurisprudence and Philosophy*, Oxford: Clarendon.

Kelsen, H. 1978. *Allgemeine Theorie der Normen*. Wienna: Manz.

McIlwain, Ch. 2008. *Constitutionalism: Ancient and Modern*, Indianapolis: Liberty Fund.

Marmor, A. 2002. "Exclusive Legal Positivism", in *The Oxford Handbook of Jurisprudence and Philosophy of Law*, ed. Coleman and Shapiro, Oxford: Oxford University Press.

Schmitt, C. 1969. *Gesetz und Urteil*, 2nd ed., München: Beck.

Searle, J. 1991. *Minds, Brains, and Science*, London: Penguin.

Chapter 2
Judicial Activism: Clearing the Air and the Head

Lawrence A. Alexander

I've never liked the term "judicial activism." It is usually—but not always—a term of opprobrium, a pejorative, a complaint. But the opposite of judicial activism would seem to be judicial passivism—or because passivism, not to be confused with pacifism, is not actually an English word, judicial passivity. But judicial passivity seems equally to be something undesirable, I think we need a better term than judicial activism if it is to capture a valid complaint about judicial behavior.

So let me reframe the discussion of judicial activism this way. Let us begin with I should hope to be a banal, obvious point. Judges should follow and apply the law. That is why we have judges, to do just that. And we will have valid complaints about the judiciary when they fail to do what they are supposed to do, namely, follow and apply the law.

Notice that judges can fail in their duty in two different ways. They can fail to follow the law, and they can fail to apply it. So in place of the vague charge of judicial activism, I recommend the following two different indictments of judicial behavior: judicial usurpation and judicial abdication.

Let me begin with the latter indictment, as we hear less about it than the former one. Judicial abdication occurs when judges refuse to apply the law that governs the case before them. Judicial abdication leaves the party legally entitled to a remedy without one. It leaves the party legally required to provide that remedy free from legal compulsion to do so. Actors legally in the wrong can act with impunity, or at least impunity within the legal system. Actors legally in the right must take their causes elsewhere than the courts—perhaps to other branches of government or to the "court" of public opinion—or else resort to self-help, an always dangerous course and one that may result in their breaching legal duties that *will* be judicially enforced.

So judicial abdication is a serious matter, and judges should be condemned for it. Their job is an extremely important one, and they should do it. Fortunately, however, judges rarely abdicate, and surely not as a general policy. They, of course, make mistakes and believe they are applying the law when they are not. And some

L.A. Alexander (✉)
University of San Diego School of Law, 5998 Alcala Park, San Diego, CA 92110, USA
e-mail: larrya@sandiego.edu

L.P. Coutinho et al. (eds.), *Judicial Activism*,
Ius Gentium: Comparative Perspectives on Law and Justice 44,
DOI 10.1007/978-3-319-18549-1_2

can be corrupted and take bribes to refrain from applying the law in particular cases, or be cowed by public reaction or by the wrath of powerful parties into refraining from applying particular laws or laws in particular cases. Still, all in all, judicial abdication is not frequent nor an overweening concern.

So let me turn to the other judicial sin, that of usurpation. Usurpation occurs when judges follow, and apply, not the law, but norms of their own making, norms that they are not legally authorized to make and enforce. I suspect that when the term "judicial activism" is used pejoratively, the speaker is usually referring to judicial usurpation.

Now judicial usurpation comes in degrees. Total usurpation occurs when the judges, without legal authorization to do so, just make up a norm and enforce it as law. There are plenty of examples in American constitutional law of judges engaging in total usurpation.

Usurpation, however, can be less than total. Partial usurpation occurs when there is a legal authorization for the judges to fashion a norm, but the judges do so immodestly, asserting more expertise relative to other government actors than they, as judges, can rightly lay claim to.

At this point I believe a short digression on legal norms may be useful. It is commonplace, but nonetheless useful, to divide legal norms into two ideal types—rules and standards. I call them ideal types because all rules will have vague, standard-like margins; and all standards will operate within domains bounded by rules. And most legal norms will have some rule-like features and some standard-like features.

Rules are determinate, algorithmic norms. Everyone, regardless of his or her values, will apply them identically. Once it is ascertained what the rule-maker intended the algorithm to be, the application of the rule will be clear, or at least will be so in the absence of factual uncertainties.

Standards are the mirror opposites of rules. A standard invites those subject to it to apply and act upon first-order practical reasoning within boundaries fixed by rules. If people have differing values, then the verdicts of their practical reasoning will differ and thus so will their application of the same standard. Marxists and monarchist can all agree on what a stop sign requires; they will likely disagree over the meanings of standard-like terms such as "reasonable," "fair," and "just."

When judges apply standards, they must employ first-order practical reasoning in order to give content to the standards they are applying. They must translate the standard either into a set of more determinate rules or at a minimum into a determinate judgment about the specific case before them. That is not judicial usurpation.

The problem comes when judges apply the standard to invalidate the actions of other governmental actors, as when they apply a standard in the Constitution to strike down legislation passed by Congress or by a state legislature. For when judges do so, they are claiming that their first-order practical reasoning is superior to that of the legislators. Yet, judges are not, as a group, selected because of their superior abilities as practical reasoners. Their legal training is neither necessary nor sufficient for superior ability in discerning and applying moral and prudential norms. Moreover, judges typically do not have the democratic warrant buttressing the verdicts of their practical reasoning that legislators have for theirs; nor do they have the fact-finding resources that legislatures possess, at least with respect to the kinds of facts upon which first-order practical reasoning must rely.

Consider the form of judicial review of governmental action extolled in many quarters, that of proportionality review. In order to execute proportionality review, judges must assess the legitimacy and importance of the governmental interest at stake as well as the legitimacy and importance of the interests of those challenging the government's action. Legitimacy and importance will, of course, themselves be contentious matters about which reasonable people can disagree. Then the judges must ask whether there are other, less restrictive means for accomplishing the government's purposes. I say purposes, plural, because legislation is always furthering a mix of purposes, including administrative convenience. So the judges must ask if there is a Pareto superior government action to the action in question. Finally, the judges must weigh the marginal benefits of the law (relative to alternatives) against the marginal harms to the challengers. The bottom line is that there is little reason to think that judges will on average perform these tasks better than the government officials whose action is being challenged.

One would think, therefore, that judges should be extremely modest with respect to asserting the superiority of their practical reasoning to that of other governmental actors. They should be hesitant to strike down the actions of those government actors under the authority of a vague standard. They should be extremely deferential toward those other governmental actors.

In large domains of American constitutional law, that has been the case. Judges have applied constitutional standards quite deferentially. This is what is called minimal scrutiny or rationality review.[1] Only egregious instances of arbitrary, corrupt, or non-public-interested governmental acts are struck down. Indeed, sometimes the courts label the meaning of a constitutional standard to be a "political question," one not fit for judicial elaboration at all.[2] Deference to other governmental actors is then total. (Some believe "political questions" are a form of judicial abdication; the rationale for "political questions" is, however, that such questions are not really legal ones that are fit for judicial resolution.)

Nonetheless, there are exceptions to this picture of judicial deference, some clear examples of improper judicial immodesty. More about them in a moment.

Judicial deference is not called for when the legal norm is a rule. Judges are quite well-suited to ascertaining the meaning of rules. They are trained in the art of interpreting canonical legal texts. And when the legal text is a rule, applying it does not call for great skill in practical reasoning.

---

[1]See, e.g., United States v. Carolene Products Co., 304 U.S. 144 (1938); Ferguson v. Skrupa, 372 U.S. 726 (1963); New York City Transit Authority v. Beazer, 440 U.S. 568 (1979).

[2]See, e.g., Pacific States Telephone & Telegraph Co. v. Oregon, 223 U.S. 118 (1912); Nixon v. United States, 506 U.S. 224 (1993).

When it comes to rules, then, there is no need for judicial modesty. What is required, however, is for the judges to follow the rule and not to convert it into a standard that they can then apply to cases beyond the scope of the rule. For treating a limited rule as if it were a standard is judicial usurpation, pure and simple. Judges are enacting legal standards without the legal authority to do so. Arguably, this has sometimes occurred in American constitutional law. More about this below as well.

The reader may believe that in my inventory of legal norms, I have omitted some that are not either rules or standards. For I have said nothing about "principles," legal norms that are not rules but are not, as I have described standards, invitations to general first-order practical reasoning. Principles, at least as adumbrated by such theorists as Robert Alexy and Ronald Dworkin, are more specific than standards as I have described standards. They embody specific focal values—for example, freedom of expression, equality, non-cruelty, freedom of religion. And they have weight.[3]

Now I do not deny that there are *moral* principles, and that these may have weight.[4] And whenever a standard was in play, all of these moral principles and their weights would have to be taken into account in applying the standard. For one way to see standards is as injunctions to "do the right thing" within the spaces not covered by rules. And doing the right thing necessarily requires making sure that all moral principles and their weights are taken into account.

The problem with legal principles as conceptualized by people like Alexy and Dworkin is that they may not be identical with moral principles.[5] So if, for example, there is no moral principle of freedom of expression, then any "legal principle" of freedom of expression cannot be referring to such a moral principle.[6] And if "freedom of expression" is not a rule and is not a standard as I have described standards, what kind of norm is it, and how is its "weight" to be derived?

I contend that there are no such norms that can play the role that Alexy and Dworkin would have legal principles play. Legal principles, if they are not rules, standards, or moral principles, do not exist. They have no referent. And weight cannot be enacted. I have written about this elsewhere at length and so shall rest my case here on the skeletal argument I have just given.[7]

I should add, however, that I have the same misgivings about another similar claim that Dworkin makes, namely, that some terms in the constitution refer to "concepts" and not to the constitutional authors' "conceptions" of those concepts. I am extremely dubious that concepts exist apart from peoples' conceptions about the meaning of the terms they use.[8]

Let me return then to judicial usurpation. One form it takes is precisely that licensed by Dworkin and Alexy, namely, judges taking a term in a constitution that

[3]See Alexander (2012).

[4]See Alexander (2013).

[5]See Alexander (2012).

[6]See Alexander (2005).

[7]See Alexander (2012), Alexander and Kress (1995).

[8]See Alexander (2013).

had a particular meaning to its authors and calling the term a "principle" or a "concept" that can then be given a meaning by the judges that is different from the meaning intended by the authors. For when judges say that such and such a concept really means X, or that principle P outweighs some other principle or policy and demands a particular outcome, *there are no truthmakers for such assertions.*[9] The judges are making up legal norms, that is, usurping others' legal authority.

Let me conclude with some examples of judicial usurpations drawn from American constitutional law.

There are lots of examples of improper judicial immodesty. Take the issue of abortion. The central question in terms of whether laws against abortion violate the Constitution is whether the state has a sufficiently compelling interest in preserving the life of the fetus. That in turn requires asking whether fetal life is morally protectable, a difficult philosophical question. If its answer is "yes," then clearly states have a compelling interest in preventing abortions. And given the consequences of incorrectly answering the question "no" versus those of incorrectly answering "yes," surely judges should defer to legislatures that answer the question "yes." Yet, in *Roe v. Wade*,[10] that is precisely what the U.S. Supreme Court did *not* do. It acted immodestly. It told legislatures that their practical judgment about the protectability of fetal life was, for constitutional purposes at least, erroneous.

A similar point can be made about the courts and same-sex marriage. It surely takes a good deal of judicial immodesty to say that a legislature that adheres to a traditional and widely-held definition of marriage violates the vague and quite contestable standard of "equality."[11]

Indeed, given Peter Westen's apt description of "equality" as an empty idea, a vessel that can be filled with a lot of different values but that is not itself one of those values, a lot of constitutional law in the U. S. can be characterized as judicial usurpations, not just as judicial immodesty.[12] For if there is no equality "principle," and no equality "concept," then the equal protection clause of the Fourteenth Amendment really has no meaning beyond what its authors believed it would do. And we know what they did *not* believe it would do, including affecting who can vote[13] and eliminating sex discrimination.[14] Yet, the Supreme Court held otherwise.[15] (And if it was not intended to eliminate sex discrimination, could it plausibly have been intended to require same-sex marriage?)

[9]See Alexander (2012), (2013), Alexander and Kress (1995).

[10]410 U.S. 113 (1973).

[11]See, e.g., Perry v. Schwarzenegger, 704 F. Supp.2d 921 (N.D. Cal. 2010); Perry v. Brown, 671 F. 3d 1052 (9th Cir. 2012).

[12]See Westen (1982).

[13]See, e.g., the dissent of Justice Harlan in Reynolds v. Sims, 377 U.S. 533 (1964).

[14]See, e.g., Bradwell v. Illinois, 83 U.S. 130 (1872); Muller v. Oregon, 208 U.S. 412 (1908).

[15]See Reynolds v. Sims, 377 U.S. 533 (1964) (voting); Reed v. Reed, 404 U.S. 71 (1971) (sex discrimination).

Other examples of what are arguably judicial usurpations in U.S. constitutional law include reading the free speech clause as prohibiting laws other than prior restraints—that is, laws requiring official approval in order to publish[16]; reading the establishment of religion clause to do more than merely deny the federal government the power to outlaw state established religions[17]; and reading the cruel and unusual punishment clause to apply to penalties other than those that are *both* cruel *and* unusual.[18] In at least the first two of these examples, and arguably with respect to the Equal Protection Clause's extension beyond racial equality, the Court has illicitly converted a rule into a standard.

So judicial activism is an ambiguous charge. It is not a criticism if it refers to judges enforcing legal rules and not abdicating their responsibility to do so. It is a criticism, however, if it refers to judges acting immodestly under standards or converting rules into standards. Judges are well trained for interpreting but have no advantage in skill when it comes to first-order practical reasoning.

Acknowledgments Thanks to Steve Smith for his comments on an early draft, to Luís Pereira Coutinho for inviting me and organizing the conference on judicial activism at which this paper was originally presented, to all the participants at the conference for their comments, and to the Universidade de Lisboa for hosting the conference. And thanks to Sieun Lee for her assistance.

References

Alexander, Larry and Kress, Kenneth. 1995. Against Legal Principles. In *Law and Interpretation: Essays in Legal Philosophy*, ed. Andrei Marmor. New York: Oxford University Press.

Alexander, Larry. 2005. *Is There a Right of Freedom of Expression?* Cambridge: Cambridge University Press.

Alexander, Larry. 2012. Legal Objectivity and the Illusion of Legal Principles. In *Institutionalized Reason: The Jurisprudence of Robert Alexy*, ed. Matthias Klatt. Oxford: Oxford University Press.

Alexander, Larry. 2013. The Objectivity of Morality, Rules, and Law: A Conceptual Map. *Alabama Law Review* 65:501–517.

Claus, Laurence. 2004. The Anti-Discrimination Eighth Amendment. *Harvard Journal of Law & Public Policy* 28:119–168.

Levy, Leonard. 1960. *Legacy of Suppression*. Cambridge: Belknap Press of Harvard University.

Smith, Steven. 1995. *Foreordained Failure*. New York: Oxford University Press.

Westen, Peter. 1982. The Empty Idea of Equality. *Harvard Law Review* 95:537–596.

[16]See, e.g., Levy (1960).

[17]See, e.g., Smith (1995).

[18]See, e.g., Claus (2004).

Chapter 3
Judicial Activism and "Reason"

Steven D. Smith

3.1 Introduction

I discuss in this paper the justifications or rationalizations for judicial activism. You will join with me, I hope, in recognizing that this is an impossible task. In the United States, at least since *Brown v. Board of Education*, 347 U.S. 483 (1954), and especially since the controversial Warren Court decisions of the 1960s, scholars and jurists have been at work devising justifications for judicial activism. (I'll say more about that troublesome term—"judicial activism"—in a moment.) It would not be much of an exaggeration to say that this—namely, the justification of judicial activism, in general or in specific areas—has been *the* principal project of American constitutional theorists for two or three generations. By now these efforts have produced a massive body of sophisticated or at least abstruse work that, depending on your perspective, may be a thing of beauty or, conversely, a sort of intellectual monstrosity.

For today, therefore, I want to make only one main point about only one of the main themes in that beautiful or monstrous body of work: about the theme (presented in various ways) which claims that judicial activism is a good thing because

S.D. Smith (✉)
University of San Diego, Warren Hall 304d, 5998 Alcalá Park, San Diego, CA 92110-2492, USA
e-mail: smiths@sandiego.edu

L.P. Coutinho et al. (eds.), *Judicial Activism*,
Ius Gentium: Comparative Perspectives on Law and Justice 44,
DOI 10.1007/978-3-319-18549-1_3

the courts are somehow an instrument of "reason" in governance.[1] More specifically, I want to consider how, in the context of "activist" judging, a discourse that aspires to the ideal of "reason" degenerates into the opposite of reason. Some years ago, citing "a substantial number of Supreme Court decisions, involving a range of legal subjects, that condemn public enactments as being expressions of prejudice or irrationality or invidiousness," Robert Nagel argued that "to a remarkable extent our courts have become places where the name-calling and exaggeration that mark the lower depths of our political debate are simply given a more acceptable, authoritative form" (Nagel 1993). I want to consider the cultural dynamics that produce the sort of *ad hominem* argumentation that Nagel perceived. And I will suggest that the United States Supreme Court's recent decision in *United States v. Windsor,* 133 S. Ct. 1675 (2013), nicely confirms this diagnosis of our situation.

3.2 What is "Judicial Activism"?

Before taking on "reason," though, I should try to clarify the notion of "judicial activism." The term is used often, usually pejoratively, and by proponents of a variety of political and constitutional positions. But what one person condemns as "activism," another praises as statesman-like or Solomonic judicial wisdom. Thus, conservatives complain of "activism" when the courts intrude into governance to strike down traditional marriage laws or abortion restrictions; progressives cry "activism" when the judges intervene to protect the free speech rights of corporations against campaign finance regulations.

These various and conflicting characterizations may lead may lead skeptics to dismiss claims about judicial activism as empty rhetoric, and to conclude that the term "judicial activism" is a purely polemical one that people use to describe judicial decisions that they disagree with in substance. Acknowledging the looseness of the

[1]This theme complements what I view as the other main theme, which we could call the hermeneutical theme. Hermeneutical theory attempts to show that "interpretation"—and everyone agrees that judges are supposed to "interpret" law—is not the straightforward and relatively commonsensical reading of texts and precedents that humble non-lawyers may suppose it to be. Rather, interpretation is a much more complex and creative enterprise. But just by itself, this hermeneutical conclusion could serve to undermine rather than enhance judicial prestige and power. It could be that we are willing to give judges the formidable power to, for example, strike down democratically enacted laws so long as we think the judges are just reading and enforcing what our constitutions objectively permit and forbid; but once we realize that interpretation is actually a much more open and creative adventure than we had supposed, we might not see any good reason to entrust judges with this power. (By "we," here I of course mean something like "we citizens"—not "we members of the legal profession." The latter "we" may be more than happy to expand judges' power—and thus our own.) So the hermeneutic-type arguments operate to justify and *expand* judicial power, I think, mainly when they are explicitly or tacitly accompanied by the claim that judges, in contrast to ordinary politicians and officials, are somehow a voice of "reason".

term, though, I think that we can continue to use it, and that we can understand it in terms of two factors.

The first factor is the revisionary impact—or, as you might say, the meddlesomeness—of a judicial decision. Narrowly crafted decisions invalidating laws or practices that not many people care about will seem less activist than more sweeping decisions—and decisions can be sweeping either in their rationales or in the remedies ordered—striking down laws or practices of widespread public concern.

The second factor is the extent to which a judicial decision cannot be persuasively justified without going beyond conventional legal reasoning. The more a decision seems well supported by obvious or natural readings of the relevant constitutional text, or by well-settled precedent, the less "activist" it will seem—and vice versa.

Both of these factors are obviously matters of degree, and also of judgment, but I think they are meaningful enough to permit our conversation to proceed. And sometimes there will even be agreement in characterizing a decision as "activist." Thus, some Americans revere and others revile the Supreme Court's decision in *Roe v. Wade*, 410 U.S. 113 (1973), but nearly everyone has agreed, first, that the decision has had a powerful impact on American law and politics and, second, that the decision was difficult to justify purely in terms of conventional legal reasoning (e.g., Ely 1973). Brown v. Board of Education, 347 U.S. 483 (1954), is an even starker example. That is precisely why *Roe*, *Brown*, and other analogous decisions have generated a major academic project calculated to supply such justifications. As this example reflects, this understanding also shows that to classify a set of decisions as "activist" is not automatically to condemn such decisions (although, to be sure, critics are more likely to use the label "activist," given its generally pejorative connotations). The question is whether adequate justifications for such activism can be developed.

As I have noticed already, one of the most powerful sets of justifications attempts to defend judicial activism based on the premise that activist courts are an instrument of "reason" in governance. The basic proposition would go something like this: It is a good thing (at least sometimes) for courts to render decisions that have a significant revisionary impact and that cannot be persuasively justified in terms of conventional legal reasoning because this is a way in which "reason" can be given a decisive role in governance.

How persuasive is that proposition? That is the question I want to address in this talk.

3.3 Courts as Institutions of "Reason"?

I should start by acknowledging the appeal of the proposition. Given that ordinary politics is so often messy, and also mercenary, the idea that law might instead be the product of something more pristine and exalted like "reason" can seem almost irresistible. The aspiration goes back at least to Plato's *Republic*, and probably beyond that. In addition, at least in the abstract, there are grounds for supposing that courts might come closer to approximating this ideal than ordinary politics can. Judges are at least officially non-partisan, the process that they administer involves an orderly presentation of evidence and argument, and the main participants in the process—namely, lawyers and judges—are required to have attained a certain level of education. And the decisions that are rendered are by custom required to be accompanied by an explanation that considers the various arguments that have been offered and seeks to justify the acceptance of some of those arguments and the rejection of others. If reason can be brought to bear on governance, isn't this what it would look like?[2]

If we move from the abstract to the experiential, unfortunately, the results can be disappointing. Some years ago, the prominent constitutional scholar Daniel Farber observed that the opinions of the American Supreme Court are "increasingly arid, formalistic, and lacking in intellectual value." The opinions seem "almost seem designed to wear the reader into submission as much as actually to persuade." (Farber 1994: 157). Farber's former and more exuberant colleague Michael Paulsen made the point in less restrained terms: Supreme Court opinions, Paulsen thought, are "arid, technical, unhelpful, boring, ...unintelligible," "formulaic gobbledygook." (Paulsen 1995: 677). These are somewhat dated observations, and it is possible that in the intervening years the opinions have gotten better. But although I devote no more time to reading Supreme Court opinions than duty demands (in part because I share Farber's and Paulsen's judgments), my occasional browsings give me no reason to think the situation has improved.

So then why has the reality fallen so far short of what may have seemed like sensible hopes? One possibility is that, precisely by insisting on standards of propriety and rationality, constitutional discourse has filtered out voices and perspectives that would make for richer, more fully informed, and ultimately wiser conversation and decision-making. If so, the public conversation associated with "politics," though (or because) it is more rambunctious than legal discourse, is also ultimately and in the aggregate more rational than the more staid and limited discourse of the courts (Waldron 1999: 152–62). Another possibility is that however notorious and even celebrated the fact of judicial activism may be, judges still feel constrained to present their decisions as if these were the product of conventional legal reasoning. The consequence may be dissimulation: the judges are guilty, as Ronald Dworkin suggested, of "a costly mendacity." (Dworkin 1996: 37). And mendacity is more or less the opposite of the open honesty we associate with "reason."

Without in any way rejecting these explanations, I want to explore a different kind of explanation—one premised on what we may call the "discursive situation"

[2]For a classic statement of this view, see Fiss (1979). Cf. Rawls (1996: 235) (asserting that "the court's role is... to give due and continuing effect to public reason by serving as its institutional exemplar... It is the only branch of government that is visibly on its face the creature of that reason and of that reason alone.").

in which contemporary courts operate. The point I want to make is that this discursive situation works to transform decisions that attempt to ground themselves and to present themselves as the product of "reason" into something like the opposite of "reason."

3.4 Unmoored Morality and Ad Hominem Discourse

We should start by noticing one conspicuous and crucial feature of normative discourse today—namely, its radical pluralism.[3] On key questions of public policy —abortion, same-sex marriage, the distribution of wealth and opportunity, the granting of preferences based on race or ethnicity, and so forth—people obviously differ significantly in their conclusions; but beyond the disagreements at this level, people disagree as well in their normative premises and approaches.

One influential diagnosis of this situation was offered a generation or so ago in Alasdair MacIntyre's book *After Virtue*. Reciting common pro and con arguments on issues including just war, abortion, and governmental support for equality, MacIntrye suggested that these various arguments may seem perfectly cogent on their own terms (MacIntyre 1985: 6–7). Paradoxically, though, while the pro and con arguments lead to opposite conclusions, the arguments themselves do not really engage with each other. That is because they proceed from different premises and different conceptions of morality. Consequently, the ostensible adversaries talk past each other, and there is accordingly no way to achieve resolution of the disagreements.[4]

The incommensurability described by MacIntyre need not preclude meaningful moral discussions within communities of like-minded people—of economists, or utilitarians, or Kantians, or Catholic natural law theorists. But as we move into more public discourse, incommensurability becomes problematic. That is because in public discourse it comes to seem important that discussion proceed on *shared* premises. After all, how can people converse and debate profitably if they cannot agree on the fundamental premises or objectives?[5] Meaningful discussion and debate in such a situation is difficult.

---

[3]The discussion that follows closely tracks and borrows from Smith (2015).

[4]See MacIntyre (1985: 8):

> Every one of the arguments is logically valid or can easily be expanderd so as to be made so; the conclusions do indeed follow from the premises. But the rival premises are such that we possess no rational way of weighing the claims of one as against another. For each premise employs some quite different normative or evaluative concept from the others, so that the claims made upon us are of quite different kinds.

[5]But see Smith (2010: 220–23) (arguing that discussion is possible even among people with different comprehensive worldviews).

This predicament applies with particular force to courts—once, that is, they stray beyond the comfortable confines of constitutional text and precedent and conventional legal reasoning. If courts have any excuse for wielding authority outside their conventional domain, it is that they are not merely advancing some partisan or sectarian agenda, in the way more openly political actors are, but rather are acting more on the basis of some sort of detached "reason." This makes it all the more imperative that courts act on the basis of some more generally accepted values or premises. But in a radically pluralistic normative world, where are such values or premises to be found?

This problem, I believe, underlies two of the most common but unfortunate forms of normative discourse today. One common practice, which I have discussed at length elsewhere,[6] is to invoke some premise that is widely venerated precisely because it so abstract as to be virtually devoid of any intrinsic substantive content, and then to smuggle one's more substantive commitments into that revered but empty receptacle. Thus, a great deal of contemporary argumentation consists of appeals to and ostensible derivations from the idea of equality. Equality happens to be an ideal that nearly everyone in our society respects; more than that, it is a ideal that no one *can* sensibly reject. That is because, as Peter Westen's famous article in the *Harvard Law Review* explained, the normative ideal of equality merely means that "relevantly like cases should be treated alike"—a virtual tautology. The unfortunate corollary, as Westen also explained, is that equality is substantively "empty." (Westen 1982). Its content has to be imported from sources other than equality. Consequently, although advocates may purport to be deriving conclusions from the ideal of equality, in reality they are often merely engaging in sophisticated question-begging.

Much the same is true of arguments framed in terms of liberty. Liberty is a value that would seem to command widespread support in our society. But the apparent consensus is largely illusory, covering over deep disagreements about what sort of liberty or freedom, and whose freedom, is to be valued. My freedom to live as I want to, or your freedom to live in the sort of neighborhood that is conducive to your preferred lifestyle? One person's freedom to play loud music, or another's freedom to enjoy peace and quiet? Michael Klarman may overstate the matter—but not by much—when he observes that "[f]reedom. … is an empty concept. To say that one favors freedom is really to say nothing at all." (Klarman 2000: 270–71).[7]

---

[6]See Smith (2010: 26–38).

[7]In much the same way, arguments framed in terms of the celebrated "harm principle" turn out, upon closer inspection, to be artful exercises in gerrymandering the concept of harm so as to include the sorts of injuries that support regulations one favors, and to exclude—as "hurts" but not "harms", as Joel Feinberg put it, in his massive explication of the harm principle—the sorts of injuries that would support regulations one does not favor. Indeed, as Feinberg also acknowledged, without this sort of a priori disqualification of many real human concerns and grievances from the calculus, the harm principle would turn out to be not so much an instrument of liberty as a license for authoritarianism (Feinberg 1984: 33–34).

Beyond the illusion of agreement about values such as equality and liberty, however, there *is* in fact something approaching universal support for one proposition that is actually substantive, and this proposition leads to a second common form of contemporary normative discourse. More specifically, a proposition that people of virtually all moral positions can endorse is that it is wrong to act from hatred or malevolence or ill-will toward others.

This proposition is the converse or corollary of set of related propositions that can be stated more affirmatively. Thus, Kantians may affirm that we are required to treat all people as *ends*, not *means* (Kant 1959: 46–49). Political liberals may assert that we should treat all people with equal *respect*, or that we must recognize everyone's human *dignity* (see Dworkin 2011: 330; Minow and Singer 2010: 905). Utilitarians maintain that everyone is entitled to be counted equally in the utilitarian calculus (Blackburn 2001: 89). Christians teach that we should *love* everyone, both neighbors and enemies (Matthew 5: 38–48). Devout Jews believe that every person is a child of God, and hence of infinite worth (Steinberg 1947: 75–76). These affirmative propositions are not identical. But however the affirmative value is articulated, a similar prohibition seems to follow: it is wrong to act from hatred or ill-will toward others.

Unfortunately, the effect of this thoroughly sensible counsel on public discourse can be counterproductive. If the one normative proposition that virtually everyone agrees on is that it is wrong to act from hatred or ill-will, then in debates over public issues a potentially effective form of rhetoric will be to argue that your opponents are acting from hatred or ill-will. That is the one kind of argument that can potentially appeal to everyone. By contrast, arguments invoking utility, or universalizability, or religiously-informed conceptions of virtue and goodness will fail to engage the views and premises of large sections of the public audience—even if the arguments are persuasive on their own terms. But practically everyone will concur in rejecting a position or party that is deemed to be motivated by hatred or ill-will towards others.

Should we expect courts to be immune to this sort of demonizing argumentation? I don't see why. On the contrary, courts might be expected to be peculiarly receptive to this kind of *ad hominem* argumentation. After all, courts routinely resolve disputes by convicting an accused party of wrongdoing often involving some sort of guilty mind or *mens rea*. This focus on culpable mindsets or motives is most conspicuous in criminal cases, but it occurs as well in many tort cases and other kinds of cases.

The courts' institutional capacity to ascertain bad motives or purposes would seem easily to exceed their ability to perform other sorts of tasks sometimes assigned to them. Ronald Dworkin sometimes proposed that courts should decide cases by doing moral philosophy, for example. But what reason is there to suppose that judges, trained in law, would be good at that arcane task? Or it is often suggested that courts should "balance" competing interests. But in fact judges and scholars have never even seriously attempted to address the factual and methodological questions that any serious attempt at balancing would immediately present (see Aleinikoff 1987). Although lacking the training, experience, or methodology that would equip them for philosophizing or balancing, however, courts are well practiced in resolving conflicts by declaring that one or another party has been guilty of acting badly and from a bad motive.

And so it seems fitting and natural that prominent constitutional doctrines not only permit but indeed demand this sort of *ad hominem* argumentation. Under equal protection doctrine, for example, the Supreme Court has ruled that, by itself, disparate impact on the basis of race or sex will not invalidate a law. Rather, in order to obtain a declaration of unconstitutionality, advocates must show that the law was adopted for a discriminatory purpose (Washington v. Davis, 426 U.S. 229 (1976)). The requirement is understandable. If disparate impact alone were enough to invalidate a law, huge numbers of laws might go by the boards: given demographic disparities, numerous laws defining crime or regulating taxation or education are likely to affect different groups differently. Nonetheless, the effect of this doctrine is to force advocates challenging a law to argue that it was adopted for hateful or discriminatory purposes.[8]

3.5 Animus in the Judiciary

The United States Supreme Court's decision last year in *United States v. Windsor,* 133 S. Ct. 1675 (2013), provides a nice, because egregious, illustration of this analysis. In *Windsor*, the Court struck down the section in the federal Defense of Marriage Act, or DOMA, that provided that for purposes of federal law "marriage" would be considered to be a union between a man and a woman. The Court might have tried to justify this conclusion on various grounds, but in fact the primary rationale given was that the law was unconstitutional because it was enacted from "a bare congressional desire to harm a politically unpopular group," or from a "purpose …to demean," "to injure," and "to disparage." (Id. at 2693–95). Justice Kennedy and the Court thereby in essence accused Congress—and, by implication, millions of Americans—of acting from pure malevolence.

The "animus" ascribed to these millions of Americans was of an especially vicious kind. There are of course situations in which a person or political faction, in the pursuit of self-interest, selfishly and unjustly tramples on the rights and interests

[8]As Cass Sunstein and others have argued, even decisions that do not overtly focus on motive or purpose but instead talk in "balancing" terms may in fact reflect a search for or judgments about illicit motivation (Sunstein 1984: 1699). That is because a minimal requirement in such contexts is that the government has acted for a "legitimate" purpose or to secure a "legitimate" interest. But the Constitution nowhere lists which purposes or interests are legitimate and which are not. Nor is there any general cultural consensus regarding such lists: purposes and interests that "progressives" might regard as within government's proper purview may be rejected by libertarians. Once again, though, and for the reasons discussed above, there is one purpose or interest that citizens of all persuasions will view as not legitimate—namely, a purpose of acting from "a bare desire to harm" some disfavored person or group. Not surprisingly, therefore, even "rational interest" balancing decisions can turn on explicit or implicit attributions of malevolent motivation.

of others. A robber kills to get someone's wallet. A political party holds up needed legislation to gain an electoral advantage. Such actions may deserve and receive severe censure, but at least the offending party has acted on some prima facie legitimate and rational interest. By contrast, the Congress that enacted DOMA was not pursuing any legitimate interest at all; it was acting from pure malice—from "the bare desire to harm" or "to injure." Or so charged the Court.

In support of this savage accusation the Court produced no evidence at all. Or, rather, the Court purported to cite some evidence, but the evidence in fact serves to subvert, not support, the Court's accusation. More specifically, the Court cited evidence from the legislative history showing that DOMA was based on judgments (a) approving of traditional marriage and (b) disapproving of homosexual conduct. Both judgments are contestable, obviously, but neither is equivalent to a "bare desire to harm." Though the Court somehow equated these moral or cultural judgments with a desire to harm, this dubious equation remained wholly unexplained.[9]

Of course, the fact that a prosecutor provides no evidence of guilt does not prove that the accused is in fact innocent. At least in the abstract, it is possible that the members of Congress who enacted DOMA and the millions of Americans who have supported this and similar measures have been motivated mostly or entirely by hatred. The standard reasons given for their position—for example, that same-sex marriage will have a corrosive effect on marriage, and thus on the family, and thus on society—might be not only unpersuasive but hypocritical—thin pretexts for more base or hateful motives. Supporters of same-sex marriage often assert as much. But how could the Justices possibly know this to be so with respect to DOMA? Could they somehow look into the minds and hearts of the members of Congress, and of the millions of Americans who claim to believe that marriage should be between a man and woman, and know that all of these people were and are in fact lying or deceiving themselves, and that the various reasons offered in support of their position were and are merely pretextual? Indeed, although the Court's accusation appeals to a widespread commitment to treating all people with "equal respect," it is arguably the Justices who wholly fail to treat those who disagree with them with respect—even with the minimal respect of allowing that those people might actually believe what they say they believe.

3.6 Conclusion

Should we be surprised that five distinguished Justices of the nation's highest court would be prepared to decide a hugely important constitutional issue on the basis of unsupported, disparaging accusations perhaps more suitable for the sort of mean-spirited commentary one finds on various unfiltered political blogs? We should, I think, be disappointed—or perhaps outraged. (I am.) But as I have tried to show,

[9]I have argued this point at more length elsewhere (Smith 2015).

in a radically pluralistic discursive situation, advocates may have little choice except to smuggle their commitments into question-begging terms like equality or else to accuse their opponents of violating one of the few ethical norms that we can virtually all agree on: namely, that it is wrong to act from hatred or a desire to harm.

And thus judicial discourse, once it is detached from the mundane conventions of reading texts and precedents in accordance with their natural or commonsensical meanings, loftily aspires to be the realization of "reason" but instead ends up degenerating into a discourse of mean-spirited denigration.

References

Aleinikoff, T. Alexander. 1987. Constitutional Law in the Age of Balancing. *Yale Law Journal* 96: 943.

Blackburn, Simon. 2001. *Being Good: A Short Introduction to Ethics*. Oxford: Oxford University Press.

Dworkin, Ronald. 1996. *Freedom's Law*. Cambridge MA: Harvard University Press.

Dworkin, Ronald. 2011. *Justice for Hedgehogs*. Cambridge MA: Belknap Press.

Ely, John Hart. 1973. The Wages of Crying Wolf: A Comment on *Roe v. Wade. Yale Law Journal* 82: 863.

Farber, Daniel A. 1994. Missing the "Play of Intelligence." *William & Mary Law Review* 36: 147.

Feinberg, Joel. 1984. *Harm to Others*. New York: Oxford University Press.

Fiss, Owen M. 1979. Foreword: The Forms of Justice. *Harvard Law Review* 93: 1.

Kant, Immanuel. Lewis White Beck tr., Bobbs-Merrill 1959. *Foundations of the Metaphysics of Morals.* New York: Liberal Arts Press.

Klarman, Michael J. 2000. Rethinking the History of American Freedom. *William and Mary Law Review* 42: 265.

MacIntyre, Alasdair. 2d ed, 1985. *After Virtue*. Notre Dame IN: University of Notre Dame.

Minow, Martha & Singer, Joseph William. 2010. In Praise of Foxes: Pluralism as Fact and Aid to the Pursuit of Justice. *Boston University Law Review* 90: 903.

Nagel, Robert F. 1993. Name-Calling and the Clear Error Rule, *Northwestern University Law Review*, 88: 199.

Paulsen, Michael Stokes. 1995. Captain James T. Kirk and the Enterprise of Constitutional Interpretation. *Albany Law Review* 59: 671.

Rawls, John. 1996. *Political Liberalism*. New York: Columbia University Press.

Smith, Steven D. 2010. *The Disenchantment of Secular Discourse*. Cambridge MA: Harvard University Press.

Smith, Steven D. 2015. The Jurisprudence of Denigration, *University of California-Davis Law Review*, 48: 675.

Steinberg, Milton. 1947. *Basic Judaism*. Mariner Books.

Sunstein, Cass R. 1984. Naked Preferences and the Constitution. *Columbia Law Review* 84: 1689.

Waldron, Jeremy. 1999. *The Dignity of Legislation*. Cambridge: Cambridge University Press.

Westen, Peter. 1982. The Empty Idea of Equality. *Harvard Law Review* 95: 537.

Chapter 4
Judicial Activism and Fidelity to Law

Gonçalo de Almeida Ribeiro

4.1 'Judicial Activism'

What do lawyers and non-lawyers mean by 'judicial activism'? When the phrase was introduced in popular discourse in 1947 by American historian Arthur Schlesinger Jr. it described pejoratively an interpretive tendency within the U.S. Supreme Court (Green 2009a). Since then it became a standard term of opprobrium. When I published a few months ago an Essay under the title 'Judicial Activism Against Austerity in Portugal' (Ribeiro 2013) I surely did not mean to pay a compliment to the judges of the Portuguese Constitutional Court, and I expected my readers to perceive that immediately. 'Activism' is rarely used as a term of approbation when speaking about judging—a judge charged with 'activism' is responsible for a mischief of some sort, although clearly not something as serious as miscarriage of justice or straightforward corruption.

We know that judicial activism has something to do with judges going beyond the law in their business of settling disputes, or that it involves judges substituting their personal views of justice and policy for those of the law when they decide cases. That, at any rate, is what some of the most common definitions out there convey. According to the English-language version of Wikipedia, 'judicial activism describes judicial ruling suspected of being based on personal or political considerations rather than the existing law'. Black's Law Dictionary in turn states that 'judicial activism' is a 'philosophy of judicial decision-making whereby judges allow their personal views about public policy, among other factors, to guide their decisions' (Black and Garner 2000). The website of the conservative think tank Heritage Foundation supplies the most derogatory and muddled definition among the various I stumbled across in my perfunctory explorations: 'Judicial activism occurs when judges write subjective policy preferences into the law rather than

G. de Almeida Ribeiro (✉)
Universidade Católica Portuguesa, Lisboa, Portugal
e-mail: gar@ucp.pt

L.P. Coutinho et al. (eds.), *Judicial Activism*,
Ius Gentium: Comparative Perspectives on Law and Justice 44,
DOI 10.1007/978-3-319-18549-1_4

apply the law impartially according to its original meaning.' There is a common thread across these definitions, apart from the obvious fact that they are notoriously unsatisfactory: they imply a connection between proper judging and fidelity to law. An activist judge is one who consistently flouts his duty to decide cases or to settle disputes under the law, as opposed to any set of nonlegal or extralegal standards—often labeled 'personal' or 'political' judgments in this context.

These statements conceal a formidable difficulty. Since the definition of activism as a form of judicial mischief turns on the concept of law as the set of decision-making standards which claim the allegiance of judges, we must know what the law is before we furnish ourselves with criteria to identify and charge the activists within the judiciary. In other words, thinking about judicial activism pulls us irresistibly towards the most daunting and controversial of all jurisprudential problems—what is law? What begins as a simple-minded inquiry into a mainstream notion turns into a philosophical nightmare.

It is not quite as dramatic as it sounds though. When legal philosophers and other theoretically-minded jurists ask 'what is law?' they may be pursuing a wide variety of research agendas. Max Weber famously defined law as 'a system…[that is] externally guaranteed by the possibility of (physical or psychic) coercion through action aimed at enforcing compliance or punishing violation…' (Weber 1978: 34). This is a respectable account of law from a sociological standpoint, an account which looks at law as a certain type of social arrangement, practice or institution. It is certainly not a plausible account of law from the normative or so-called internal standpoint of the judge (Hart 1994: 88–91). Law as a set of standards to which judges owe fidelity must be of such character that it *justifies* judicial activity—activity that characteristically takes the form of authoritative and enforceable settlement of disputes. Put briefly, law in this normative or internal sense is the concept of the body of reasons binding on judges *qua* judges.

Now we find ourselves walking in a circle. Judges ought to decide cases according to the law and the law is the set of standards according to which judges ought to decide cases. In order to break the deadlock, we have to examine and contrast rival conceptions or models of adjudication, that is to say, accounts of how judges *ought* to decide cases. The main contenders are what I shall call legalism, idealism and pluralism.

4.2 The Legalist Model

According to the legalist model all law is positive in nature: norms are rendered legal by virtue of being posited by law-making authorities. Such positing may, of course, take a variety of forms, from legislative enactments to past judgments. What counts as law-making depends on legal practice in general and the behavior of judges in particular, which may be theorized along the familiar lines of either a rule of recognition—a social norm holding among officials (Hart 1994: 100–10)—or the

Grundnorm—a presupposed norm that renders legal claims intelligible (Kelsen 1978: 201–205).

The philosophical subtleties should not distract us from the basic point that we have no trouble identifying sources of positive law; everyone knows that the *Grundgesetz für die Bundesrepublik Deutschland* (GG) or the *Bürgerliches Gesetzbuch* (BGB) are law in Germany and that the *Administrative Procedure Act* or *Lawrence v. Texas* are law in the United States. What fidelity to law amounts to, according to this model, is quite straightforward as a matter of principle: judges should act as closely as possible as mouthpieces of legislation and adherents to precedent, that is to say, they should defer to the judgment of positive law. Failing to do so implies substituting their own views of how the case should be settled for those of the law—precisely the defining feature of judicial activism. It is as simple as that in theory.

There are, of course, all sorts of difficulties with the simple image of the judge as the 'mouthpiece of legislation' or the 'follower of precedent'. Statutes require interpretation and judicial opinions have to be construed in order for any legal norms to see the day of light; and while there are canons of legal argument guiding judges in such processes, any moderately reflective jurist knows that there are competing theories of interpretation and precedent out there, such that judges have a significant amount of leeway in their engagements with positive law. That certainly undermines the strongest conceptions of legalism, such as statutory positivism (*Gesetzespositivismus*) or legal formalism, which assert that personal or political judgment play *no* role in legitimate adjudication. But it does not hurt the moderate legalist who qualifies his definition of fidelity to law as adherence to positive law with the clause 'as much as possible' and then proceeds to spell out the more or less numerous instances of judicial discretion. In fact, a clever legalist will argue in favor of his position that the theory enables a reasonably clear distinction between judicial application of existing law and judicial law-making (Hart 1994: 135–36, 274–75).

The main issue with legalism, however, is of a different order. It is unable to answer the following question: Why should judges follow positive law at all? This might seem like a silly concern. Judges owe allegiance to positive law, one might be tempted to say, because it is the business of judges to settle disputes according to law. Yet this is a question-begging argument (Dworkin 1978: 47). The legalist cannot assume that fidelity to law means fidelity to legislation and to precedent, or to the set of recognized sources of law, since that is precisely what he is arguing for.[1] And the fact is that, upon closer inspection, there is nothing obvious about the

[1]One may, of course, stipulate that the term 'law' should be reserved for source-based norms, and add the proviso that a norm's legal character should be carefully distinguished from any binding force it may have on judges, an issue that is moral in nature. That is the point of view of sophisticated legal positivism. See, e.g., John Gardner (2001), Joseph Raz (2004), Leslie Green (2009b). Whether or not such an account of law can be sustained, it is clear that it is immune to the primary objection directed against legalism, namely that it derives judicial duty from contingent social facts about legislative, judicial or customary activity. Clearly, though, the sophisticated

binding force of positive law. Judges are bound to offer reasons—indeed, good reasons—for their decisions because they are bestowed with the authority to settle disputes and to order the enforcement of such settlements by the executive arm of government. Invoking a legislative act or a judicial decision as a reason for a judgment that entails the loss of either property or freedom on the grounds that legislation and precedent are law without further ado, or by definition, or because that is what judges have been saying all along, is hardly persuasive (Dworkin 1986: 6–11). Surely it would be more persuasive if the judge settled the dispute on the merits, weighting impartially the claims of the parties in the lawsuit and issuing a decision that she is prepared to argue as just or fair (Raz 2004: 8). In a word, substantive justice is a better candidate than positive law for the role of defining the term law in the phrase 'judicial fidelity to law'. This leads us to the idealist model.

4.3 The Idealist Model

According to the idealist model law is right reason or substantive justice: *ius* instead of *lex*. The judge is bound by justice instead of humanly made laws. It does not follow that the latter are irrelevant in legal argument. Statutory rules, for instance, are attempts to externalize or express the demands of justice in the circumstances of their application, and as such they carry a certain measure of heuristic or persuasive value. This is a conception of law that is quite alien to us, jurists shaped by late modernity and post-modernity, although it was the dominant view in medieval jurisprudence and, to some extent, in the early modern period of the so-called 'law of reason' (Wieacker 1995: §§16–17).

Let us move backwards some eight centuries and ask: How could the *Corpus Juris Civilis*, a compilation of law books with material drawn primarily from the classical period of Roman jurisprudence and arranged under the direction of a Byzantine Emperor in the sixth century, become law in thirteenth Century Europe? Indeed it became law even in Western Europe where the authority of the Holy Roman Emperor was notoriously weak and princes and jurists alike did not pay any allegiance to the doctrine of *translatio imperii*. Roman law was received in late-medieval Europe not because it had been enacted by a law-making authority but because it was regarded as *ratio scripta*, that is, a particularly felicitous formulation of natural justice, right reason, or *ius* (Stein 1993). That is why the medieval jurists, particularly in those regions beyond the political reach of the Holy Roman Emperor, claimed that the Digest of Justinian, an anthology of maxims and

(Footnote 1 continued)

positivist view of law is of no interest in the debate about judicial activism, since it denies the very premise upon which the debate is grounded, namely that judges ought to apply the law. The account of law underlying the rhetoric of judicial activism equates law with (good or legitimate) adjudication, whereas sophisticated legal positivists insist that theories of law and theories of adjudication belong in different jurisprudential departments.

opinions formulated by Roman jurists who lived in the first two centuries of our Era, were law not *ex ratione imperii* but *ex imperio ratione*—not on account of imperial authority but on account of the authority of reason (Hespanha 2003: 104–107).

Since the function of *lex*, on this view, is to establish a bridge between the invisible order of right reason and the observable world of texts and practices, what is ultimately decisive is not the letter but the spirit. 'Textual authority', writes legal historian Paolo Grossi, 'is not something completely fixed; on the contrary, it is flexible, the text can and should be translated into the situation of its reader and user, can and should be *interpreted*' (Grossi 1996: 162). He is at pains to stress that the medieval notion of *interpretatio* is altogether different, mostly in the sense of being far more liberal, from our understanding of (statutory) interpretation. I suspect that the key connection here is furnished by the Church tradition of picking on a passage of Paul's *Second Epistle to the Corinthians*—'The letter killeth, but the spirit giveth life'—to establish that Scripture is merely the vehicle in which the Holy Spirit drives the faithful to the actual Word of God.

The nearly sacred status of the *Corpus Juris Civilis* in the Low Middle Ages is, of course, inextricably tied with the intellectual and moral humility of medieval culture, according to which the individual can only hope to overcome his imperfection within the framework of the community, both that which he forms with his living peers and that which he forms with his ancestors. That is what lies behind both the veneration the medieval jurists held for their Roman counterparts and the idea that the standard of correctness of legal arguments is the community of experts —the *opinio communis doctorum*. If we fast-forward a mere three centuries, we stumble across Grotius mockery of the 'scholastic subtlety' (Grotius 2005: 1761) of medieval compendiums and Barbeyrac's impatience with the 'barbarous language' (Gordley 1991: 126) of the jurists affiliated with the *mos italicus iura docendi*. For them, authors of the great law of reason or modern natural law treatises, law is a matter of natural reason and therefore any educated person can study it and write about it in clear and elegant language (Gordley 1991: 129–32).

It is tempting to interpret this idealist conception of law as licensing just about any form of judicial activism. It appears that, on this view, so long as a judge follows his sense of justice and is prepared to articulate arguments in its favor he is exhibiting all the fidelity to law required from him. Yet even within the idealist framework there is room for a certain form of activism: the judge who takes advantage of his position to further an agenda of social policy at the expense of doing justice in the dispute at hand. Imagine that in the case of a boat collision involving a careless fisherman and a rich yacht owner the judge denies damages to the latter on the grounds that while the fisherman is responsible for the accident the yacht owner is richer than the fisherman by a margin that widely exceeds what the judge's sense of distributive justice can support. Or imagine a judge in one of those standard 'industrial revolution' cases of train sparks damaging a farmer's crops deciding for the railway company on account of the significance of railway development for economic growth.[2] In these cases, even an idealist would have no trouble condemning the judge as an activist. Yet it is quite clear that within this model of adjudication the leeway of the judge is much greater than that which is afforded by the legalist view.

Moreover, idealism is patently problematic. Judges owe allegiance to legislation and other forms of positive law for far more pervasive and important reasons than their heuristic or persuasive excellences. Indeed, the latter are at least doubtful, as Bismarck flagged with the famous aphorism that statutes are like sausages in that it is better not to see them being made. Judges owe allegiance to legislation and other so-called sources of the law for a variety of fundamental reasons of certainty, legitimacy, equality and prudence that must be balanced against considerations of substantive justice. That is exactly what the third model that we shall consider—pluralism—stresses.

4.4 The Pluralist Model

According to the pluralist model judges are bound by a set of *prima facie* equally fundamental principles: justice, certainty, legitimacy, equality, and prudence. Justice requires giving to the parties to the dispute what a perfectly just legal system would provide. Certainty requires predictability in social life. Legitimacy requires deferring to the judgment of authorities holding the comparatively better title to settle controversial issues. Equality requires consistency with past decisions understood in terms of 'treating like cases alike'. Finally, prudence requires proper consideration of the consequences of a judgment for the long run realization of the law.

These are *principles* and they are *fundamental*. They are principles in the relatively technical sense in which the notion was developed by legal theorists in the late twentieth century (Dworkin 1978: 22–28; Sieckmann 1990: 52–87; Alexy 2002a, b: 44–68). They embody values that can be fulfilled in varying degrees and have varying weight depending on the circumstances; consequently, their application involves the mediation of a judgment balancing them against competing principles. They are fundamental, on the other hand, in the sense that they are the ultimate criteria of legal justification, the standards to which good legal argument ultimately harks back. In other words, they are the basic 'value facts' of the law (Greenberg 2004)—the deep source of valid legal reasons.[3] Let me examine each of them in somewhat greater detail.

[2]According to Morton Horwitz's controversial 'legal subsidization' hypothesis, American courts transformed the common law during the antebellum period in order 'to create immunities from legal liability and thereby to provide substantial subsidies for those who undertook schemes of economic development' (Horwitz 1977: 99–100).

[3]It is understandable why pluralism might be seen as a 'third way' in relation to legalism and idealism. However, it is certainly not a 'middle road' in relation to the views of law as social fact or as part of morality. The champion of such an intermediate view was, for a long time, Ronald

Justice. We expect courts to deliver justice rather than charity, piety, magnanimity, or paternal oversight. Justice is the only branch of morality that is ordinarily taken to justify the use of force that the judiciary is entitled to command. In other words, duties of justice are the only subset of moral duties that it is morally appropriate to enforce. That is why justice is usually regarded as the 'political' among the manifold moral virtues, and why duties of justice are said to constitute an independent domain of so-called 'political morality'.[4]

The association of coercion with justice is fairly intuitive (Hart 1955: 178). Most people believe that force may be legitimately deployed against a trespasser of private property or against a recalcitrant taxpayer, but that it should not be used against an uncharitable millionaire or to remedy someone's impoverished lifestyle. Why the difference? To a very large extent it lies in the special connection between justice and society: norms of justice concern the very structure of human coexistence in the finite world that we are fated to share. They determine our entitlements and burdens—what we owe each other—as participants in the joint venture of collective life. Securing them is thereby an unavoidably public concern (Waldron 1999: 105–6, 159–60).

There is of course a long way from justice considered in general to justice as it bears on a particular dispute brought before a court of law. A judge should not decide a torts dispute involving a wealthy driver and a poor pedestrian on the basis of their income sheets, even though his Ralwsian conception of justice may require large scale redistribution of income and wealth in the society in question. There are numerous other factors, including the wrongfulness of the defendant's conduct and the effects of the decision in future activity, that possibly should play a significant role in the fair assessment of the dispute; disregarding these other factors will yield the decision not just inadequate but unjust. Judges are bound by justice as it bears on the case before them, not as if they were supreme architects well positioned to implement large scale social reforms.

Certainty. Social life would be hopelessly unpredictable if the citizenry could not count on any guidance but that which is provided by trying to figure out individually what justice requires or by trying to predict future judicial rulings. This is true for two basic reasons. First, people disagree about the requirements of justice, meaning that two reasonable individuals are unlikely to come to the same conclusions as they engage with the plethora of issues of justice entangled in their

(Footnote 3 continued)

Dworkin (1978, 1986), who argued over his career for slightly different versions of the view of law as a normative domain straddled between the two realms. Dworkin appears to have evolved in his latest work towards a view of law as part of morality (Dworkin 2011: 400–15). That is also the view underlying the pluralist model of adjudication articulated in this section.

[4]This view is typically modern and can be traced back to Kant (1996), who distinguishes sharply between (duties of) right (*Recht*) and (duties of) virtue. An earlier conception, well represented by Aquinas (1947: II–I, q. 96, a. 2), was that morality is not divided into different 'departments' but embodies a *continuum* of obligation, with the range of enforceable duties determined by context-bound prudential judgments.

ordinary affairs (Waldron 1996: 1538–40). Moreover, the mental burden of unrestrained moral reflection about each and every issue of justice would prove exhausting even to the most resilient citizen. Second, there are numerous collective action or coordination problems that cannot be settled rationally but only through the *fiat* of some authority—say, decisions about whose vehicle should be given priority at an intersection, concerning the maximum time after a legally relevant event to initiate the corresponding proceedings, or to create administrative agencies devoted to the provision of public goods (Raz 1993: chs. 2–4).

The force of these reasons is the measure of the value of certainty and of its independent weight in judicial decision-making. Judges ought to defer to past decisions or practices because by doing so they provide conduct guidelines to the citizenry and enable the creation of coordination benefits. Such decisions and practices command greater deference, other things being equal, if they exhibit certain formal properties that improve their value as guides to conduct, namely the familiar 'rule of law' virtues of publicity, clarity, determinacy, prospectivity, and the like. What makes these distinctively 'legal' is that they are creatures of positive law, for certainty is a value yielded once norms of justice are embodied in such things as statutes, rulings, customs, and other conventional legal sources. But certainty is not merely a surplus yielded by the incorporation of justice into positive law; it has an independent value that justifies more or less significant judicial departure from the requirements of substantive justice.

Legitimacy. There are reasons of a different nature pulling judges towards deference to past decisions, particularly those issued by the elected branches. Such reasons fall into two basic categories. The first concerns the title or right to settle controversial issues of political morality. Citizens disagree about justice and they do so in good faith (Waldron 1999: 1–4, 10–16, 176–186, 306–312). The elected branches are typically endowed with a comparatively strong title to decide which among the rival conceptions of justice should be given preference because they possess good democratic credentials (Wollheim 1969). In most legal systems, judges are neither politically accountable nor representative of the ideological pluralism across the community. The elected branches, on the contrary, are chosen by the addressees of their power, the citizenry itself, acting as free and equal persons.

The second category comprises considerations of functional competence. Courts are comparatively ill-equipped to make certain types of judgment, namely empirical assessments involving complex prognoses—e.g., what are the effects of shifting from negligence to strict liability in the area of accidents caused by defective products?—and judgments of policy aimed at the public interest or general welfare —e.g., what goal should be given precedence in case of conflict, full employment or price stability? Judges have good reason to defer to the decisions of the elected branches on these issues because the latter are more likely to get things right. The expertise of the judiciary lies not in technical questions that implicate the deployment of instrumental rationality but in what Dworkin calls 'matters of principle' (Dworkin 1978: 82–84), which involve primarily normative judgments concerning the content and weight of competing claims over some disputed resource, opportunity or competence.

Equality. Yet another reason for deferring to past decisions flows from the requirement to 'treat like cases alike'. This is the principle underlying the central role played by analogy not only in legal argument but in ordinary moral reasoning as well. Formally speaking, it determines that two cases should be treated alike in the exact proportion of their relevant similarity—e.g., if A is sentenced to pay a fine x for committing offense y, B ought to be sentenced to pay a proportionately higher fine for committing offense $y + 1$.

Equality is a value as pervasive as it is mysterious, so we may profit from a down-to-earth illustration of its normative force. Imagine a parent that gives a certain amount of money to one of his teenage twin children on a given day, only to realize in a few hours that he should have been less profligate. On the next day he is approached by the other twin who, in similar circumstances, asks the same amount of money from him. He was wrong in his first decision, but does he not have a *prima facie* reason to repeat it on this occasion? I believe so. The second twin is likely to claim not only that he relied upon the past decision, but that her standing in the family requires from the parental authority equal treatment in relevantly similar circumstances.

Admittedly, there are various complications built into the idea of equality, notably the tension between what we might call bare consistency and consistency of principle (Dworkin 1986: 219–224). Does equality require that a past decision inconsistent with the principle(s) governing issues of a similar type (what the Roman jurists called *jus singulare*) be followed or, on the contrary, it requires principled decision-making, hence that the anomalous exception be abolished? The latter route is apparently more attractive from a normative standpoint and is quite congenial to the role that analogy ordinarily plays in legal reasoning. The issue is complicated, and cannot be pursued any further on this occasion.

Prudence. Courts might have good reason to depart from the best judgment according to the four preceding principles for reasons that we might describe as prudential. Their responsibility is not exhausted by the duty to deliver justice in the case at hand, comprising as well the institutional obligation of ensuring the basic conditions for the continuing realization of the law. What that requires from them is a permanent concern with the *consequences* of a ruling for the rule of law. The force of this point may be conveyed through an example.

The jurisdiction of the International Court of Justice to adjudicate a dispute between sovereign states depends on their consent, i.e. it is voluntary instead of compulsory. This is undoubtedly a major flaw of the international legal order, since it gives leeway for states to act as judges in their own cause. There are plenty of compelling arguments—to begin with, the principle of *nemo iudex in causa sua*—for the ICJ to claim compulsory jurisdiction over states. But the political backlash of such a decision, however correct as matter of principle, is likely to be of such character as to undermine instead of furthering the Court's effective authority to enforce international law. Powerful states would not take lightly what would amount to unconsented loss of sovereignty, ultimately challenging instead of submitting to the Court's unilateral claim to authority. At the end of the day, an imperfect legal order could very well degenerate into a state of nature subject to the ruthlessly unstable and unprincipled rule of naked power and self-interest.

Prudence is the basis of what Alexander Bickel called the 'passive virtues' of judicial power (Bickel 1961-62).[5] It reminds judges that they are not insulated from the real world, where decisions often have unintended consequences that require an openness to compromise grounded in the 'ethic of responsibility' (Weber 1991: 119–27).

4.5 Stare Decisis

Let me illustrate the interplay of these principles with a basic example: the doctrine of precedent. In its so-called historical as opposed to hierarchical dimension—involving past and future decisions of a superior court instead of decisions by higher and inferior courts—precedent is the doctrine according to which a court is bound by its past rulings on the issue to be decided. Now it is important to distinguish carefully the binding force of precedent from its persuasive value. No doubt judges deciding a case are likely to find in the records of past decisions a rich source of insight about the issues it raises and how to handle them properly. There are very good reasons of economy (saving time and energy) and method (learning from past experience) to use past cases as guidance to decide those of the present day, and there is every reason to adhere to previous rulings whenever these prove persuasive on the merits. But that is the spirit in which a judge might turn to the writings of Aristotle or to foreign case law in his search for the right answer to a challenging issue; it does not mean that the *Nicomachean Ethics* or the case law of the Canadian Supreme Court are law in Portugal or in South Africa. *Stare decisis* implies that precedent is binding even if the court is now persuaded that the issue was wrongly decided in the past.[6] Why should such an apparently odd doctrine be accepted? Should we not join Oliver Wendell Holmes when he complains that 'it is revolting to have no better reason for a rule of law than that so it was laid down in the time of Henry IV' (Holmes 1997: 1001)?

Holmes' point is entirely sound from the standpoint of justice alone. If the duty of a judge were to decide each case according to what a perfectly just legal system would provide, the force of precedent would be exhausted by its substantive merit.

[5]For more on this subject, see the contribution of Luís Pereira Coutinho in this volume.

[6]To expand on the point above, the doctrine of precedent is (nearly) redundant when the present day court believes that the matter was correctly decided in the past. It might sound paradoxical, but *stare decisis* makes a greater difference in legal argument precisely when the judge of today believes that his predecessor made a mistake as to the law. This might be taken to be an argument against the 'declaratory theory' of precedent, the view that judges declare instead of making law. But the issue is usually ill-conceived (Zander 2004: 298–99). Judges do (should) not make law (understood, of course, in the non-legalistic or pluralistic sense advocated here) when they decide a case; their job is to settle the dispute according to the law as it stands. They cannot deliberately change the law, like legislatures regularly do. But in deciding a case as they ought to, by trying to figure out the law, they unintentionally change it by introducing a new element—the decision—in the body of relevant legal materials.

There would still be plenty of reason for judges to engage with the records of past decisions in their search for a just resolution to the dispute at hand, but they would not take themselves to be legally bound by anything decided by their predecessors on the job. If anything, justice is a principle that counts against *stare decisis*—it furnishes a *prima facie* reason to overrule incorrect or unjust precedents. If precedent has any legal force at all, then, it must be in virtue of other fundamental principles.

Certainty is surely one of them. Past decisions known to bind courts in the future encourage the reliance of persons acting in similar circumstances, and in so doing they increase the predictability of social life by improving the ability of the citizenry to foresee the consequences of a given course of action. This proposition might be doubtful if we take precedent to mean a single case, for 'standing alone [no case]… can give you…guidance as to how far it carries, as to how much of its language will hold water later' (Llewellyn 2008: 46). Can we infer any guiding principle regarding the scope of First Amendment (freedom of expression) rights exercised in someone else's property from a decision to disallow the use of trespassing laws to prevent the distribution of religious materials on a sidewalk of a privately owned company town?[7] Does the ruling imply anything for a case involving a shopping center owner barring union members from peacefully picketing in front of a store?[8] What about a case concerning the distribution of handbill invitations to a political meeting in a shopping mall?[9] The answer to these queries is obviously negative. Past judicial decisions offer guidance for the future when they form clusters or lines of cases, that is to say, when each case can be read against the background of a number of others lying in its vicinity (Llewellyn 2008: 46–54).

Are there grounds of legitimacy to follow precedent? That is hardly the case. Neither do past judges hold better credentials than those of the present day to settle controversial issues of political morality, nor do they exhibit any functional advantage over their identically positioned successors. On the contrary, there is reason to think that the current generation is more legitimate simply because it was appointed more recently. Whatever method of judicial appointment is adopted in a given jurisdiction, the most recent nominee to the bench is in theory, barring unusual circumstances of political systems degenerating over time, the most legitimate judge, since he benefits both from the fresher democratic legitimacy of whatever elected officials were involved directly or indirectly in his appointment and from the most up to date technical preparation for the job.

The connection between equality and precedent is more ambiguous. It is standard law talk that the principle 'treating like cases alike' is one of the foundations of the doctrine of precedent. That is certainly true. But the same principle is also the source of a deep tension within the doctrine between arguments for strict adherence to precedent and for distinguishing the case at hand from a line of previous cases or

[7]*Marsh v. Alabama*, 326 U.S. 501 (1946).

[8]*Amalgamated Food Employees Union Local 590 v. Logan Valley Plaza*, 391 U.S. 308 (1968).

[9]*Lloyd Corp. v. Tanner*, 407 U.S. 551 (1972).

for abolishing unprincipled exceptions to general standards. Equality, as we saw earlier, may be taken to imply either bare consistency with the past or consistency of principle, and the choice between one and the other is far from inconsequential in this area. Consistency of principle pushes judges in the direction of forcing coherence upon the case law, either by abolishing unjustified exceptions or by introducing distinctions that might have been overlooked or even disallowed in the past. Bare consistency, on the other hand, requires strict adherence to the rules laid down, even if these do not add up to what Ronald Dworkin calls 'a coherent scheme of principle' (Dworkin 1986: 214).

Prudence, at last, should usually be counted as a reason for precedent. Courts, particularly the highest in a jurisdiction, are moral persons in the eyes of the public, not simply collections of individual judges belonging to this or that jurisprudential tendency or this or that generation. Much of their authority is based on the integrity of the case law they produce over time. Shifts of opinion are perfectly appropriate and often necessary but unless they take place against the background of reasoned engagement with the record of past decisions, the judiciary can be easily brought into disrepute. Accordingly, prudence places the burden of proof with the reformist.

It is an open question how to balance these rival considerations. Reflective and responsible judges will adhere to stricter or more flexible conceptions of precedent depending both on the relevant empirical circumstances of their legal system—say, whether there is a deep seated practice of precedent that encourages the reliance of the citizenry on past judgments—and the relative value they ascribe to the fundamental principles pulling them in opposite directions. Precedent, like all law, is riddled with tension and controversy. That explains why any mature legal culture where the doctrine is taken seriously recognizes not just *stare decisis* but also the countervailing technique of distinguishing and the power to overrule. The latter, for instance, is properly exercised in those circumstances where the standpoints of substantive justice and legitimacy take precedence over competing considerations of certainty, equality and prudence.

4.6 Varieties of Activism

The pluralist view is thus that law, understood as the appropriate ground of a judicial decision, is the outcome of the all-things-considered judgment balancing the fundamental principles of legal justification in the circumstances of the dispute. If this view is correct, it is quite silly to draw any sharp distinction between law and politics, or legal and personal judgment, or to adhere to Montesquieu's misleading account of the judiciary as a neutral or void power (Montesquieu 1955: 68). Proper judging—that is, according to law—is unavoidably political in two respects. First, it is political in the general sense of the term: law engages the judge's sense of justice in proportion to the role that the principle of justice plays in legal argument; and the judge's sense of justice obviously translates into his ideological commitments in a public culture characterized by the fact of reasonable pluralism (Rawls 2005:

36–39, 54–66). Second, it is political in a specific sense tied to legal argument: engagement with the fundamental principles implies balancing judgments which are inevitably complex and controversial, leading to genuine and reasonable disagreements among lawyers about the law (Dworkin 1986: 4–5, 112–113).

Does that mean we are left empty handed in our search for criteria to define judicial activism? Not at all. Even if we accept the jurisprudential conception embodied in the pluralist model, there are perfectly intelligible and appropriate deployments of the concept of judicial activism. Let me outline the main three, along a spectrum going from the most serious or blatant form of activism to the lighter and subtler.

First, there is judicial activism in the sense that even the idealist jurist recognizes. Judges are expected to settle cases: they owe justice to the parties. If they use their power to advance a broader policy agenda, such as redistribution of wealth or economic growth, of the sort illustrated previously, they usurp the authority of the legislature and compromise the separation between legislative and judicial power.

Second, judges who operate within an idealist conception of law are activists of two possible sorts: they may be 'outliers' acting as vigilantes unrestrained by anything but their sense of justice or 'rogues' who lack integrity in that they deploy legal arguments strategically. A 'rogue' in particular is a judge who is committed to idealism but pretends otherwise, mastering legalist or pluralist techniques in order to bolster or conserve his legitimacy. It is the sort of judge who will turn to this or that account of precedent or this or that theory of statutory interpretation depending on which one yields the outcome he favors (Kennedy 1986; Posner 1991), with the implication that his record of decision-making is a patchwork rather than a coherent narrative (Dworkin 1986: 228–232, 400–407).

Finally, there is activism as a notion within the realm of pluralist adjudication. It is the charge directed against a relatively liberal judge by a more conservative jurist (Dworkin 1986: 357–359) that he did not give sufficient weight to the principles that counsel restraint. 'Activist' in this sense is the judge who is more prone than the average to accord weight to justice vis-à-vis legitimacy, certainty, equality and prudence—the judge who is likely to deploy frequently doctrines such as teleological reduction and analogical extension in the field of statutory interpretation or distinguishing and overruling in the field of precedent. Or the judge who is prepared to, if push comes to shove, issue a straightforward *contra legem* ruling grounded in the doctrine of *lex injusta* (Radbruch 2006; Alexy 2002b: 40–68). Activism in this sense is part of the ordinary business of adjudication, an offspring of the inevitably political dimension of judicial power.

4.7 Judicial Review of Legislation

I have focused in the previous sections on ordinary adjudication of the type involved in any standard civil or criminal case, or for that matter in most instances of judicial review of executive action. It is by far the more general case in the theory of adjudication. But I should like to make a few brief remarks by way of conclusion about the somewhat special case of judicial review *of legislation*, perhaps the field where the charge of judicial activism is laid with more frequency—and appropriately so, since it is the area where the temptation to derail from the path of the law is felt more intensely.

There is indeed an important difference between ordinary (let me use this label for the general case of adjudication) and constitutional adjudication. Not that 'the law' is something fundamentally different for judges deciding one and the other types of case; the pluralist model of adjudication, and specifically the five basic legal principles, hold all the same when judges are called to decide on the validity of legislation. The relevant differences concern the nature of the task and the very form of judicial power it entails. Put briefly, they can be reduced to the following three points:

Scope of Power. Ordinary adjudication concerns the resolution of disputes between particular (natural or moral) persons. The authority of the court is bound to the case, in the sense that the job of the judge(s) is to settle *that* one dispute. Constitutional adjudication, on the other hand, places courts in the position of what Hans Kelsen called a 'negative legislator', empowered to *strike down* legislation (Kelsen 2008). It is the nature of the beast itself that requires judges to cast a much wider net, so wide that it places the judiciary in a territory that has traditionally been regarded as the province of the legislature: general prescription (Gény 1919: 74–92).

Function Served. Ordinary adjudication serves a necessary function, in the sense that if a court refuses to settle a dispute the issue will remain disputed and will eventually have to be settled privately. That is why in any mature legal system judges cannot refuse to decide a case on account of the complexity, ambiguity or unclarity of the situation; such prohibition of so-called *non liquet* judgments is a fairly straightforward implication of the principle *nemo iudex in causa sua*. On the contrary, constitutional adjudication is a safeguard against legislative defects, and in that sense it plays a secondary role. Legal systems without judicial review of legislation are perfectly conceivable, and indeed a reality both historically and in some contemporary liberal democracies.[10]

Positive Constraints. Constitutions are far more open-textured than ordinary legal sources, namely statutes. Many constitutional provisions embody principles instead of rules, meaning that their application involves an ad hoc balancing judgment which is likely to be controversial. The leeway of a constitutional judge is hence, even where fundamental principles pull him towards the material of positive law, much greater than that which ordinary judges enjoy. No wonder that

[10]New Zealand is the contemporary example that I am acquainted with. Notice that the list is much longer if we decide to include in it all the systems which lack strong judicial review of legislation, i.e. in which courts can declare that a statute is unconstitutional but lack the power to strike it down. The most prominent example of this later type of system is the U.K. regime of 'declaration of incompatibility' under the Human Rights Act of 1998. For a fine summary of the differences between systems of strong and weak review, see Waldron (2006: 1554–57).

constitutional theory has been haunted for so many decades with what is misleadingly labeled the 'counter-majoritarian difficulty'.[11]

Legal theorists tend to overlook these differences, although they yield important consequences for the theory of constitutional adjudication.[12] I have argued elsewhere that the proper scope of constitutional justice in a liberal democracy is quite narrow (Ribeiro 2013, 2014). This is not the occasion to restate or to refine the argument. The point that I wish to stress here is that the differences listed above justify a much broader endorsement of the virtue of self-restraint in constitutional than in ordinary adjudication.

References

ALEXY, Robert. 2002a. *A Theory of Constitutional Rights*, translated by Julian Rivers. Oxford: Oxford University Press.

ALEXY, Robert. 2002b. *The Argument from Injustice*, translated by Bonnie L. Paulson and Stanley L. Paulson. Oxford: Oxford University Press.

AQUINAS, Thomas. 1947. *Summa Theologica*, translated by the Fathers of the English Dominican Province. URL: http://www.sacred-texts.com/chr/aquinas/summa/index.htm.

BICKEL, Alexander. 1961-62. The Supreme Court 1960 Term — Forward: The Passive Virtues. *Harvard Law Review* 75: 40.

BICKEL, Alexander. 1986. *The Least Dangerous Branch*. New Haven: Yale University Press.

BLACK, Henry and GARNER, Bryan. 2000. *Black's Law Dictionary*. St Paul: West Publishing Co.

DWORKIN, Ronald. 1978. *Taking Rights Seriously*. Cambridge, Mass.: Harvard University Press.

DWORKIN, Ronald. 1986. *Law's Empire*. Cambridge, Mass.: Belknap Press of Harvard University Press.

DWORKIN, Ronald. 2011. *Justice for Hedgehogs*. Cambridge, Mass.: Belknap Press of Harvard University Press.

FERRAJOLI, Luigi. 2009. *Garantismo*, translated by Andrea Greppi. Madrid: Editorial Trotta.

GARDNER, John. 2001. Legal Positivism: 5 1/2 Myths. *American Journal of Jurisprudence* 46: 199.

GENY, François. 1919. *Méthode d'Interprétation et Sources en Droit Privé Positif*, vol. II. Paris: Librairie Générale de Droit et de Jurisprudence.

GORDLEY, James. 1991. *The Philosophical Origins of Modern Contract Doctrine*. Oxford & New York: Oxford University Press.

GREEN, Craig. 2009a. An *Intellectual History of Judicial Activism*, Emory Law Journal 58: 1195.

[11]The term was coined by Alexander Bickel (1986: 16–23). It is misleading because, as Jeremy Waldron (2006: 1391–93) stresses, courts are majoritarian institutions as well. What they normally lack is electoral accountability and popular representativeness.

[12]Italian legal theorist Luigi Ferrajoli (2009: 96), for example, argues that the reason to have a majority of unelected judges second-guessing legislative judgments about controversial issues concerning the content and weight of fundamental rights is no different from the basic separation-of-powers reason for having unelected ordinary judges deciding hard cases. In addition to confusing the separation of powers with the democratic principle—the former prescribes that legislation and adjudication should be entrusted to different actors while the latter prescribes a particular method (free and open elections) for selecting officials—Ferrajoli overlooks all the important differences between ordinary and constitutional adjudication. His appeal to Montesquieu (*Id.*: 97), who believed in a neutral judiciary, is particularly misguided.

GREEN, Leslie. 2009b. Legal Positivism. *The Stanford Encyclopedia of Philosophy*, ed. Edward N. Zalta, URL = http://plato.stanford.edu/archives/fall2009/entries/legal-positivism/.

GREENBERG, Mark. 2004. How Facts Make Law. *Legal Theory* 10: 157.

GROSSI, Paolo. 1996. *L'Ordine Giuridico Medievale*. Roma: Editori Laterza.

GROTIUS, Hugo. 2005. *The Rights of War and Peace*, Book III, translated from the French of Jean Barbeyrac and edited by Richard Tuck. Indianapolis: Liberty Fund.

HART, H. L. A. 1955. Are There Any Natural Rights? *Philosophical Review* 64: 175.

HART, H. L. A. 1994. *The Concept of Law*. Oxford & New York: Oxford University Press.

HOLMES Jr., Oliver Wendell. 1997. The Path of the Law. *Harvard Law Review* 110: 991.

HESPANHA, António Manuel. 2003. *Cultura Jurídica Europeia: Síntese de um Milénio*. Lisboa: Europa-América.

HORWITZ, Morton. 1977. *The Transformation of American Law: 1780-1860*. Cambridge: Harvard University Press.

KANT, Immmanuel. 1996. *The Metaphysics of Morals*, translated by Mary Gregor. Cambridge & New York: Cambridge University Press.

KELSEN, Hans. 1978. *Pure Theory of Law*, translated by Max Knight. Berkeley: University of California Press.

KELSEN, Hans. 2008. *Wer soll der Huter der Verfassung sein?* Tübingen: Mohr Siebeck.

KENNEDY, Duncan. 1986. Freedom and Constraint in Adjudication: A Critical Phenomenology. *Journal of Legal Education* 36: 518.

LLEWELLYN, Karl. 2008. *The Bramble Bush*. Oxford: Oxford University Press.

MONTESQUIEU. 1955. *Œuvres Complètes, De L'Esprit des Lois*, t. II. Paris: Les Belles Lettres.

POSNER, Richard. 1991. What has Pragmatism to Offer Law? In *Pragmatism in Law & Society*, ed. Michael Brint and William Weaver. Boulder: Westview Press.

RADBRUCH, Gustav. 2006. Statutory Lawlessness and Supra-Statutory Law, translated by Bonnie L. Paulson and Stanley L. Paulson. *Oxford Journal of Legal Studies* 26: 1.

RAWLS, John. 2005. *Political Liberalism*. New York: Columbia University Press.

RAZ, Joseph. 1993. *The Morality of Freedom*. Oxford: Oxford University Press.

RAZ, Joseph. 2004. Incorporation by Law. *Legal Theory* 10: 1.

RIBEIRO, Gonçalo de Almeida. 2013. Judicial Activism Against Austerity in Portugal, *I-CONnect — Blog of the International Journal of Constitutional Law*. URL - http://www.iconnectblog.com/2013/12/judicial-activism-against-austerity-in-portugal/.

RIBEIRO, Gonçalo de Almeida. 2014. O Constitutionalismo dos Princípios. In *O Tribunal Constitutional e a Crise*, ed. Gonçalo de Almeida Ribeiro and Luís Pereira Coutinho. Coimbra: Almedina.

SIECKMANN, Jan-Reinard. 1990. *Regelmodelle und Prinzipienmodelle des Rechtssystems*. Baden-Baden: Nomos.

STEIN, Peter. 1993. Justinian's Compilation: Classical Legacy and Legal Source. *Tulane European & Civil Law Forum* 8: 1.

WALDRON, Jeremy. 1996. Kant's Legal Positivism. *Harvard Law Review* 109: 1535.

WALDRON, Jeremy. 1999. *Law and Disagreement*. Oxford & New York: Oxford University Press.

WALDRON, Jeremy. 2006. The Core of the Case Against Judicial Review. *The Yale Law Journal* 115: 1346.

WEBER, Max. 1978. *On Law in Economy and Society*, translated by Edward Shils & Max Rheinstein. New York: Simon and Schuster.

WEBER, Max. 1991. Politics as a Vocation. In *From Max Weber: Essays in Sociology*, ed. H. H. Gerth & C. Wright Mills. London: Routledge.

WIEACKER, Franz. 1995. *A History of Private Law in Europe, with Particular Reference to Germany*, translated by Tony Weir. Oxford & New York: Oxford University Press.

WOLLHEIM, Richard. 1969. A Paradox in the Theory of Democracy. In *Philosophy, Politics and Society*, ed. in Peter Laslett and W. G. Runciman. Oxford: Basil Blackwell.

ZANDER, Michael. 2004. *The Law-Making Process*. Cambridge: Cambridge University Press.

Chapter 5
Adjudication as Grammatication: The Case of French Judicial Politics

Pierre Legrand

> *Law, says the priest with a priestly look,*
> *Expounding to an unpriestly people,*
> *Law is the words in my priestly book,*
> *Law is my pulpit and my steeple.*
> —Auden (W.H. Auden, "Law Like Love", in *Collected* Poems, ed. by Edward Mendelson (London: Faber and Faber 1976 [1939]): 208).

There is compelling empirical evidence to the effect that over the long term France fashioned legal configurations which at certain junctures supplied important models across Europe and beyond, not least through military conquest or colonization. A mainstay of French legal culture, indeed one of its most famous exports, concerns a singular articulation of adjudication marked by a primordial tension between the *overt* legal/constitutional enframing *of* the judge and the *covert* practical/interpretive performing *by* the judge. In this text, I wish to consider aspects of this entrenched paradox.

Officially, the French judge is bereft of any law-making attribution and wields no political power at all. Not only does Article 5 of the 1804 *Code civil* expressly emphasize this restricted existential condition, but the 1958 Constitution draws a formal distinction between the judiciary which, though mentioned, does not feature as a power (or "*pouvoir*") while the executive and the legislature expressly do.[1] In this regard, the 1958 document follows earlier constitutions which had either expressly confined the judicial role (as in 1791, 1793, 1795, 1814, and 1830) or remained silent on the topic of judges (as in 1852 and 1946). Already, a 1790

[1]In this regard, the French Constitution closely follows Montesquieu who held that the executive and the legislature were the only two powers. Discussing the act of judging and addressing "judicial power" (in his words, "*la puissance de juger*"), he called it "in any way non-existent": Montesquieu, *De l'esprit des lois*, in *Œuvres complètes*, ed. by Roger Caillois, vol. II (Paris: Gallimard, 1951 [1748]), bk XI, ch. 6: 401 ("*en quelque façon nulle*").

P. Legrand (✉)
Ecole de droit de la Sorbonne, 12, place du Panthéon, 75005 Paris, France
e-mail: Pierre_Legrand@orange.fr

L.P. Coutinho et al. (eds.), *Judicial Activism*,
Ius Gentium: Comparative Perspectives on Law and Justice 44,
DOI 10.1007/978-3-319-18549-1_5

post-revolutionary statute had introduced the "legislative reference" ("*référé législatif*") in order to compel judges to solicit a decision from the legislature whenever they believed the interpretation of a statute to be necessary. This procedure, which became increasingly cumbersome over time, lasted well until 1837. But its abolition, though freeing the judiciary from an awkward bureaucratic burden, did not in any way signify a revision of the official understanding of the judge as "the mouthpiece that utters the words of the statute"—which Montesquieu famously defended in his 1748 *De l'esprit des lois*.[2]

The fame of Montesquieu's metaphor notwithstanding, theoretical credentials justifying a reductionist view of adjudication deserve to be attributed in substantial part to Rousseau and to his *Contract social* argument from indivisible sovereignty. For Rousseau, the advocates of separation of powers are not unlike what he calls these "charlatans from Japan" who, he recounts, are said to dismember a child before throwing his limbs up in the air so as to have the child fall back alive and fully assembled.[3] Rousseau scorns political theorists who likewise purport to be able to dismember sovereignty while somehow pretending to preserve its unity. It is not, says Rousseau, that sovereignty features discrete parts, but that it boasts various "emanations".[4] However, state reservation of power from judicial hands is hardly a modern phenomenon as Justinian's Christianization of Roman law fifteen centuries ago well illustrates.

Having had the supreme deity repeatedly vouchsafe for his *Digest*,[5] Justinian also theorized the divine provenance of his own imperial power. It followed from this holy warrant that, in Justinian's own words, "the Emperor shall justly be regarded as the sole maker and interpreter of the laws" ("*tam conditor quam interpres legum solus imperator iuste existimabitur*").[6] And such uncontested imperial preeminence meant that no alternative legal power, whether doctrinal or praetorian, would be countenanced—the terms "interpretations", "perversions",

[2]Montesquieu, *supra*, note 1, bk XI, ch. 6: 404 ("*la bouche qui prononce les paroles de la loi*").

[3]Jean-Jacques Rousseau, *Du contract social*, in *Œuvres complètes*, ed. by Bernard Gagnebin and Marcel Raymond, vol. III (Paris: Gallimard, 1964 [1762]), bk II, ch. 2: 369 ("*charlatans du Japon*").

[4]*Id.*: 370 ("*émanations*").

[5]Thus, Justinian's *De conceptione digestorum*—his instructions to Tribonian, his chief compiler—begins with the famous words "By the authority of God" ("*Deo auctore*"), a phrase which can arguably be offered as an early formulation of the European idea of theocracy: *Deo auctore*, pr. [530]. For a currently authoritative English translation of the *Digest*, see *The Digest of Justinian*, ed. by Theodor Mommsen, Paul Krueger, and Alan Watson, transl. by Alan Watson et al., vol. I (Philadelphia: University of Pennsylvania Press, 1985): xlvi [hereinafter *Digest* (*Watson*)].

[6]*Codex*, 1.14.12.5 [529]. For a published English translation of the *Codex*, see S.P. Scott, *The Civil Law*, vol. XII (Cincinnati: Central Trust, 1932): 89. See also *Novels*, 72, pr. [538], where Justinian mentions "those to whom permission has been given by God to enact laws" ("*eis qui proferendi leges a deo licentiam*"). He adds: "We mean by this him who is invested with sovereignty" ("*dicimus autem de eo qui imperat*"). Justinian is, of course, referring to himself. For a published English translation of the *Novels*, see S.P. Scott, *The Civil Law*, vol. XVI (Cincinnati: Central Trust, 1932): 269.

"confusion", and "discredit" being used by Justinian in his second preface to the *Digest* to cast negative aspersions on all commentative initiatives which he deemed, so to speak *ex ante*, to operate contrapuntally.[7] While he relegated legal scholars to the subordinate role of "priests" of the law ("*sacerdotes*"),[8] he confined the judge to behave as a ventriloquist in as much as he would be acting strictly as the law's "living voice" ("*viva vox*").[9] Only reverential repetitions of the *Digest*—after all, knowledge of the law was "a most hallowed thing" ("*res sanctissima*")[10]—would ensure that "no offense arises through interpretation".[11] Interestingly, nearly six hundred years before the coming into force of the *Digest* as imperial law, Cicero, in his *De legibus*, had already defended the idea that the judge is the voice of the statute, "a speaking law" ("*magistratum esse legem loquentem*").[12]

Montesquieu's relegation of the judge to the role of "mouthpiece" is thus in important respects but an avatar of a Roman understanding of adjudication, itself very much reflecting a biblical attitude towards the text of the law regarded as sacred, which antedates the French Revolution by many centuries.[13] To be sure, the events of 1789 significantly amplified the French distrust of judges on account of the defiant displays of judicial autonomy that had been increasing in the provinces over many centuries and that would now be curbed (hence, for instance, the "legislative reference" I mentioned earlier).[14]

---

[7] *Tanta*, 21 [533]. For these English translations, see *Digest* (*Watson*), *supra*, note 5, vol. I: lxii–lxiii.

[8] *Digest*, 1.1.1. For this English translation, see *Digest* (*Watson*), *supra*, note 5, vol. I: 1.

[9] *Digest*, 1.1.8. For this English translation, see *Digest* (*Watson*), *supra*, note 5, vol. I: 2.

[10] *Digest*, 50.13.5. For this English translation, see *Digest* (*Watson*), *supra*, note 5, vol. IV: 929.

[11] *Deo auctore*, 12. For this English translation, see *Digest* (*Watson*), *supra*, note 5, vol. I: xlix.

[12] *De legibus*, III.1. For this English translation, see Cicero, *The Republic [and] the Laws*, ed. by Jonathan Powell and transl. by Niall Rudd (Oxford: Oxford University Press, 1998 [*c*. 52 BCE]): 150.

[13] In his work, historian Pierre Legendre (the historical garb being one of Legendre's many scholarly guises) probes the profoundly theocratic fabric of French legal culture. In particular, see Pierre Legendre, *L'Amour du censeur*, 2d ed. (Paris: Le Seuil, 2005). See also Peter Goodrich, "Historical Aspects of Legal Interpretation", (1986) 61 *Indiana Law Journal* 331.

[14] In the main, such initiatives took two forms. First, a superior provincial court—then known as a "*parlement*"—could issue decisions that went beyond the specific facts of the case and addressed a problem in general terms. Such judgments, akin to legislative measures, were called "*arrêts de règlement*" (a possible translation would be "regulative judicial decisions"). Secondly, a superior provincial court could refuse to register, and therefore to apply, a royal ordinance which it felt did not conform to existing provincial law. From the XIIIth to the XVIIIth centuries, fourteen superior provincial courts were established which steadfastly imposed themselves as an evermore significant alternative to royal power. In 1790, soon after the Revolution, all judges sitting in these superior provincial courts, who had owned their offices and been regarded as nobility, were replaced by judges named by the state. In this way, revolutionary leaders sought to overcome centrifugal forces and tame arbitrariness.

Law is a profoundly traditionary practice,[15] and in any ascertainable legal culture examples of iterations over the *longue durée* are legion. Yet, it cannot be easy to devise a case of cultural earnestness more firmly embedded in legal history than the French desire to continue to keep the judge firmly bereft of any law-making power. Indeed, it is hard to imagine a more unifying rallying cry in France, whether within the legal community or beyond, than the call against the "*gouvernement des juges*" ("government by judges")—a translinguistic and transcultural transposition (though not an equivalence) of "judicial activism".[16] This expression is said to work as a "*repoussoir absolu*", the word "*repoussoir*" being derived from the verb "*repousser*", which means "to repel" or "to repulse". The idea, then, is that the terms "*gouvernement des juges*" would act to generate "absolute repulsion".[17] Incidentally, the formula "*gouvernement des juges*" itself is not as old as may be assumed since it was devised by Edouard Lambert, a professor of comparative legal studies in Lyon, who used it as the title of his 1921 book on U.S. constitutional adjudication.[18] But Lambert was translating "government by judiciary"—the name of a 1911 article in the *Political Science Quarterly*[19]—and "government by

[15]If scholarly authority be needed, see Martin Krygier, "Law as Tradition", (1986) 5 *Law & Philosophy* 237.

[16]Only the most naive appreciation of translation, whether strictly linguistic or more generally cultural, would indulge the existence of "equivalences". For an extensive theoretical account with specific reference to law, see Simone Glanert, *De la traductibilité du droit* (Paris: Dalloz, 2011). See also *Comparative Law—Engaging Translation*, ed. by Simone Glanert (London: Routledge, 2014). Briefly, the argument against the idea of "equivalence" can be said to run as follows. In order to have an "equivalence", the singularity of each language-term has to be weakened, but cannot be entirely lost: since something must be equivalent to something else, the two terms cannot collapse into unity. However, if the singularity of each language-term continues to obtain, no matter how minimally, there cannot be an equivalence. Differential meaning is therefore a condition of possibility of an equivalence, but at the same time it stands as a prohibition on it.

[17]The expression is on the Wikipedia page devoted to "*Gouvernement des juges*": http://fr.wikipedia.org/wiki/Gouvernement_des_juges. I accessed the site on 19 July 2014 and kept a pdf of the text. For other uses of the word "*repoussoir*", see Séverine Brondel, Norbert Foulquier, and Luc Heuschling, "D'un non-sujet vers un concept scientifique", in *Gouvernement des juges et démocratie*, ed. by Séverine Brondel, Norbert Foulquier, and Luc Heuschling (Paris: Publications de la Sorbonne, 2001): 11; Bastien François, "Pourquoi et comment les juges gouvernent? Prolégomènes problématiques", in *Gouvernement des juges et démocratie*, ed. by Séverine Brondel, Norbert Foulquier, and Luc Heuschling (Paris: Publications de la Sorbonne, 2001): 327. In countries like Austria or Germany, the expression "*Richterstaat*", which is far from being in common use, can be deployed in a laudative sense. A well-known illustration is in René Marcic, *Vom Gesetzesstaat zum Richterstaat* (Vienna: Springer, 1957).

[18]Edouard Lambert, *Le Gouvernement des juges et la lutte contre la législation sociale aux Etats-Unis: l'expérience américaine du contrôle judiciaire de la constitutionnalité* (Paris: Giard, 1921; repr. Dalloz, 2005).

[19]L.B. Boudin, "Government by Judiciary", (1911) 26 *Political Science Quarterly* 238. A Russian-born lawyer and activist in socialist and communist politics, Boudin (1874–1952) was a foremost authority on Marxism and a leading contributor to scholarly journals on Marxist theory. His 1911 article arguing the usurpation of the people's democratic rights by the judiciary led to a book by the same title in the same year and prompted a subsequent two-volume work, again bearing the identical designation, in 1932.

judges"—the title of a 1914 address by Chief Justice Walter Clark.[20] (Perhaps because of my interest in the transnational scene, I find it fascinating that an expression like "*gouvernement des juges*", which has become such a significant cultural marker in France, should have been imported from the common-law world.)

For what anecdotal-empirical evidence is worth, it is clear to me on the basis of the nearly twenty years that I have spent as a postgraduate student or teacher in French law faculties that the currency of Montesquieu's oral metaphor remains unimpeachable in today's France, and that it is in fact unimpeached. Indeed, adjudication, being apprehended along the lines of an evil the necessity of which is only most reluctantly conceded,[21] is openly and incessantly disdained.[22] However, upon a close reading of any judicial decision, it ought to be apparent that, irrespective of all desire and all denial, the French judge wields enormous power, including political power, at the very least in the sense in which judicial decisions reveal discretionary determinations, and therefore inherently value-laden decisions, regarding the regulation or administration of the *polis*—or so I want to claim. Now, the idiosyncratic workings of French adjudication raise, it seems to me, three threshold questions.

First, as a matter of political theory the French concern with "*gouvernement des juges*" can largely be traced to the fact that, in a country where judges are civil servants having graduated soon after the completion of their basic law degree from a school specifically designed for the training of aspiring judges, judicial interventionism of any kind is regarded as profoundly anti-democratic. No French judge is elected or subjected to hearings before elected representatives of the French people. Though a consensual definition of "democracy" seems implausible, in France the idea of the "general will" ("*volonté générale*") as theorized by Rousseau supplies what remains a widely-accepted understanding of the term. According to Rousseau, it is essential that there should not be an alternative

[20]Clark (1846–1924), a Chief Justice of the Supreme Court of North Carolina, argued the unconstitutionality of judicial review as devised by the U.S. Supreme Court in *Marbury* v. *Madison* (1803). For the text of his speech delivered in New York on 27 January 1914, which later made its way into the U.S. Senate papers, see http://famguardian.org/Subjects/LawAndGovt/LegalEthics/govtbyjudges.pdf. I accessed the site on 19 July 2014 and kept a pdf of the text.

[21]Montesquieu expressly uses the words "a necessary evil": *supra*, note 1, bk VI, ch. 1: 308 ("*un mal nécessaire*").

[22]Speaking on "France 2", a French public television network, on Sunday, 7 October 2007 in response to questions from the presenter of "Vivement dimanche prochain", one of France's most popular programmes, President Nicolas Sarkozy, making reference to French "supreme court" (or *Cour de cassation*) judges, called them "peas in a pod" ("*petits pois*")—the idea, it appears, being to underline through this belittling characterization, the matter of judicial indifferentiation, the irrelevance of the judge as individual, and ultimately the insignificance of the act of adjudication. I am certainly not claiming that every analyst in France would subscribe to those specific words, but the very fact that the President of the Republic feels able to express himself in this way before millions of viewers says much about the low regard in which French judges are generally held. No doubt, this fact also reveals something about the French President.

regulatory body—such as the "judicial body" (or "*corps judiciaire*")—operating within the state that would, in the pursuit of an alternative interest, seek to supplant the (democratic) state as a source of law.[23] Such a body would, perforce, prove non democratic. It is not difficult to correlate this distrust of alternative locales of power with the revolutionary ban on corporate bodies (the word "corporate" being understood in the widest terms), which was to find its expression within thirty years of *Du contract social*'s release first in Article 3 of the 1789 *Déclaration des droits de l'homme et du citoyen* to the effect that "no body" ("*nul corps*") can wield an authority "that does not emanate expressly" ("*qui n'[...]émane expressément*") from the state, and then in a famous statute dated 14 August 1791 known as "*loi Le Chapelier*". The French take anti-corporationism very far, so that in contemporary France it continues to be the case that "hatred of the 'corporate spirit' must prevail everywhere".[24] In fact, the matter is primordial: "To fashion society under the shape of the One allows for [...] the expression of difference from the *Ancien régime*".[25] It follows that "the right to the last word" would be denied to the judge in the name of democracy.[26] But it seems relatively easy to reply that in the end, no matter how activist the judge, it is always open to the French legislature to enact a statute nullifying a judicial decision.[27] In other terms, the judge never has the last word, and it therefore becomes difficult to see, as a matter of political theory, how judicial interventions, no matter how bold, can genuinely be regarded as anti-democratic.

If the French problem is that of "*gouvernement des juges*", one must ask—and here is the second issue that I want to address—whether there is, properly speaking, an act of "*gouvernement*" manifesting itself within a given adjudicative configuration. In order to ascertain if there is indeed such an instance of "*gouvernement*" being deployed—which according to French official discourse would make the judgment *ex hypothesi* objectionable—it becomes necessary to consider the semantic extension of the verb "*gouverner*". What must a French judge do to be engaged in what it is to "*gouverner*", so that he can be said to be indulging in what is deemed to be a reprehensible act of "*gouvernement*"? The answer calls for some observations on the question of interpretation.

Arguably, any interpretive situation, as it features ascription of meaning to words, must involve, structurally so to speak, a measure of latitude, of lee-way, of room, of play, which the interpreter cannot but bring to bear on the words awaiting

[23]Rousseau, *supra*, note 3, bk II, ch. 4: 372.

[24]Patrick Savidan, *Le Multiculturalisme*, 2d ed. (Paris: Presses Universitaires de France, 2011): 49 ("*la haine de l''esprit de corporation' [doit] partout prévaloir*").

[25]Pierre Rosanvallon, *Le Modèle politique français* (Paris: Le Seuil, 2004): 28 ("*Figurer la société sous la forme de l'Un permet [...] d'exprimer sa différence avec l'Ancien régime*"). The "One" Rosanvallon has in mind is, of course, the state.

[26]Brondel, Foulquier, and Heuschling, *supra*, note 17: 17 ("*[l]e droit du dernier mot*").

[27]In France, a famous legislative intervention took place in 2002 openly countermanding a 2000 judicial decision that had vindicated a claim for wrongful birth. See Olivier Cayla and Yan Thomas, *Du droit de ne pas naître* (Paris: Gallimard, 2002). Such French legislative reaction to a judgment is not an isolated instance.

interpretation. The alternative would involve regarding words as harbouring meanings that would exist *an sich*, that is, irrespective of time and place and moreover that would impose themselves *an sich*, that is, irrespective of who the interpreter happens to be—a view which the most cursory examination of the matter must regard as unsustainable. Is, then, the practice of interpretation, as the judge inevitably inserts himself within the semantic play that is structurally inherent to any exercise in ascription of meaning to law-texts, an instance of "*gouvernement*"? One could answer affirmatively by claiming that even as he purports to be confining any interference with the text as much as he possibly can, to be deploying but the "[m]eremost minimum" interpretation,[28] the judge is always already partaking of the normative order in as much as, even as he seeks to implement this limited-intrusion policy, he is inescapably involved in the formulation of what will be the applicable law-text.[29] Even assuming that the degree zero of interpretation could somehow be achieved, to not-interpret would still be to interpret in the sense at least that the judge would still be applying the allegedly non interpreted text with a view to the words carrying a certain meaning—an outcome it would be open to him to circumvent through ascription of an alternative meaning, the decision not to avoid a particular semantic result implying at least a tacit endorsement of it and therefore a choice in its favour.

On the question of the assemblage between law-text and judicial interpreter so that the two are ultimately seen to form part of one integrated configuration, a very fruitful line of reasoning, it seems to me, is Peter Sloterdijk's. As the judge transports himself away from himself towards the law-text, as he puts himself outside himself, *hors de lui*, as the law-text becomes the medium of his expansion, he creates a space of co-existence, an interior, a solidarity, a sphere of intimacy embracing the text. In Sloterdijk's language, the judge's exoteric mission resolves itself as "an act of sphere formation".[30] This situation, which has nothing to do with "a merely dominating control by a subject over a manipulable object mass",[31] involves the law-text being ascribed a meaning through a breathing-in of inspiration. There takes place an arousal of the law-text to animated life so that it can be

---

[28]Samuel Beckett, *Worstward Ho*, in *Company/Ill Seen Ill Said/Worstward Ho/Stirrings Still*, ed. by Dirk Van Hulle (London: Faber and Faber, 2009 [1983]): 82.

[29]The interlacing between "interpretation" and "application" is one of the most important themes in Hans-Georg Gadamer, *Truth and Method*, 5th ed., rev'd Eng. transl. by Joel Weinsheimer and Donald G. Marshall (New York: Continuum, 2004 [1986]): 321: "[A]pplication is neither a subsequent nor merely an occasional part of the phenomenon of understanding, but codetermines it as a whole from the beginning" ("*die Anwendung [ist] nicht ein nachträglicher und gelegentlicher Teil des Verstehensphänomens […], sondern [bestimmt] es von vornherein und im ganzen [mit]*"]; p. 385: "[T]he experience of meaning that takes place in understanding always includes application" ("*die Erfahrung von Sinn, der derart im Verstehen geschieht, [schließt] stets Applikation*").

[30]Peter Sloterdijk, *Spheres*, vol. I: *Bubbles*, transl. by Wieland Hoban (Los Angeles: Semiotext(e), 2007 [1998]): 12 ("*eine Sphärenbildung*").

[31]*Id.*: 40 ("*[einer] bloß herrschaftliche[n] Verfügung eines Subjekts über eine manipulierbare Objekt-Masse*").

seen "as a *canal* for breathing by an inspirator".[32] But there is mutuality at work. In other words, "a reciprocal, synchronously interchanging relation between the two breath poles [the breather and the one breathed on] comes into effect as soon as the infusion of the breath of life into the [other] is complete".[33]

In effect, therefore, because the law-text, "a hollow-bodied sculpture awaiting significant further use",[34] "only awakens to its destiny" on account of the judicial attribution of meaning to it,[35] the interpretive process "expresses itself as a correlative duality from the start".[36] It is "a dyadic union from the start, a union that can only last on the basis of a developed bipolarity. The primary pair floats in an atmospheric biunity, mutual referentiality, and intertwined freedom from which neither of the primal partners can be removed without canceling the total relationship".[37] In other words, there exists an entity like the-law-text-and-the-judge, and "[t]he two are bonded by an intimate complicity".[38] Because "there cannot possibly be such a sharp ontological asymmetry between the inspirator and the inspired",[39] it may help to think of "a relationship of pneumatic reciprocity", to envisage a "pneumatic pact".[40]

But this understanding suggests that there would be taking place an act of "*gouvernement*" every single time the merest judicial interpretation materializes. And since the judge is unceasingly interpreting, even when he is approximating something like the degree zero of interpretation, what could he do that would not amount to an act of "*gouvernement*"? Or is it that the judge would have to engage in, say, "heavy" interpretation in order for his intervention to be castigated as "*gouvernement*"? But if a distinction were to become operational between something like "minimal" interpretation—which would not count as an instance of "*gouvernement*"—and other forms of interpretation, a criterion would need to be identified. It quickly becomes awkward to ascertain what such a criterion could be and who would be the arbiter overseeing its deployment. Would commentators such as law professors determine whether a particular interpretation falls on the hither or

[32]*Id.*: 39 ("*[als ein]* Kanal *für Einblasungen durch einen Inspirator*") [emphasis original].

[33]*Id.*: 40 ("*so tritt doch, sobald die Eingießung des Lebensatems in [den Text] vollzogen ist, eine reziproke, synchron hin und her gespannte Beziehung zwischen den beiden Polen der Hauchung [dem Hauchenden und dem Angehauchten] in Funktion*").

[34]*Id.*: 33 ("*eine Hohlkörperplastik, auf die eine signifikante Weiterverwendung wartet*").

[35]*Id.*: 36 ("*zu seiner Bestimmung [...] erwacht*").

[36]*Id.*: 42 ("*bekundet sich von Anfang an als korrelative Zweiheit*").

[37]*Id.*: 42–43 ("*von Anfang an eine dyadische Union, die nur bei entfalteter Zweipoligkeit Bestand hat. Das primäre Paar schwebt in einer atmosphärischen Zweieinigkeit, Aufeinanderbezogenheit und Ineinandergelöstheit, von der sich keiner der Urpartner abtrennen läßt, ohne das Gesamtverhältnis aufzuheben*").

[38]*Id.*: 44 ("*Zwischen beiden herrscht eine intime Komplizenschaft*").

[39]*Id.*: 40 ("*zwischen dem Inspirator und dem Inspirierten [kann] unmöglich ein so scharfes ontologisches Gefälle herrschen*").

[40]*Id.*: 41 and 44, respectively ("*ein Verhältnis pneumatischer Gegenseitigkeit*"/"*pneumatische[r] Pak[t)]*").

tither side of "*gouvernement*"? As rapidly becomes apparent, one is back to the matter of interpretive latitude as one encounters the age-old infinite-regress problem (while a commentator interpretively pronounces on whether a given instance of adjudication counts as "*gouvernement*", a second commentator will interpretively pronounce on the first commentator's interpretive pronouncement while a third commentator will interpretively pronounce on the second commentator's interpretive pronouncement while …, and so on and so forth).

I claim that it is much more reasonable to accept that whenever a judge undertakes to interpret a law-text, which must be done for all intents and purposes every time there is a case of adjudication, he is in effect engaging in an act of "*gouvernement*", no matter how seemingly innocuous. It is a matter of *inherence*. In other words, the reading and application of law-texts is inherent to adjudication; interpretation is inherent to the reading and application of law-texts; decision or choice is inherent to interpretation; and in the specific context of adjudication where judgments have an inherent impact on the regulation or administration of the *polis*, decision or choice means there is "*gouvernement*". That the act of "*gouverner*" should be inherent to adjudication is emphatically not to say that judges can do whatever they want. To take a silly example, it is hard to imagine a judge who would adjudicate on a medical liability case by drawing on a statute governing shareholders' rights. Adjudication, no matter how daring, remains framed on account of the legal materials before the court: the judge must work with the law-texts at hand, which he cannot transgress.[41] Adjudication is also constrained, though less visibly, through an assemblage of strictures such as the exercise of self-control by the judge on account of a concern for one's reputation or for the judicial institution's credibility (or, ultimately, for fear of disciplinary sanctions); the demands of collegiality; and the stock of available arguments deemed persuasive within the legal community.[42] What French official discourse therefore contests as it opposes "*gouvernement des juges*" is a feature of the act of adjudication that is inherent to it, structurally so. Even as it is systematically stigmatized, "*gouvernement des juges*" is inevitably happening every time a judge decides on a case.

In effect, what French official discourse would want to efface is therefore the very idea of adjudication. And there is indeed a long tradition, conventionally known as "*mos geometricus*" (or "geometrical wont"),[43] that has been aiming for the mathematization of the law so that all adjudication would become superfluous. Jean Domat (1625–1696), a scholarly figure who continues to be regarded as one of France's most distinguished lawyers—every French jurist today would be "a child

[41]"[T]he reading […] cannot legitimately transgress the text toward something other than itself": Jacques Derrida, *De la grammatologie* (Paris: Editions de Minuit, 1967): 227 ("*[la lecture] ne peut légitimement transgresser le texte vers autre chose que lui*").

[42]For a detailed analysis of the various constraints impacting on judicial behaviour in the United States, see Richard A. Posner, *How Judges Think* (Cambridge, MA: Harvard University Press, 2010): 125–268.

[43]For a useful account, see James Gordley, *The Jurists* (Oxford: Oxford University Press, 2013): 165–94.

of Domat"[44]—was adamant that law must aim to be as geometry.[45] While intellectual influences over Domat ranged from Ramus (1515–1572) to his close friend Pascal (1623–1662), it is arguably Descartes (1596–1650) who exercised the greatest philosophical ascendancy. Perhaps one can begin with a few of Descartes's choice metaphors as he repeatedly sought to inscribe his radical lack of faith in man's epistemological processes. In the *Discours de la méthode*, Descartes thus talks about razing buildings to their foundations.[46] Elsewhere, he mentions wiping bad paintings clean.[47] In yet another text, he suggests emptying the whole basket of apples.[48] As two of Descartes's best-known and most authoritative commentators observe, Descartes's method emphatically illustrates a "general mathematicization of reality",[49] "a grasp at once mathematical and technical of reality".[50] Descartes's theory, "named *mathesis universalis*" in one of his posthumously released texts,[51] left one in no doubt that for him mathematics reigned supreme on account of the

[44]The quotation is from Laurent Aynes, Pierre-Yves Gautier, and François Terré, "Antithèse de 'l'entité'", D.1997.Chron.229: 230.

[45]For samples of Domat's statements on "law-as-geometry", see Jean Domat, *Les Quatre livres du droit public* (Caen: Université de Caen, 1989 [1697]), bk I, tit. XVII: 307; Jean Domat, *Les Loix civiles dans leur ordre naturel* (Paris, 1689), "préface" ("foreword"). On Domat's mathematics, see André-Jean Arnaud, *Les Origines doctrinales du code civil français* (Paris: LGDJ, 1969): 142–47. Later, Chancellor d'Aguesseau (1668–1751) would say of Domat that "according to the method of the geometers after which this author had trained himself, he first formulated rules and something like general axioms that influence all the parts of the law": D'Aguesseau, "Première instruction [à son fils aîné sur les études propres à former un magistrat]", in *Œuvres de M. le chancelier d'Aguesseau*, vol. I (Paris: Les Libraires associés, 1759 [1716]): 274 ("*suivant la méthode des Géometres sur laquelle cet Auteur s'étoit formé, [il] établit d'abord des regles & comme des axiomes généraux qui influent sur toutes les parties de la Jurisprudence*"). For an interesting discussion of Domat's adhesion to mathematization as a response to what he perceived to be the demands of his Christian faith, see Marie-France Renoux-Zagamé, *Du droit de Dieu au droit de l'homme* (Paris: Presses Universitaires de France, 2003): 83. On the relationship between geometry and religion, see generally Robert Lawlor, *Sacred Geometry* (London: Thames and Hudson, 1982).

[46]Descartes, *Discours de la méthode*, in *Œuvres philosophiques*, ed. by Ferdinand Alquié, vol. I (Paris: Garnier, 1997 [1637]), II: 581 (hereinafter *Discours*).

[47]Descartes, *La Recherche de la vérité par la lumière naturelle*, in *Œuvres philosophiques*, ed. by Ferdinand Alquié, vol. II (Paris: Garnier, 1999 [1701]): 1116.

[48]Descartes, *Septièmes réponses*, in *Œuvres philosophiques*, ed. by Ferdinand Alquié, vol. II (Paris: Garnier, 1999 [1647]): 982.

[49]Alexis Philonenko, *Relire Descartes* (Paris: Grancher, 1994): 120 ("*mathématisation générale du réel*").

[50]Ferdinand Alquié, *Leçons sur Descartes* (Paris: La Table ronde, 1955): 81 ("*une saisie à la fois mathématique et technique du réel*").

[51]Descartes, *Regulae ad directionem ingenii*, in *Œuvres de Descartes*, 2d ed. by Charles Adam and Paul Tannery, vol. X (Paris: Vrin, 1986 [1628]): 378 ("*Mathesim universalem nominari*"). Descartes never finished his text which was published in its incomplete state in 1701, more than fifty years after his death. On Descartes and *mathesis universalis*, see Gilles Olivo, *Descartes et l'essence de la vérité* (Paris: Presses Universitaires de France, 2005): 72–80. For a detailed exploration of "*mathesis universalis*" (a notion that long precedes Descartes), see David Rabouin, Mathesis Universalis (Paris: Presses Universitaires de France, 2009).

reliability it could offer: "Whether I stay awake or I sleep, two and three put together will always give the number five and the square will never have more than four sides".[52] Accordingly, Descartes's goal was unabashedly to philosophize like a geometer, specifically, to formulate the "long chains of all simple and easy reasons that geometers are in the habit of using in order to achieve their most difficult demonstrations".[53] For his part, Spinoza (1632–1677) went so far as to geometrize ethics in his posthumously released *Ethica, Ordine Geometrico demonstrata* (or *Ethics, Demonstrated in Geometrical Order*). Domat would also have found guidance in the work of some notable jurists who came before him. Thus, François Le Douaren (1509–1559) was one of many French law professors who held that "the elements of law, the bases of its maxims and of its fundamental problems are like the points, the lines, and the surfaces in geometry".[54]

No doubt on account of the law's deeply traditionary character—French legal culture's staunch commitment to formalism demonstrably showing France's law-world to be, on the whole, even more traditional than would be the case in many other places[55]—precisely the same craving for mathematization appears in a late-twentieth-century French introduction to legal methodology where the author claims that "ideally, *of course*, the solution to any litigation would be mathematically deduced from clearly defined legal rules".[56] To be sure, the tropism towards mathematization can express itself in more subtle fashion. Christian Atias, a leading French scholar, thus writes that "[t]he judge is there to ascertain the right answer and to impose it".[57] The author's verb to designate the basic task he assigns to the judge is "*retrouver*", which translates awkwardly into English on account of a range of senses it may carry. But whatever meaning one wishes to ascribe to the French verb, it subordinates the judge to an act of discovery or identification of "the right answer" and denies any judicial initiative or creativity in the production of it—a process immediately evocative of the resolution of mathematical problems.[58]

[52]Descartes, *Première méditation*, in *Œuvres philosophiques*, ed. by Ferdinand Alquié, vol. II (Paris: Garnier, 1999 [1641]): 408 ("*Car, soit que je veille ou que je dorme, deux et trois joints ensemble formeront toujours le nombre de cinq, et le carré n'aura jamais plus de quatre côtés*").

[53]Descartes, *Discours*, *supra*, note 46, II: 587 ("*longues chaînes de raisons, toutes simples et faciles, dont les géomètres ont coutume de se servir, pour parvenir à leurs plus difficiles démonstrations*").

[54]François Le Douaren, *In primam partem Pandectarum, sive Digestorum, methodica enarratio*, in *Opera omnia*, vol. I (Lucca, 1765 [1561]): 3.

[55]I am fully confident that I could persuasively marshall any number of indicators to substantiate this claim. Suffice it to mention the persistent and pervasive ascendancy of formalism, which one illustration can establish. I refer to Appendix I.

[56]E.S. de la Marnierre, *Eléments de méthodologie juridique* (Paris: Librairie du Journal des notaires et des avocats, 1976), no. 91: 193-94 (emphasis supplied).

[57]Christian Atias, *Devenir juriste* (Paris: LexisNexis, 2011): 3 ("*Le juge est là pour retrouver la bonne réponse et pour l'imposer*").

[58]Perhaps it bears adding that this formalistic thesis has nothing to do with Ronald Dworkin's argument by the same designation which is to the effect that there exists objective moral truth.

In France, the commitment to the mathematization of law must be seen as one instantiation amongst many of the larger argument to the effect that law is a scientific configuration and that the study of law is a scientific pursuit. The list of quotations from French legal scholars in support of the idea that law exists as science and legal scholarship as a scientific venture is literally endless, and I have to limit myself to three brief statements which I regard as epistemologically significant in as much as they display the *obviousness* of French law and of French legal scholarship's scientificity for French jurists.[59] According to Jean-Louis Bergel, "[l] aw is uncontrovertibly a science",[60] and leading French theoretician André-Jean Arnaud observes that "[t]he assertion of the scientificity of [l]aw [...] has become a truism".[61] Unsurprisingly, perhaps, it has been said that "one will not dwell on a refutation [of the claim against scientificity], since it is so convenient to show that the approach of the jurist is scientific at every step of the way".[62]

While French arguments for the mathematization or scientificization of law correlate closely with the refusal of any law-making power to the judge in as much as they deploy at once a remorseless desubjectivization and a relentless depoliticization of the act of adjudication, there is another way for legal analysts to parry "*gouvernement des juges*", and it is to deny, not that there is "*gouvernement*" (this is the question that I just addressed as my second theme), but that there is a "*juge*". The claim that the adjudicator is not a "*juge*" takes me to the third of the three issues I want to raise.

It is Hans Kelsen who makes what has become a famous claim to the effect that when a court annuls a statute—which is arguably the most consequential act of judicial "*gouvernement*" possible—what is taking place is not the work of a "*juge*", but of a second legislator, albeit a "negative legislator".[63] Now, when the act of judicial "*gouvernement*" unfolds in plain view, so to speak, and when French jurists are content to engage in a Kelsenian pirouette with a view to arguing that, well, "a government by judges remains something conceptually impossible",[64] I submit that one is either pushing formalism beyond any plausible configuration or else must be

[59]For a more detailed examination from a comparative standpoint, see Pierre Legrand and Geoffrey Samuel, "Brèves épistémologiques sur le droit anglais tel qu'en lui-même", (2005/54) *Revue interdisciplinaire d'études juridiques* 1.

[60]Jean-Louis Bergel, *Méthodologie juridique* (Paris: Presses Universitaires de France, 2001): 34 ("*le droit est incontestablement une science*").

[61]André-Jean Arnaud, *Les Juristes face à la société* (Paris: Presses Universitaires de France, 1975): 195 ("*[l]'affirmation de la scientificité du Droit [...] est devenue un poncif*") (emphasis omitted).

[62]Henri Roland and Laurent Boyer, *Introduction au droit* (Paris: Litec, 2002), no. 284: 109 ("*on ne s'attardera pas [...] à la réfutation, tant il est commode de montrer que la démarche du juriste est scientifique à chacune des étapes de son activité*").

[63]Hans Kelsen, "La garantie juridictionnelle de la constitution (La justice constitutionnelle)", (1928) *Revue du droit public et de la science politique* 197: 226 ("*législateur négatif*").

[64]Otto Pfersmann, "Existe-t-il un concept de gouvernement des juges?", in *Gouvernement des juges et démocratie*, ed. by Séverine Brondel, Norbert Foulquier, and Luc Heuschling (Paris: Publications de la Sorbonne, 2001): 49 ("*un gouvernement des juges demeure quelque chose de conceptuellement impossible*").

said to be navigating perilously close to the shoals of "bad faith" (I use the expression roughly in Duncan Kennedy's sense to refer to a situation where one is openly making an assertion while at once denying the claim to oneself).[65]

To summarize, I argue that no matter how unpleasant to the French, the fact is that adjudication is inherent governance, if only on account of a necessary moment of undecidability, an instance of instability preceding the making of any judgment. Formalist circumventions that persist in denying the judge's agency ring hollow—as does the claim that judicial governance would be undemocratic, as long as it is open to the legislature to cancel a judgment. To say, as I do, that adjudication is legal governance, that it is political governance also, is not to defend the view that adjudication is only politics or that adjudication and politics are interchangeable or that judicial governance is not different in significant ways (including discursive ways) from other types of governance. And it is not to say either that it is a good thing that the political be present within adjudication. Rather, I reject the implausible assumption that adjudication French style can be neatly delineated from political determination, which means that I refute the idea that there could be a judicial decision that would be purely a matter of law (though I find it impossible to understand what "pure law" indicates, I think it gestures towards strictly conceptual and systemic outcomes that would somehow be sealed from any infiltration by the political and therefore prove value-neutral). If you will, within adjudication I claim the absence of an ascertainable border between law and politics, *even in France*.

Ultimately, then, French judges are to be seen as fully-fledged political agents—though in France it remains *sacrilegious* to say so. I use the word "sacrilegious" advisedly given that the outrage being perpetrated is against a *theological* order, that is, a system which seeks, through primary texts, hierarchically to map and control an epistemological space by instituting in censorial fashion the authoritarian motifs of reverence and repetition. To be sure, the "religious" is not located in the contents of the primary texts themselves. However, it is very much to be found in the material conditions of the primary texts' enunciation, in the forms in which these texts are communicated and applied through a structured relation which purports to link ("*religare*") law-giver to law-receiver—the unique and authoritative, and uniquely authoritative, sender standing above the plurality of subordinated recipients. To this day, in France, the exegetical and hermeneutic traditions of legal interpretation as religious interpretation, survive, live on—and are meant to survive, to live on—so as to support the persistent status of law as definite written text, as univocal inscription of a sovereign will. Accordingly, it is properly sacrilegious to suggest that judges are in effect subverting the biblical attitude that they are supposed to uphold, and that there is anything in effect existent as a matter of adjudication that would look like a "*gouvernement des juges*".

While judicial legal/political power is deployed on a daily basis from Calais to Arles and from Biarritz to Strasbourg, it manifests itself covertly. Instead of the

[65]See Duncan Kennedy, *A Critique of Adjudication* (Cambridge, MA: Harvard University Press, 1999): 23–38.

spectacular policy statements associated with adjudication practice in the common-law world, French judicial law-making occurs most significantly under the guise of what I shall style "grammatical" interventions. There is at work a grammatical logic, a *grammatology*.[66]

The deeply-ingrained French unwillingness to countenance "*gouvernement des juges*", that is, judicial activism, is everywhere visible. Consider a typical French "supreme court" (or *Cour de cassation*) decision as printed in the official law reports. Most strikingly, it is short, sometimes as short as three paragraphs only. From a common-law standpoint, a French judgment is in fact *shockingly* short. There is just enough institutional room to allow for a brief statement of the material facts and of the ground for appeal (which are both lifted from the record), to permit a mention of the relevant legislative text, and to register in the most formulaic terms what is offered as the syllogistic application of the statute to the case. This discursive strait jacket, which leaves the judgment bereft of any expression of even the merest policy consideration, purports to avoid any personalization of the opinion and by extension to obviate any personalization of the law and ultimately any self-fashioning of the law, that is, any appearance of any fabrication of the law.

On the subject of the institutional structures built into the judicial system so as to foster a brand of adjudication that would seem to be hovering around the degree zero of judicial activism, one could also mention the anonymity of every court opinion (the reader never knows who authored the judgment) and the impossibility of a dissent. Through such commitment to the bureaucratization of adjudication, on account of an "administrative conception" of the judge (think of the way in which one's entitlement to a social security card ought not to be allowed to vary depending on who happens to be the clerk staffing the desk on any given day),[67] the proclaimed official view is that, both descriptively and prescriptively, the individual person of the judge ought not to matter in the least, that judges ought to be perfectly interchangeable.[68] In the words of Pierre Legendre, "the personality of the judge is supposed not to count and Justice descends from Heaven".[69] The postulate about the irrelevance of any particular judge connects with an appreciation of the law as being in the process of working itself scientific, as being on the way to achieving logical self-evidence, not unlike mathematics.

Imagine a case having to do with an entitlement to damages for breach of contract. Addressing a law of contract deemed to be scientifically, mathematically foreordained (have scholars not been hard at work over a very long time through the writing of countless textbooks and monographs, dissertations and articles?), the

---

[66]It is no doubt unnecessary to trace the currency of this word to Derrida, *supra*, note 41.

[67]Pierre Legendre, "Qui dit légiste, dit loi et pouvoir", (1995/32) *Politix* 23: 31 ("*conception administrative*").

[68]In the words of leading political scientist Lucien Jaume, "[i]t is very difficult and socially risky, in France, to speak in one's own name": Lucien Jaume, *L'Individu effacé* (Paris: Fayard, 1997): 456 ("*Il est très difficile, et socialement risqué, en France, de parler en son nom propre*").

[69]Pierre Legendre, *Trésor historique de l'Etat en France* (Paris: Fayard, 1992): 247 ("*La personnalité du juge est censée ne pas compter et la Justice descend du ciel*").

judge, whoever the individual happens to be, is meant to slot the material, pre-existing facts in the proper, pre-existing law-box so as to generate the irresistible outcome. Given the scientific or mathematical inevitability of the operation, any argument or discussion becomes pointless—hence 350-word judgments. After all, what is there to argue or discuss in the face of scientific, mathematical evidence? The brevity of the judgment purporting to confer upon it the air of sententiousness befitting an objective ascertainment of what would be the semantic truth of the matter, one is reminded of Descartes who, in a 1640 letter, held that "our mind is of such a nature that it cannot help assenting to what it clearly conceives".[70]

A decision such as the French "supreme court"'s (or *Cour de cassation*'s) opinion of 17 December 1997 pronouncing on whether a tenant's homosexual partner is legally entitled to remain on the rented premises after the tenant's death provides a typical illustration of the way in which the French judge engages in governance or activism under cover of what would appear to be the strategy least suggestive of any effective governance or activism.[71] What, indeed, could be more seemingly innocuous than a grammatical discussion, a "grammatication"? As one reads a French "supreme court" (or *Cour de cassation*) decision, it shows itself typically to be about the composition of law-texts—with a focus on clauses, phrases, and words—or, more abstractly, about the composition of the conceptual legal system—with a predilection for qualifications, categories, and distinctions. In the 17 December 1997 case, the court would have its readers believe that the issue is exclusively about "the" meaning of the word "*concubin*" which, it says, can *only* refer to a relationship involving a male and a female. As any good French dictionary will show, however, the etymology of the word "*concubin*" ("*concumbere*", "to sleep with") reveals that it can refer to any person having regular sexual intercourse with any other person irrespective of the sex of the partners. As it substitutes its preferred, reductive interpretation for the word's acknowledged broader meaning, the court is engaging in a grammatical motion which is effectively a deed of legal/political governance, an instance of judicial activism. As the court pronounces on the semantic extension of a definition or delineates the limits of a category, as it makes decisions objecting to any idea of semantic heterogeneity in

---

[70]Descartes, [Letter to Regius], in *Œuvres de Descartes*, 2d ed. by Charles Adam and Paul Tannery, vol. III (Paris: Vrin, 1988 [24 May 1640]): 64 ("*mens nostra est talis naturae, ut non possit clare intellectis non assentiri*").

[71]I refer to Appendices II and III where this decision appears both in the original French and in my English translation. The judgment is the work of the French "supreme court" as regards matters falling within "private law" (or *Cour de cassation*) as this category is understood in France. In particular, the opinion is by the Third Civil Chamber ("*Troisième chambre civile*") specializing in real estate law. Note that in terms of the posited law, this judgment has been superseded by Article 515-8 of the *Code civil* which came into force on 1 January 1989 and states that "[c]oncubinage is a de facto relationship, characterized by a cohabitation presenting a character of stability and of continuity, between two persons, of different sex or of the same sex, who live as a couple" ("*Le concubinage est une union de fait, caractérisée par une vie commune présentant un caractère de stabilité et de continuité, entre deux personnes, de sexe différent ou de même sexe, qui vivent en couple*").

pursuit of fixation of meaning, there takes place, on each occasion, not only an exercise in lexical control but also a discretionary—and therefore a partisan—determination regarding the regulation or administration of society, of the *polis*: "The law becomes a sort of reality imposed upon the social data, shaping it, and in short becoming in the end more 'real' than the facts".[72] In other words, judicial grammatology is judicial governance or judicial activism—no matter how much the institutions of French law (and the desire of French lawyers and of French society at large) aim to deny it. Emphasizing what judges would most willingly not deny doing—grammatication—I contend that the provision of "grammatical" solutions registers as governance or activism, that it therefore counts as a politics.

Fascinatingly, even as the court issues its decision, it acts so that its judgment refuses to locate itself in a fully autonomous analytical space. As one considers the opinion one can see that the key wording is framed in apodictic language very much in the way one expects a statute to operate. In other words, the court is content to claim that it is offering a reprise or a restitution of the statute (it will tell the legal community *the* meaning of the statute) and certainly not an interpretation of it, which would be tantamount to proclaiming judicial independence from it through the adoption of some meta-language. In the way it writes *ex auctoritate*, the court very much wants to behave, and to be seen to behave, like the legislator instead of suggesting itself as the author of an independent speech. Even as it effectively dilutes the distinction between *interpretandum* and *interpretans* (as befits interpretation), the court continues to act as if the statute was intangible and as if it deemed it to be such. Effectively, though, the judicial decision will graft itself to the statute so that the statute will no longer be able to signify without it. The selfhood of the statute will henceforth consist in part of the otherness of the judgment.

The French judicial system, as it is structured, as it is said officially to work, as it is practiced, as it is taught in law faculties, as it is oh so relentlessly defended by French legal actors and within French society at large,[73] offers a striking illustration of institutional bad faith in as much as the massive smoke-screen that has been draped over French courts and French judges simply cannot hide the fact that in every single case—of which the "supreme court" (or *Cour de cassation*) alone hears approximately 30,000 each year—in every single case, then, the French judge engages in an act of legal/political governance, of judicial activism—that is, he does precisely what he is officially claimed not to be doing, what he is said not to be

[72]Jacques Ellul, *Histoire des institutions*, 9th ed., vol. III (Paris: Presses Universitaires de France, 1982): 27 ("*Le droit devient une sorte de réalité imposée au donné social, le mettant en forme, et finissant en somme par devenir plus 'vrai' que les faits*").

[73]In France, teaching and scholarship are largely reduced to the exposition of the state's laws in "connivence" with the state itself: Philippe Jestaz and Christophe Jamin, "L'entité doctrinale française", D.1997.Chron.167: 172 ("*connivence*"). To my knowledge, such a critique of French legal academia by two prominent French legal scholars—what by the light of local standards of obsequious collegiality would have been perceived as a vitriolic attack—remains well-nigh unique. It is, in fact, so inhabitual that even these academics' subsequent publications fail to sustain it.

allowed to be doing, and what he is desired not to be doing. If it were a matter of a sentence to say, then, I would claim that in the way in which it is structured with a view to promoting a certain set of beliefs about the passivity of the French judge, and given the manner in which these beliefs are obediently disseminated by legal agents, the French institutional system tells a resounding lie. The empirical fact is that the French judge is not passive but active, that he is politically active also, every word of the way—all strategies of dissimulation notwithstanding.

Appendix I

French Legal Culture and the Preponderance of Formalism

I must begin with a few words about what the French know as the "*concours d'agrégation*" ("the aggregation competition"). A mid-nineteenth-century institution, the "*agrégation*" (the Latin source means "herd" or "flock" as in "gregarious") is relentlessly—and unquestioningly—promoted in France as the "incarnation of the egalitarian ideal"; specifically, "[t]he *concours d'agrégation* uproots candidates from what is vaguely felt as evil (the provinces, the land, the local particularisms) to transform them completely into missionaries of the public spirit and of the state".[74] In law, the two major "*concours*" concern private law ("*droit privé*"), held every other year, and public law ("*droit public*"), conducted on a quadrennial basis (incidentally, such structure assumes an evident and meaningful distinction between the two spheres). For each "*concours*", the jury consists of a president directly appointed by the state, who selects six fellow jurors (who must be confirmed by the state). A "*concours*" spans an entire academic year during which each of the candidates, barring elimination along the way, undergoes four examinations, all of them oral. At the end of the year, a ranking of successful candidates is issued. A characteristic feature of a "*concours*" is that the list of successful candidates is made to match exactly the number of vacant posts. If, in response to the many requests submitted by the various French law schools, the state has authorized thirty professorships in private law to be opened in a given academic year, the relevant "*concours*" will generate thirty successful candidates exactly, ranked (publicly) from one to thirty. In the order of their rank, the new "*agrégés*" ("aggregated individuals")—those who, literally, are joining the herd or flock—then proceed to select the law school where they want to teach. Importantly, the law schools themselves have no say whatsoever in the selection of posts by *agrégés*, the controlling idea being, again, to avoid localism. As often as not, the last-ranking candidate will inherit a post in one of the universities located in France's overseas departments, such as La Réunion (*Université de la Réunion*) or the French West

[74]Vincent Descombes, *Le Même et l'autre* (Paris: Editions de Minuit, 1979): 16 ("*incarnation de l'idéal égalitaire*"/"*le concours d'agrégation arrache les candidats à ce qui est vaguement ressenti comme le mal (les provinces, les terroirs, les particularismes locaux) pour les métamorphoser en missionnaires de l'esprit public et de l'Etat*").

Indies and French Guiana (*Université des Antilles et de la Guyane*). On account of state regulations, it is impossible to move from one's chosen post, except with special permission, for an initial period of three years. Being a public servant, each "*agrégé*", now a "*professeur des universités*" ("professor in the universities"), can decide to occupy the chosen professorship until retirement. Very many do.

Allowing for the fact that exemplarity is never simple in as much as it entails its elisions, its conflations, that is, its folds—the case of Julie Klein, who placed first in the 2011 "*agrégation*" in private law, is instructive in a number of respects. Before all else, one must be clear that in France to rank first at the "*agrégation*" is a most signal honour that attaches to one for the entire duration of one's career. In a country where there is no tradition of prestigious scholarships, this distinction is, in effect, the greatest badge of recognition available to a young academic. Now, amongst the many signals it sends, the conferment of the first rank at the "*agrégation*" acts as a heightened form of institutional validation of the candidate's (necessarily anterior) doctoral dissertation. In fact, the doctorate is very much the exclusive or near-exclusive focus of the first "*agrégation*" examination. While this examination bears on all of the candidate's written work, it is unlikely that anyone will have written anything apart from a doctorate, except perhaps one or two case-notes, if only because French law professors actively discourage early publication. For various reasons revolving around the perceived inadequacy of the doctoral dissertations under consideration, a substantial number of candidates fail at this preliminary stage. To be sure, the candidate who will, in time, be ranked first by the jury will have had to offer not only what counts in the eyes of the jurors as an excellent doctoral dissertation, but will also have had to deliver superior performances in the other three "*agrégation*" examinations. Yet, it remains fair to say that no one can conceivably rank first at the "*agrégation*" without the jury deeming the candidate's doctorate to be excellent. In other words, Klein's doctorate, given the official recognition that she earned at the "*agrégation*", offers a compelling indicator of what the French academic establishment values as a noteworthy exercise in the construction of legal knowledge and, indeed, as meritorious legal scholarship. As I shall argue presently, this doctorate also attests to French academia's unstinting commitment to unalloyed formalism.

Klein's 644-page typewritten dissertation, which she wrote at a leading Paris law school and defended in May 2010, is entitled, *Le Point de départ de la prescription*, or "The Starting-Point of Limitation Periods". As befits French legal scholarship, the argument is divided into two parts. These are respectively entitled, "*Le constat du désordre*", or "Attesting to Disorder", and "*La mise en ordre*", or "Putting Into Order". In a legal culture where formal aesthetics is most highly valued, neither the semantic contrapunct nor the assonance are accidental. The first part of the dissertation offers a detailed inventory of the various points of departure of the different limitation periods to be found in French private law and is supplemented by a fifteen-page chart tabulating this data; the second part aims at a rationalization of the author's findings. In this regard, Klein adopts what she styles a "functional" approach, which prompts her to reject the idea of a unitary function or goal that would characterize all limitation periods under scrutiny. Rather, she asserts that one must accept that different limitation periods fulfil different functions. Klein then articulates those functions under two headings according to whether they are common to all limitation periods or specific to given limitation periods (pp. 507–581 and 475–505, respectively). She identifies three instances—the question of statutory warranties; the matter of professional liability; and the cases having to do with the avoidance of the debtor's ruin—where the limitation period's function can properly be said to be specific. Her conclusions, which are summarized over three-quarters of a page in the epigrammatic mode typical of the peremptory and formulaic French civil code, are meant to operate *de lege ferenda*. They enunciate a general proposition to the effect that the limitation period would start to run "from the origin of the right to sue" (p. 589: "*à compter de la naissance du droit d'agir*"). This statement is followed by three further provisions that would govern the three exceptions mentioned previously with respect to which three specific criteria would obtain.

Apart from an early literary allusion to Flaubert and a perfunctory nod to Henri Bergson's work on time (though it fails to earn a quotation)—two French, established, "safe" figures—the dissertation does not include any source material from any discipline other than law (as traditionally understood in France). Just as typically, the text does not, if one excepts half a dozen cursory references or so, purport to address any law other than French law. Some of the rare mentions of foreign law are strikingly outdated, not to say embarrassingly ill-informed, as when a French comparatist writing in 1970 is quoted as saying that "for the English, the law consists […] essentially of rules of procedure" (p. 461, not. 2: "*pour un Anglais le droit consiste […] essentiellement en des règles de procédure*"). (The fact that such a reductive assertion would not alarm Klein's supervisor says much concerning the knowledge that circulates about foreign law within French law schools, on the one hand, and reveals the utter lack of interest in the matter shown by French law professors, on the other. Indeed, after fifteen years of teaching "comparative law" in Paris, I have come to the firm conclusion that the local significance of this undertaking ranks on a par with what I can imagine to be the relevance of the teaching of "The Thought of Simone de Beauvoir" in Khartoum or of "Oceanography" in La Paz.)

In sum, Klein's doctoral dissertation is thoroughly "French legal", that is, it is informed by an abiding respect for the clear semiotic boundaries assumed to be afforded by disciplinary palisades, a deep concern for the kind of doctrinal exposition that allows her to remain homogeneous with the existing discursive hegemon through the re-organization of extant information into new forms located well within the doctrinal box, and a keen preoccupation with systematic integrity and logical rectitude. Having mortgaged her thesis, in the names of certainty and predictability, to the ideas of conceptual amelioration and formalist reconciliation, Klein externalizes all other discourses, whether originating from other fields or other laws. Meanwhile, her text is profoundly animated by a formalistic epistemological drive as revealed by her relentless desire for enhanced terminological clarity, improved logical consistency, and reinforced systematic coherence—that is, for optimized formalization of the law. It is precisely that effort that the 2011 "*jury d'agrégation*" in private law proceeded to reward in such compelling terms thus reminding observers of what matters as a matter of French law.

Appendix II

Cour de cassation
Chambre civile 3
Audience publique du mercredi 17 décembre 1997
N° de pourvoi: 95-20779
Publié au Bulletin **Rejet.**

Président: M. Beauvois, président
Rapporteur: M. Toitot, conseiller rapporteur
Avocat général: M. Weber, avocat général
Avocats: la SCP Waquet, Farge et Hazan

Texte intégral
REPUBLIQUE FRANCAISE
AU NOM DU PEUPLE FRANCAIS

Sur le moyen unique

Attendu, selon l'arrêt attaqué (Paris, 22 mars 1995), que Mme Z… a donné un appartement à bail à M. X…; qu'après le décès du locataire, son ami, M. Y…, qui vivait avec lui et était demeuré dans les lieux, a assigné la bailleresse en transfert du bail à son profit;

Attendu que M. Y… fait grief à l'arrêt de le débouter de sa demande, alors, selon le moyen, qu'aux termes de l'article 26 du Pacte international relatif aux droits civils et politiques, publié par décret n° 81-76 du 29 janvier 1981, la loi doit interdire toute discrimination et garantir à toutes les personnes une protection égale et efficace contre toute discrimination, notamment de race, de couleur, de sexe,… ou de toute autre situation; qu'en estimant que l'article 14 de la loi du 6 juillet 1989, qui dispose que « lors du décès du locataire, le contrat de location est transféré (…) au concubin notoire (…) qui vivait avec lui depuis au moins 1 an à la date du décès », ne visait que le cas de concubinage entre un homme et une femme, alors que ce texte ne contient aucune restriction autre que celle tenant à la durée du concubinage, la cour d'appel a violé les textes précités, ensemble l'article 8, alinéa 1er, de la Convention européenne de sauvegarde des droits de l'homme et des libertés fondamentales;

Mais attendu qu'ayant retenu, à bon droit, que le concubinage ne pouvait résulter que d'une relation stable et continue ayant l'apparence du mariage, donc entre un homme et une femme, la cour d'appel n'a violé ni l'article 26 du Pacte international relatif aux droits civils et politiques, ni l'article 8, alinéa 1er, de la Convention européenne de sauvegarde des droits de l'homme et des libertés fondamentales;

D'où il suit que le moyen n'est pas fondé;
PAR CES MOTIFS:
REJETTE le pourvoi.

Appendix III

Cour de cassation
Civil Chamber 3
Public Hearing of Wednesday 17 December 1997
Petition No.: 95-20779
Published in the *Bulletin*[75] **Rejection**.

President: Mr Beauvois, President
Reporter: Mr Toitot, Reporting Judge
Advocate General: Mr Weber, Advocate General
Lawyers: SCP Waquet, Farge & Hazan

Full Text
THE FRENCH REPUBLIC
IN THE NAME OF THE FRENCH PEOPLE

On the single ground

Whereas, according to the challenged decision (CA Paris, 22 March 1995), Mrs Z… leased an apartment to Mr X…; after the death of the tenant, his friend, Mr Y…, who lived with him and had remained on the premises, sued the landlady for [being granted] the transfer of the lease to his benefit;

Whereas Mr Y… claims against the decision to refuse his request even as, according to the ground, pursuant to article 26 of the International Covenant on Civil and Political Rights published by decree no. 81-76 dated 29 January 1981, the law must prohibit all discrimination and guarantee all persons an equal and efficient protection against all discrimination, for instance that arising from race, color, sex, … or from any other circumstance; in estimating that article 14 of the statute dated 6 July 1989, which lays down that "upon the death of the tenant, the contract of lease is transferred (…) to the recognized cohabitee (…) who had lived with him for at least 1 year at the time of death", concerned the case only of concubinage between a man and a woman, while this text contains no limitation other than that concerning the duration of the concubinage, the appeal court has violated the aforementioned texts together with article 8, paragraph 1, of the European Convention on the Protection of Human Rights and Fundamental Freedoms.

But whereas having held, lawfully, that the concubinage could result only from a stable and continuous relationship having the appearance of marriage, therefore between a man and a woman, the appeal court has violated neither article 26 of the International Covenant on Civil and Political Rights nor article 8, paragraph 1, of

[75]The *Bulletin des arrêts des chambres civiles* is one of the court's official law reports. Only a fraction of the total number of decisions are retained for publication in the *Bulletin* every year. Unofficially, these are the only judgments that are deemed to be worthy of reference as a matter of law.

the European Convention on the Protection of Human Rights and Fundamental Freedoms.

Whence it follows that the ground is not well-founded;

FOR THESE REASONS:

REJECTS the petition.

Part II
Judicial Activism in Perspective

Chapter 6
The Activist Judge—Vanity of Vanities

James Allan

Oh that I were made judge in the land, that every man that hath any suit or cause might come unto me, and I would do him justice! (King James Bible 1769: 2 *Samuel* 15:4).[1]

I, for one, certainly believe that over the last four or five decades the developed democratic world—or, I plead ignorance, perhaps just the common law part of that world—has seen a marked increase in judicial activism. In my latest book, just out in June, 2014, I argue that unelected judges have been eating into the scope for democratic decision-making (Allan 2014). They have done this in various ways including through the adoption of new approaches to constitutional interpretation that impose few (if any) external constraints on what qualifies as the correct or right answer; through how they use and appeal to transnational law; through the ways in which they treat international treaties and international customary law; and through the ways in which (in the United Kingdom and New Zealand, in particular) newly enacted statutory bills of rights are being interpreted.

Of course judges have not done these things in a vacuum. Sometimes the Executive colludes in a display of last-word judicial power as in Canadian-style reference cases to their Supreme Court on gay marriage[2] or Quebec separatism[3] or in the United States when California refuses to defend in court the constitutionality of the law of the jurisdiction, in the knowledge and with the hope that the Courts might strike down the law as a result.[4] Sometimes, okay more than sometimes, plenty of legal academics are there to cheer on these new style 'hero judges' (Gava 2001).[5] And sometimes segments of society that cannot for the moment convince a majority of their fellow citizens of the desirability of some policy or other that they

[1]The reference in the title is to *Ecclesiastes* 1:2.
[2]See *Re Same Sex Marriage* [2004] 3 SCR 698.
[3]See *Reference re Secession of Quebec* [1998] 2 SCR 217.
[4]See *United States v Windsor*, 570 US 12 (2013).
[5]The term is John Gava's.

J. Allan (✉)
C7o TC Beirne School of Law, University of Queensland,
Brisbane St Lucia, QLD 4072, Australia
e-mail: j.allan@law.uq.edu.au

L.P. Coutinho et al. (eds.), *Judicial Activism*,
Ius Gentium: Comparative Perspectives on Law and Justice 44,
DOI 10.1007/978-3-319-18549-1_6

happen to relish are happy to have the top judges execute an end-run around the elected branches—as can be seen in the United States with, say, abortion,[6] gay marriage (in California, not New York State),[7] and possibly in the future euthanasia and (again) capital punishment or in Australia with prisoner voting[8] and other electoral matters,[9] or in Canada with prisoner voting,[10] prostitution[11] and very possibly quite soon euthanasia[12] (to say nothing of the slightly different case of the top judges in Canada rather unbelievably telling the Executive whom it can and cannot appoint to the Supreme Court).[13]

Nor am I in any way at all alone in perceiving this marked increase in judicial activism. Not too dissimilar laments, to take just a few other names, have been made by Grant Huscroft and Bradley Miller in Canada (2011), by John Finnis (2011) and Richard Ekins (2013) in the United Kingdom, by Jeffrey Goldsworthy (2007) and Tom Campbell (2003) in Australia, and by Richard Posner (2006), Robert Bork (2003) and Jeremy Waldron (2006) in the United States.

And there are the political scientists, the Ran Hirschls (2007) and Frederick Mortons and Rainer Knopffs (2000), who note this very same trend from a slightly different vantage.

All that said, it is no doubt true that the charge of 'judicial activism' requires that the term be defined, that the abuse or grievance that it is meant to cover be spelt out in some circumscribed way. I do not propose to spend too much time doing that here, though I do want to claim that the sin of 'judicial activism'—and surely the term is overwhelmingly used as a pejorative one, connoting undesirable conduct—is not one that can be identified in some magical way that is free of the exercise of value judgement. Judicial activism, then, is not something that can be spotted in a purely factual manner, by just looking to see if the Court reached result X rather than Y.

No, the sin of judicial activism, or so it seems to me, is one that depends on *why* the Court reached result X or Y in some particular case. That means that any attempt by someone to create a judicial activism scorecard based solely on when laws are struck down or invalidated by top judges (Ringhand 2007)[14] is misconceived or wrong-headed. You simply cannot equate judicial activism to a willingness to overturn

---

[6]See *Roe v Wade*, 410 US 113 (1973).

[7]See *In re Marriage Cases*, 43 Cal 4th 757 (2008).

[8]See *Roach v Electoral Commissioner* (2007) 233 CLR 162. And see Allan (2012).

[9]See *Rowe v Electoral Commissioner* (2010) 243 CLR 1. And see Allan (2012).

[10]See *Sauvé v Canada (Attorney General)* [2002] 3 SCR 519.

[11]See *Canada (Attorney General) v Bedford* [2013] SCC 72.

[12]Just before this chapter went to press the Supreme Court of Canada went and did just that, striking down the ban on doctor assisted suicide (though not immediately but in a year from now to give the legislature some time to respond, if it can). See *Carter v Canada (Attorney General)* 2015 SCC 5.

[13]See *Reference re Supreme Court Act 1985* [2014] SCC 21.

[14]Ringhand purports to make the charge of 'judicial activism' a factual or objective one by simply counting how often a judge invalidates a federal law, or state law, or over-rules a past precedent. In effect you get a score by making the number of instances of over-ruling the numerator and then putting that over the number of cases heard, as the denominator. You can then make that a

legislation in some 1:1 sense. The reasons why a law is being struck down matter. Depending upon a particular jurisdiction's constitutional specifics—whether it has a written constitution, whether it be a Westminster or Presidential/republican system, how great its attachment to the Separation of Powers ideal, its particular form of federalism (if any), the content and nature of its bill of rights (if any), the body of past precedents and whether there is a commitment to *stare decisis*, and a whole lot more besides—the correct course of action for top judges can sometimes be to invalidate or strike down a law. And I mean 'correct' here as in 'doing so in this instance is *not* judicial activism'. Or put the other way round, a Court can in certain circumstances be activist when it declines to strike down a law. Just imagine a scenario where the clearly most plausible reading of a federalist written constitution is that this is an area of State law-making into which the national legislature has intruded, and yet the Court decides not to invalidate the national law—thereby in effect rewriting the federalist constitution to be less federalist.[15]

And note that I make that point that activism can be a sin of omission not just of commission as someone who is himself perfectly at home in and largely in favour of a New Zealand-style out-and-out parliamentary sovereignty, unwritten constitution-type set-up where the elected legislature has no legal (but only moral and political) constraints on what laws it can pass.[16] But one's first-order druthers were he to imagine that he was drafting a constitutional order from scratch is not the same thing as what one's proper job is as a top judge appointed to decide cases in an established system where, say, there is a constitutionalized bill of rights and a federalist division of powers.[17]

The take-away point here is that for me the charge of judicial activism really has to be understood as a prescriptive or normative or value-laden one.

In that vein, Black's Law Dictionary defines this sin as occurring when 'judges allow their personal views about public policy, among other factors, to guide their decisions' (Black and Garner 2000). This amounts to a 'wrongful use of power' type definition, which more-or-less gets at the heart of the grievance though the focus on the judge's personal views is problematic.[18] So I prefer what I have

(Footnote 14 continued)
percentage score out of 100, the higher the score the more 'activist' you are according to this sort of thinking.

[15]Just such a scenario has played out in Australia, in my view, over the past eight or nine decades. I make the argument at length in Allan and Aroney (2008).

[16]In other words I would structure my preferred constitutional set-up so that judges overwhelmingly kept their hands off the work of the elected legislature, with the proviso that I am not adverse to federalism-type constraints on the national legislature. See, for example Allan (2010).

[17]I consider what such a judge ought to do in Allan (2008).

[18]For one thing a particular law might enact a vague, amorphous standard, say 'award custody based on the best interests of the child', in which case the law is in effect delegating (or abdicating) decision-making to the point-of-application interpreting judge. For another matter, talk of 'personal views' is ambiguous (or does not specify) between (a) the judge's personal views of what the law means or requires and (b) the judge's personal views of what is the most desirable outcome in this case, all things considered including non-law things. The first of these is inevitable whenever humans are involved in any decision-making procedure.

elsewhere suggested as a working definition of judicial activism, something along these lines:

> [T]he gist of the judicial activism complaint, then, is a complaint about what the unelected top judges are doing — that they are gainsaying or second-guessing or circumscribing or redirecting the elected branches of government *without any legitimate warrant or grounds for doing so*.... Notice, however, that [the judicial activism charge] does not necessarily connote bad faith. The gainsaying, second-guessing and circumscribing can be done not only to achieve what are believed to be good substantive outcomes (which can motivate even bad faith judicial activism), but also in the belief the constitutional materials and jurisdiction's rules of recognition do allow such actions. The latter belief, in other words, can be honestly held by the judges. It is just that disinterested observers may disagree and think such a belief far-fetched in the particular circumstances. (Allan 2012: 744).

So judicial activism, for me, is not limited to charges of bad faith or dishonest judging; it also encompasses judging that relies on implausible and unconvincing reasoning undertaken in good faith. And almost always, as a matter of contingent empirical fact, judicial activism involves increasing—not decreasing—the moral and political input of judges themselves at the point-of-application.

That, then, is my working understanding of the sin of judicial activism. It is a sin, as I said to start, that I think has been on the increase, markedly so, these past four or five decades. Yet from the point-of-view of some particular judge accused of activism there might exist replies that he could give that would take most or all of the sting out of how blameworthy such activist judging is perceived to be. These possible replies can be thought of as partial defences or mitigating factors that might come close to exculpating the activist judge. Or at least that would be so if these replies were considered to be persuasive or well-founded. If so, the sin of judicial activism would not really be that sinful—at most a minor or summary offence, not overly difficult to shrug off or brush aside.

I can think of two such possible replies that might plausibly be pled in mitigation by the judge accused of judicial activism. Considering each in turn will take up the remainder of this paper. I give little away, I suspect, if I indicate upfront that neither exculpatory reply is to my mind attractive or persuasive for those of us lucky enough to be living in the long-established democratic world.

6.1 What is the Purpose of Our Written Constitution?

Let me take the less abstract or less theoretical possible reply first. Here we are considering the judge in a certain sort of jurisdiction only. I think it goes almost without saying that the charge of judicial activism only has force or bite in the democratic world. In the authoritarian states of the world, governed by one party or by a theocracy or by a military junta the judiciary is not independent in any meaningful sense. Citizens in such jurisdictions have plenty of things to worry about, but judicial activism is not one of them. So my consideration of judicial activism generally is confined to the democratic world. Yet that is not all. In considering this first possible rebuttal or plea in mitigation to the charge of judicial activism, I am considering only a sub-section of the democratic world, albeit a very, very large sub-section.

This is the portion of the democratic world whose jurisdictions possess a written constitution. I am here explicitly putting to one side the few parliamentary sovereignties that exist, most obviously New Zealand and somewhat less obviously the United Kingdom (because of its membership in the European Union) and Israel. But in this now slightly circumscribed democratic world one possible defence (or plea in mitigation) to the charge of judicial activism might follow on from how one answers the question 'What is the purpose of our written constitution?'.

To be more precise, I want to consider the two and a half most plausible answers to this question, and then to concede that all but one of those answers to this question significantly undermines or diminishes the charge of judicial activism. These other answers allow the activist judge to shrug off the activist label. So in any discussion of judicial activism it really matters which of those two and a half answers one gives to the question 'What is the purpose of our written constitution?'.

6.1.1 Plausible Answer #1

The answer here is that the purpose of a written constitution is to lock certain things in, say an enumeration of State and Federal powers, or some rules on how the top judges are to be selected and for how long or an amending procedure or a set of citizens' moral entitlements, enunciated in the form of a bill of rights. These things, or others, will be taken off the parliamentary sovereignty or majoritarian table and be made harder than usual to alter or change. They will be locked in, meaning that change will require a super-majoritarian procedure (in some jurisdictions, for some matters, a near on impossible one ever to achieve[19]).

You can think of the motivation for doing this as being in opposition to what motivates New Zealand-style parliamentary sovereignty, namely the desire to leave each generation to decide all important social policy-making issues for itself by simple Act of Parliament or legislative enactment. As Larry Alexander puts it, the locking things in purpose of a written constitution follows on from deciding that 'risking rigidity rather than risking security' (Alexander 1998: 4)[20] is the better bet as regards these matters that have been taken off the majoritarian table.

Or as Justice Antonin Scalia puts it:

> It certainly cannot be said that a constitution naturally suggests changeability; to the contrary, its whole purpose is to prevent change – to embed certain rights in such a manner that future generations cannot readily take them away. A society that adopts a bill of rights

---

[19]Take Canada for instance. See *Constitution Act 1982*s 41, for matters that require the unanimous assent of provincial legislatures.

[20]See also, Kay (1998: 16).

> [for instance] is sceptical that 'evolving standards of decency' always 'marks progress,' and that societies always 'mature' as opposed to rot (Scalia 1997: 40–41).

Of course outside of these particular locked-in provisions, there is parliamentary sovereignty. So the purpose of the written constitution is to lock in some few things, but to leave all the rest to the democratic process, to letting-the-numbers-count majoritarianism.

Now it is true that the locking things in understanding of the purpose of a written constitution can in some circumstances be characterised as a form of 'ancestor worship' (Kirby 2000). After all, on this understanding you are taking off the majoritarian table at least some matters that in New Zealand would still be on that table. Indeed, that is the core purpose of the written constitution; that is why you opted to have one.

That said, critics of 'ancestor worship' can no doubt be prone to overstating what is being taken off the democratic table, especially as regards any constitutionalised, locked-in bill of rights. The fact is that these sort of constitutionalized rights provisions are overwhelmingly locked in floors, not ceilings. So if modern understandings of 'cruel and unusual punishment' or 'marriage equality' have evolved, there is nothing in the locked in view of a constitution that prevents the elected legislature from passing a statute to get rid of capital punishment or to extend the scope for who can marry—to widen the scope of what is now seen as rights protections by legislation.

All that means that if you buy the 'locking things in' answer to the purpose of a written constitution, then you are buying an unchanging portion of the democratic pie being taken away. It does not get to be extended over time, at least not without some future constitutional amendment. No, as regards the rest of that pie (the part not originally locked away from the reach of the elected legislature) you just have decision-making by the elected legislature, otherwise known as democracy, or what you have for the whole pie, all the time, in New Zealand.

It will be clear by now, I think, that it is this first 'to lock things in' answer to the question of 'What is the purpose of our written constitution?' that leaves present day judges wide open to the charge of judicial activism should they opt to intrude into (or grab by judicial fiat a further piece of) that portion of the pie that was originally meant to stay on the democratic table. As regards what was locked in we may have ancestor worship, or opting for judicially supervised rigidity to secure us against what we fear might happen in a New Zealand-style legislative sovereignty arrangement. But if the judges step over the line of what was locked in, trespassing into what was not locked in, then that is judicial activism.[21] Yes, we can argue over the historical evidence for what was and was not meant to be locked in. And in some instances it may be wholly unclear and highly debatable what that in fact is. But uncertainties about the historical evidence aside, this *answer #1* gives you a line

[21]Just as it can be judicial activism deliberately to allow the locked in portion of the pie to shrink, though as an empirical matter it seems to me that this is at present not something that often happens or a cause for worry.

of sorts. Or rather it gives you that unless you imagine the weird and extremely unlikely situation of constitutional founders opting to lock in a system that simply abdicates or delegates holus bolus to future judges the power to decide for themselves what important social policy decisions they can and will make.[22] And on this locking things in understanding it is an unchanging line. Crossing it is judicial activism.

Accordingly this *plausible answer #1* offers no defence, no plea in mitigation, to the present day judge accused of judicial activism. She needs some other plausible answer to the 'What is the purpose of our written constitution?' question.

6.1.2 Plausible Answer #2

The answer here is that the purpose of a written constitution is to set out 'a statement of our most important values and [be] the vehicle through which these values are created and crystallised' (Schaeur 2004).[23] Hence on this second answer a constitution is *not* about locking anything in, or not mainly about that. No, this answer focuses instead on seeing the purpose of a written constitution as setting out a relatively amorphous, indeterminate list of guidelines and values—a list that will need updating, changing and altering as society 'advances' and grows.

Yes, this second sort of answer presumes a rather Whiggish set of presuppositions about the inevitably of societal progress, which is far from self-evidently correct. And yes, this second sort of answer allows us to evade the charge of Ancestor Worship, but at the cost of Juristocracy or Kritarchy because the irony is that the voters will in the end be locked in anyway, only this time it will be to the moral and political druthers of present day judges rather than to those of some founding ancestors (so that use of the pronoun 'we' as regards who will be doing all this updating and redesigning is more than a little misleading).

But most relevantly here—and of course this is only the case if you find this *answer #2* more convincing than *answer #1* above, which I do not—this second sort of answer basically dissolves away the sin of present day judicial activism. Take the focus away from locking things in when it comes to the point of having a written constitution and instead put it on the articulation of warm, fuzzy aspirations and values and moral abstractions that everyone knows going in will evolve and mutate over time in any instances in which they have to be applied to specific controversies, and it becomes very difficult to see what the fuss about judicial activism is all about.

At the very least this second sort of answer gives any present day judge accused of activism a strong plea in mitigation and maybe even a full defence. What, on this

---

[22]This 'having your cake and eating it too' position is essentially the line Dickson CJ adopted in Canada in *Hunter v Southam* [1984] 2 SRC 145. See Grant Huscroft's critique in Huscroft (2004).

[23]Summarised, but not endorsed, by Schauer.

second answer, is making any particular judicial decision today an illegitimate one? What are the criteria for saying this opinion or judgment was a wrongful use of the judge's power but that one was not? At any rate what are the criteria as long as the judge remembers to refer in passing to those vague, amorphous values articulated up in the Olympian heights of constitutional abstractions in the course of deciding some case or other down in the quagmire of day-to-day judging on a country's Supreme Court?

I think that this second sort of understanding of the purpose of written constitution allows, or goes a long way in allowing, the judge accused of activism simply to shrug off the charge. I also think that this second sort of understanding is nowhere near as attractive, nowhere near as defensible, as the first sort of understanding. It is not even close. Hence for me, judicial activism is a real threat, one with criteria for when it is taking place and one which carries real blameworthiness and stigma.

But all that requires that you first make the case for *Plausible Answer #1*. For anyone who finds the second sort of answer I have just sketched more attractive, more persuasive, then to that extent the charge of judicial activism will largely dissipate.

6.1.3 Plausible Non-Answer #2½

Thus far when setting out the first two plausible answers I have engaged in the polite fiction that all of us have been lucky enough to be born in a country with a long-standing democratic tradition. And I have pretended that the written constitution whose purpose we are pondering was brought into being by means of some process that today still seems legitimate—not necessarily fastidiously perfect, but good enough. In the common law world I am talking about the Canadas and Australias and United States of the world. (Remember, long-standing democracies with unwritten constitutions have been put aside.)

However that is plainly not the case for many people in many jurisdictions that happen also to have written constitutions. And here we have the situation which I am characterising as giving rise to a non-answer or half-answer to the question 'What is the purpose of our written constitution?'. This relates back to the point made in the last paragraph about the need for some core level sense of legitimacy about the source and binding nature of one's country's written constitution. So if we imagine situations such as those where the departing colonial power leaves in its wake a written constitution, or the Japan-like one where following defeat in war the victors write, and impose, a constitution on the country, then in those sort of situations I think it may prove very difficult indeed to make the charge of judicial activism stick against any present day judge.

Put bluntly, you have to care what the constitution makers thought and wanted and intended as well as thinking that what they produced is legitimate and worthy of fealty to be at all concerned with what they were trying to lock in (assuming you would otherwise opt for my *answer #1* above over *answer #2*). And in some situations, perhaps the ones I raised above and perhaps others, it is not at all clear to me why you should be. And if you and the preponderance of today's citizens in such a jurisdiction think the written constitution has little or no legitimacy, for whatever reason, then it does not seem to me that charges of judicial activism can ever carry much weight; it does not seem that in such situations blame is easily attached to those judges who stray into territory that was not intended to be theirs (at least not on the ground that they strayed, in and of itself, rather than on the ground that they are somehow out of sync with today's populace).[24]

There then are two and half plausible answers to a question about the purpose of a written constitution in today's democratic world. Only one of those answers, or so it seems to me, grounds the charge of judicial activism. As it happens, it is the answer that I think is the most plausible and persuasive one in all long-standing democracies. *Answer #2* leaves me cold; it is far-fetched. Hence for me, judicial activism is a real threat.

But I concede that if you happen to live in a jurisdiction in which *non-answer 2½* is plausible, then judicial activism for you is a much harder accusation to make stick. It may not be worth the bother even to try.

That finishes my consideration of the first sort of avenue open to a present day judge seeking to evade the charge of judicial activism. I turn now to the other possible reply this judge might try to give as a plea in mitigation.

6.2 Can the Case Be Made for Rule Utilitarianism, or for Better Consequences Flowing from Always Following the Rules?

Here we enter deep waters. And these are waters that Larry Alexander some time ago charted and surveyed, insightfully and in depth, in arguing that we can often achieve better overall outcomes by the indirect pursuit of the good rather than by attempting to maximize the good on a case-by-case basis (Alexander 1985). So take what I say next as being in addition to that.

---

[24]Here is a variant on this possibility. It occurs where a new constitution is introduced, but only after the colonial power has departed. An example is India. At least that is superficially so. Britain imposed no constitution on India before departure. Instead, a constituent assembly devised one for itself over the next three years. Much of this 1950 Constitution is taken word-for-word from the Government of India Act 1935—a piece of Imperial legislation that was considered longer than almost any other enactment in the history of the Westminster Parliament. However, few people today admit this. Put differently, one of the fetters against which the Indians had rebelled was, in large part, freely taken up by them later on. It is also true that the Supreme Court of India is, with the possible exception of Israel's top court, the most activist court in the world. Whether there is any causal connection to how their Constitution was adopted I leave for others. (The points in this footnote were made to me by Dyson Heydon, to whom I am most grateful.)

The basic idea, at least as I learned it, comes out of that branch of moral philosophy known as utilitarianism. In its late eighteenth century Benthamite form (Bentham 1789) the focus is on aiming to achieve the greatest good for the greatest number. And no doubt in terms of giving birth to practical reforming accomplishments, Jeremy Bentham was a man with few, if any, historical peers. His utilitarian writings and lobbying and networking can be linked to expanding the voting franchise in Britain in the First Reform Bill of 1832[25]; to prison reform[26]; to animal welfare[27]; to less harsh but just as effective criminal law penalties[28]; to repeal of the usury laws[29]; and more. This all flows from making human happiness or welfare the sole 'good-in-itself' and then aiming for those likely future good consequences that will maximize that happiness (or that will keep to a minimum unhappiness or pain in situations when only bad things are on the menu).

In effect you treat everyone (meaning everyone's happiness) as equal at the first stage and you then opt for the action that is most likely—given what you know of the world—to produce the best future consequences in terms of overall human welfare. It is a forward-looking moral theory, not a backwards-looking one. And no doubt there is much room for argument about which future consequences will end up producing that happiness.

Of course utilitarian theories are much more sophisticated today, some two centuries after Bentham. True, too, there are many critics of this way of thinking, not least Ronald Dworkin (1978: 232–238, 275–276) and John Rawls (1971). Nevertheless, utilitarianism is still today a vibrant school of thought.

I mention all this only because part of the modern day sophistication of utilitarianism involves the realization that sometimes best consequences are achieved by laying down clear rules, and always following them even though we know going in that all rules will at times produce sub-optimal results, will be over-inclusive and under-inclusive. In other words, we can accept the fact that no rule will ever have a 100 % hit rate, a perfect record of producing good consequences every single time that it is honestly applied. Yet despite that, and the less than 100 % hit rate, it will nevertheless be the case that in some situations opting for a rule will deliver better

---

[25]Bentham way back then also favoured the vote for women.

[26]Bentham was keen on a Panopticon Prison, a much more humane sort of prison than any then in existence, though with no concession at all to prisoner privacy. And the John Howard League for Prisoners (and all of its off-shoots in the Commonwealth world) can trace its roots to Bentham.

[27]The Royal Society for the Prevention of Cruelty to Animals (and all its off-shoots in the Commonwealth world) can trace its roots to Bentham. Of course for Bentham, the great critic of bills of rights and of the French Declaration of the Rights of Man, this protection is seen in terms of animal welfare, *not* in terms of animal rights.

[28]Bentham spotted what is now widely recognized, that deterrence operates more through the likelihood of being caught than through the severity of the punishment.

[29]Here Bentham was right, and quite unusually Adam Smith was wrong. The arguments for repeal, which did not happen until 1854, were virtually all Bentham's though he had by then been dead for over two decades.

overall consequences (all things considered, on average, over time) than case-by-case decision-making aimed at good consequences in each individual case.

One example sometimes given of this is a 'who can vote?' rule. Let us say a rule lays down something along the lines that 'any citizen 18 years of age and older, not declared mentally unfit by a doctor' can vote. That sort of rule clearly is sub-optimal; it clearly has a less than 100 % hit rate. There will be 17 year olds well-versed in civic education who look far more qualified to vote than scores of 19 or 50 or 60 year olds. Yet such 17 year olds will, sub-optimally, be barred. Obversely, there will be know-nothing, alcoholic 45 year olds who have not read a newspaper in 20 years. Under the rule they can vote.

Yet the point is that such a rule delivers better consequences than any non-rule alternative. To see this, imagine that you tried to decide who can vote by striking committees of people who would interview potential voters and then make decisions on a case-by-case basis. Not only would the costs of such a scheme be huge, the overall hit rate would be lower than that achieved with the rule. No real life human being, or group of human beings, will ever have a 100 % hit rate of opting for the better consequences choice any more than any rule would. Plus there are the various frailties that flow from being a limited biological creature; there is the possibility of succumbing to corruption (say, excluding from voting bunches of those obviously on the other side of politics to you); there is the chance of moral failures (say, opting to exclude blacks from voting); and more.

So Rule Utilitarianism says that sometimes (as with who can vote) you do better by having rules and just applying them. This is not true in all situations, of course. To see this just consider how we decide who can drive—here we go for case-by-case decision-making, despite knowing that that, too, is far from perfect (as you can see by noting all the teenage boys who manage to pass their driving tests).

This has clear ramifications when it comes to the issue of judicial activism. Let us assume that, like me, you accept the argument that society can often—not always, but often—achieve more welfare, better long-term consequences, greater good (articulate it as you please) by the indirect pursuit of that good via laying down rules and always applying them. Accept that and then you have another way of understanding the charge or sin of judicial activism, or rather a branch or sub-set of that sin.

On this understanding an activist judge is any judge who decides *not* to apply a rule when to do so—according to that judge's moral or political sensibilities, or sense of fairness, or case specific utilitarian weighing up of consequences, or nose for what social justice demands, or, well, you get the idea—would be sub-optimal. This judge sees this case as being one of those rare few that falls on the wrong side of the rule's hit rate; he perceives the rule here to be over-inclusive (and so one that captures a case not intended to be caught) or under-inclusive (and so one that fails to capture a case intended to be caught) and hence this judge opts to legislate from the bench. He amends the rule so that it now delivers the same result for this particular case that a direct appeal by him to best consequences (or to social justice or to fairness or to 'the good') would deliver.

Consider, for a moment, the judge who says something to the effect: 'I always apply the rule when its effects are good; it is only in a few hard cases when they are not that I opt for a direct appeal to good consequences, the rule be damned!' And notice that a policy of that sort,[30] of following the rule when it is perceived to deliver the better outcome, but not otherwise, is functionally no different from a policy of deciding each time on a case-by-case basis. The rule does no work, not really.

Here you might draw an analogy with the common law doctrine of *stare decisis*. If the ratios of past cases are going to have bite and influence in deciding this case today, then it must be true that those past rationes—at least sometimes—affect the outcome. They need to lead to a present day decision X that otherwise would have been a not-X decision. The past cases do no work unless they can at times decisively change outcomes away from what would otherwise be produced, absent consideration of those cases.

So what possible reply might this sort of judge make when charged with the sin of activism? What might she plead in mitigation to lessen the blameworthiness of occasionally shunning what the rule dictates in favour of a direct appeal to best consequences in this case?

I think the basic thrust of this judge's reply would be to the effect that it makes no sense to follow a rule when you know in the case before you that its effects are sub-optimal.

Were this judge keen on Shakespeare she might point to *The Merchant of Venice* and the debate between Bassanio and Portia over how to interpret a bond, or contract, calling for a pound of flesh to be taken from the merchant Antonio should he default to the moneylender Shylock, which of course he does. This judge might remind us of Bassanio's plea to the judge to:

> Wrest once the law to your authority:
> To do a great right, do a little wrong,
> And curb this cruel devil of his will.
> (Shakespeare: Act IV, Scene 1, lines 215–17).

Yes, Shakespeare has Portia respond the way a Rule Utilitarian would by saying:

> It must not be. There is no power in Venice
> Can alter a decree established:
> 'Twill be recorded for a precedent,
> And many an error by the same example
> Will rush into the state. It cannot be.
> (Shakespeare: Act IV, Scene 1, lines 218–22).

Nevertheless, our activist judge would be sure to point out that in the end, to please the crowd, Shakespeare has Portia, the judge who mouths the Rule Utilitarian line, find against Shylock. Shakespeare's judge cleverly finds the needed loophole, that the pound of flesh does not include any blood, and then throws

[30]One that to my mind is not dissimilar to Trevor Allan's position that the law is just a provisional guide as to what the judge should do. See Trevor Allan (2001: 216–225). Yuck!

Shylock to the wolves. It may satisfy the crowds, but this is hardly an honest upholding of the rule. And our activist judge would reply, 'it is all the better for it'. It makes no sense to follow the rule, she might say by way of reply to the charge of activism, when utility *in this case* points against doing so.

Or if no fan of Shakespeare our activist judge might offer her plea in mitigation by taking things to a higher philosophical plane and musing aloud about whether Rule Utilitarianism is even a stable concept (Lyons 1965). Is it not likely that Rule Utilitarianism will always collapse into Act Utilitarianism, and that the rule will be discarded when the unique circumstances of the case at hand point strongly in favour of ignoring it?

Take that as my second possible reply that might plausibly be offered as a defence to the charge of judicial activism. Nor is it one that can be dismissed out of hand. The obvious rejoinder to the activist judge taking this line is to claim that shunning the rule in the unusual circumstances of this particular case only looks attractive because the judge has failed to look at the longer term consequences, including the consequences of being seen not to follow the rule. Her judicial gaze has been too circumscribed, in other words.

However I do not think that rejoinder, alone, will suffice. To overcome this judge's reply we need to return to utilitarianism—to consequentialist thinking—and distinguish between (i) a moral theory aimed at guiding one's personal actions and (ii) a political theory aimed at achieving best outcomes for society.

Now Bentham certainly saw utilitarianism as doing both those things, as operating on the personal level as a forward-looking guide to what one ought to do. However Bentham also saw utilitarianism as a guide to the legislature, as offering a theory aimed at achieving best long-term consequences for society. Indeed, the vast bulk or preponderance of Bentham's efforts and thought were focused on that latter task.

This distinction between (i) and (ii) matters because the activist judge who claims that Rule Utilitarianism will ultimately collapse into Act Utilitarianism has a very strong case indeed when we are talking on the personal level, about *you* laying down rules for *you* as to what is best for *you* to do in the future. Why? Well if it happens at some point that you are sure that following a rule that you have made and laid down for yourself will in this instance produce less good results than not following it, then why follow it? True, when someone suggests that you have failed to consider enough of the long-term, or long, long-term, consequences that would show the rule's prescription to be optimal after all, that may be correct. But it is not just unlikely but flat out implausible, unconvincing and wrong to think that this 'just look at more and more of the likely consequences of the rule, further and further into the future' suggestion will every time give you grounds for thinking that the rule produces best outcomes *in this instance*. It will not. And in those instances when it does not, however rare, it does seem to me that the rule should only be treated as a mere guide to action, a rebuttable one.

Hence on the personal level rule consequentialism does appear to me to be prone to collapsing into case-by-case decision-making. Put differently, if we were focused on this personal realm of (i) above then the person seeking to defend herself against the charge of ignoring the rule in favour of doing what she thinks best *this time* would have a powerful plea in mitigation.

But we are not focused on that level (i). No, when we castigate the activist judge we are very much focused on rules that have been made for all of society, on level (ii). More relevantly still, we are focused on situations where the rule maker (and as I am still only concerned with the democratic world that means an elected legislature) is distinct from the rule applier (at the top level, an unelected judiciary charged with applying those laws). It is precisely that distinction, that unlike in the personal situation the rule maker is a different group of people from the rule applier, that to my mind undercuts the second possible reply to judicial activism that I mooted above. It is here that we see that the 'it makes no sense to follow the rule' reply to the charge of judicial activism falls down and fails to provide much of a defence. Here the long-term consequences of rule following make the charge of judicial activism stick.

Here is why. On level (i) there are no concerns with legitimacy and accountability. If it is legitimate for me to make a rule for my own future conduct, then it is also legitimate for me to decide to ignore that rule in these particular circumstances here and now. The question of legitimacy of the rule-applier opting to over-rule the rule-maker does not arise. Moreover, in such circumstances I am only accountable to myself. Nor is there any issue of relative competence, of whether the rule-maker has on average, over time, a higher hit rate for increasing utility through its rules than does the rule-applier through its determinations of when to ignore or gainsay those rules. (Or at least that is true barring such situations as when the sober me makes a rule and the drunk me over-rides it.)

By contrast, in the world of democratic politics in which those top judges accused of judicial activism are operating, all three concerns—legitimacy, accountability and relative competence—are live issues. To start, the rule-maker is the legislature, a body that is elected. Whatever quibbles one may have with its democratic credentials (perhaps related to the voting system used, or to the scope for gerrymandering, or to the existence or absence of bicameralism or federalism, or to anything else), those credentials will be massively greater than are those of the unelected judiciary. As regards democratic legitimacy, there literally is no comparison. The rule-making legislature wins hands down.[31]

Relatedly, the legislature is accountable to the voters for the rules it enacts. If they over-shoot or under-shoot some desired endpoint, the rule-makers can be replaced at the next election. Nothing like that sort of accountability is true of the point-of-application judge who decides that some rule fails to deliver good consequences (or fairness or social justice etc.) in the case at hand. If the judge errs—and remember, the case-by-case deciding will no more have a 100 % hit rate than the rule dispensing legislature will—he is not accountable to the voters. In fact, he

[31]For an opposing view see Barak (2006), where Barak argues 'there is more to democracy than majoritarianism' and asserts his view is 'substantively' democratic and pooh-poohs mere procedural requirements. Note my response in Allan (2014).

is not accountable to anyone in any tangible, real sense, though he may be quick to tell us how much he struggled with his conscience in deciding whether to over-ride the rule or not. Of course that is nothing like the same sort of accountability as the sort faced by people who might lose their jobs if they are widely seen to be wrong. Nor is it any other externally imposed sort of accountability.

There are even important issues of comparative competence at stake. We might put aside concerns about democratic legitimacy and accountability and still think that large bodies of people drawn from all corners of society are likely to have a better track record in setting down acceptable rules (as regards same sex marriage, euthanasia, abortion, capital punishment, how far the executive can go in protecting national security, how to regulate prostitution, and the list goes on), that they will have a better hit rate, than will committees of ex-lawyers, nine top judges on a Supreme Court. On the sort of issues just listed, though perhaps not on all other sorts of issues, the big group from across society is more competent than the incestuous, single background handful of people.

In that world of democratic politics, therefore, Rule Utilitarianism does not obviously or easily collapse into Act Utilitarianism. In that world the activist judge's second possible reply to the charge of activism, that 'it makes no sense to follow the rule', is far from convincing. Certainly whenever it is the judge's calculation of sub-optimality that is flying in the face of the legislature's opposing calculation (so, leaving aside instances where a rule has unexpected results that the rule-maker also does not want) it will be far from convincing. Long term, the legislature is better placed to get it right because it is accountable and on balance (for the sort of issues overwhelmingly at stake) more competent. Or that is true far more often than not when the two disagree. And the non-activist judge recognizes as much and defers.

So in my opinion this second sort of avenue potentially open to a present day judge seeking to evade the charge of judicial activism, or perhaps just to offer a convincing plea in mitigation, is overwhelmingly a dead end. As with the first mooted possible reply, this second one also fails to provide the hoped-for escape in the sort of democratic jurisdictions I am considering.

Or almost always it fails to do so. You see any discussion of judicial activism of the sort I have been offering needs at some point to admit that although judicial activism is certainly a sin, it is clearly not the worst sin going. Let me be blunt. We can all imagine situations in which a judge thinks the law, honestly interpreted, demands X but that that particular outcome is so morally egregious that she must lie and say the law means not-X. In this paper I have not focused on that sort of judicial lying branch of judicial activism. I have not focused on it because in any long-established democracy, by which I clearly mean to encompass Australia, Canada, the US, the UK, and plenty of other countries as well, as opposed to an apartheid South Africa, say, it will be so very, very rare that judicial lying is warranted and more warranted than resigning in protest too.

Nevertheless it is a possibility. It is a possibility that requires a theory of when judicial disobedience and lying are warranted in a generally well-functioning democracy. Here I simply concede that I doubt that the answer is 'absolutely never' and repeat that this manifestation of judicial activism is a very marginal one in our long-established democracies.

Accordingly, having noted that small caveat, I think I am now in a position to say that few pleas in mitigation will serve to exculpate the sin of judicial activism. At any rate that is my position on the matter.

Acknowledgments An earlier version of this paper was presented at the University of Lisbon's Centre for Research in Public Law and University of San Diego sponsored conference on judicial activism in Lisbon, Portugal held in May, 2014 at the Faculty of Law, University of Lisbon. The author thanks the many participants from across the EU and the US for their comments and criticisms. The author also wishes to thank Dyson Heydon for his comments on a later draft.

References

Alexander, Larry. 1985. Pursuing the Good – Indirectly. *Ethics* 95: 315.

Alexander, Larry, editor. 1998. *Constitutionalism: Philosophical Foundations.* Cambridge: Cambridge University Press.

Allan, James and Aroney, Nicolas. 2008. An Uncommon Court: How the High Court of Australia has Undermined Australian Federalism. *Sydney Law Review* 30: 245.

Allan, James. 2008. The Travails of Justice Waldron. In *Expounding the Constitution: Essays in Constitutional Theory*, ed. Grant Huscroft, 161. Cambridge: Cambridge University Press.

Allan, James. 2010. Not in for Pound – In for a Penny? Must a Majoritarian Democrat Treat All Constitutional Judicial Review as Equally Egregious?. *King's Law Journal* 21: 233–256.

Allan, James. 2012. The Three "R"s of Recent Australian Judicial Activism: *Roach*, *Rowe* and (no) 'Riginalism. *Melbourne University Law Review* 36: 743: 782.

Allan, James. 2014. *Democracy in Decline*. Montreal & Kingston: McGill-Queens University Press.

Allan, Trevor. 2001. *Constitutional Justice: A Liberal Theory of the Rule of Law.* Oxford: Oxford University Press.

Barak, Aharon. 2006. *The Judge in a Democracy*. Princeton: Princeton University Press.

Bentham, Jeremy. 1907. *Introduction to the Principles of Morals and Legislation*. Oxford: Clarendon Press.

Black, Henry C. and Garner, Bryan A. 2000. *Black's Law Dictionary.* St Paul: West Publishing Co.

Bork, Robert. 2003. *Coercing Virtue: The Worldwide Rule of Judges.* Washington D.C: America Enterprise Institute.

Campbell, Tom. Judicial Activism – Justice or Treason?. *Otago Law Review* 10: 307.

Dworkin, Ronald. 1978. *Taking Rights Seriously.* London: Duckworth.

Ekins, Richard. 2003. Judicial Supremacy and the Rule of Law. *Law Quarterly Review* 119: 127.

Ekins, Richard. 2004. Politicians are right to criticize judges. *The New Zealand Herald*, September 13.

Ekins, Richard. 2013. How to be a Free People. *American Journal of Jurisprudence* 58: 163.

Finnis, John. 2011. Invoking the Principle of Legality against the Rule of Law. In *Modern Challenges to the Rule of Law*, ed. Richard Ekins. Wellington: LexisNexis.

Gava, John. 2001. The Rise of the Hero Judge. *University of New South Wales Law Journal* 24: 747.

Goldsworthy, Jeffrey. 2007. Challenging parliamentary sovereignty: Past, present and future. In *Interpreting Constitutions: A Comparative Study*, ed. Jeffrey Goldsworthy. Oxford: Oxford University Press.

Hirschl, Ran. 2007. *Towards Juristocracy: The Origins and Consequences of the New Constitutionalism.* Cambridge: Harvard University Press.

Huscroft, Grant. 2004. A Constitutional "Work in Progress"? The Charter and the Limits of Progressive Interpretation. In *Constitutionalism in the Charter Era*, ed. Grant Huscroft and Ian Brodie. Markham: LexisNexis Butterworths.

Kay, Richard. 1998. American Constitutionalism. In *Constitutionalism: Philosophical Foundations*, ed. Larry Alexander. Cambridge: Cambridge University Press.

King James Bible. 1769. Cambridge: Cambridge University Press.

Kirby, Michael. 2000. Constitutional Interpretation and Original Intent: A Form of Ancestor Worship?. *Melbourne University Law Review* 24:1.

Lyons, David. 1965. *Forms and Limits of Utilitarianism*. Oxford: Oxford University Press.

Miller, Bradley and Huscroft, Grant, editors. 2011. *The Challenge of Originalism: Theories of Constitutional Interpretation*. Cambridge: Cambridge University Press.

Morton, Frederich and Knopff, Rainer. 2000. *The Charter Revolution and the Court Party.* Toronto: University of Toronto Press.

Posner, Richard. 2007. Enlightened Despot': Review of Aharon Barak, The Judge in a Democracy [2006]. *New Republic*, April 23.

Rawls, John. 1971. *A Theory of Justice*. Cambridge: Harvard University Press.

Ringhand, Lori. 2007. Judicial Activism: An Empirical Examination of Voting Behavior on the Rehnquist National Court. *Constitutional Commentary* 24: 43.

Scalia, Antonin. 1997. *A Matter of Interpretation: Federal Courts and the Law*. Princeton: Princeton University Press.

Schauer, Fredrich. 2004. Judicial Supremacy and the Modest Constitution. *California Law Review* 92: 1045.

Shakespeare, William. *Merchant of Venice.*Waldron, Jeremy. 2006. The Core of the Case Against Judicial Review. *Yale Law Journal* 116: 1346.

Chapter 7
Schmitt's Spectre and Kelsen's Promise: The Polemics on the Guardian of the Constitution

Miguel Nogueira de Brito

7.1 Introduction

Every reader who may be expected to stumble into these pages knows Hans Kelsen essentially as a legal, not political, theorist. Carl Schmitt, on the other hand, is perhaps the most politically minded theorist ever to have written about law. And yet, on the controversy between both thinkers on who should be the guardian of the Constitution the best way to cast Kelsen's argument is on the side of political theory, not legal science.[1] Conversely, in spite of the fact that Schmitt's defense of the President of the Reich as the best guardian of the Constitution remains politically unconvincing, some points of his argument are relevant from the point of view of legal science, even if his arguments are in essence political.

This can be explained in part by Kelsen's aim to turn the insights of Schmitt against him, ending up by turning them against himself. In fact, Kelsen attempted to turn against Schmitt the idea of the presence of a political element in every judicial decision, but in this attempt at domesticating the political decision he didn't make sense of the proper distinction between politics and justice. In the accurate synthesis of David Dyzenhaus, "Kelsen's strategy was an instance of liberal recognition of the reality of politics and the way that decision breaks through the normative, at the same time as it is a futile and purely formal attempt to contain that breakthrough".[2] Schmitt, on the other hand, runs the opposite risk: by trying to insulate the courts from any relevant role in the application of constitutional norms he risks turning the

[1]This is all the more perplexing if one recalls that Kelsen claimed to locate is analysis on the domain of legal science, see Kelsen (2008a, b: 104–105).
[2]See Dyzenhaus (1997: 122).

M.N. de Brito (✉)
Faculdade de Direito da Universidade de Lisboa, Alameda da Universidade, 1649-014 Lisbon, Portugal
e-mail: mnbrito@mlgts.pt

L.P. Coutinho et al. (eds.), *Judicial Activism*,
Ius Gentium: Comparative Perspectives on Law and Justice 44,
DOI 10.1007/978-3-319-18549-1_7

Constitution into a kind of a "plébiscite de tous les jours" on the hands of politicians.[3] We see no place for pure politics in Kelsen's view of the constitutional order, as we see no place for courts in constitutional conflicts for Schmitt.

There is anyway more to the debate between Schmitt and Kelsen on the guardian of the Constitution than the sheer presentation of their ideas on the subject, as profound and interesting as they undoubtedly are. In fact there are already plenty of excellent essays and scholarly articles on the subject. Any new text on this issue must try to answer the following questions: what is the point of this debate from the perspective of our present situation, namely regarding the so-called activism of constitutional courts? Why do we continue to read Schmitt and Kelsen on the guardian of the Constitution?

A possible answer to these questions runs, to my mind, along the following lines. On the one hand, there is a real risk of judicialization of politics in our constitutional democracies and we have to turn to Kelsen to understand that—even if this wasn't his primary concern, it is nevertheless inherent in his conception of constitutional review. Schmitt's critique of judicial review can help us understand this risk. On the other hand, we can say perhaps that there is a Schmittian spectre haunting European constitutionalism. This spectre manifests itself in two different directions: in one direction, some national courts (and not just, as alleged sometimes, the German Constitutional Court) continue to claim sovereignty along traditional lines; in another direction, the European Court of Justice accepts the "primacy of discretionary politics" in the management of the financial crisis.[4]

In what follows I shall begin by briefly stating the position of each author on the question of the guardian of the Constitution (7.2). Then I shall point out Kelsen's and Schmitt's conceptions of democracy, also showing how closely connected they are to the solution each author gives to the said question (7.3). In a third moment I shall focus on whether, according to Kelsen and Schmitt, a court's position as the guardian of the Constitution conforms to the proper characteristics of judicial function (7.4). Subsequently, I shall briefly discuss whether judicial review of legislation, in Schmitt and Kelsen's views, endangers the principle of separation of powers (7.5). Finally, I shall conclude by stressing the relevance of both thinkers to the current situation of constitutionalism in Europe (7.6).

[3]See Renan (1996: 241).

[4]See Everson and Joerges (2013: 22–23). The authors' thesis is that the discrepancy between the German Constitutional Court's commitment to the country's Constitution and the European Court of Justice's commitment to the integration project has been replaced by the converging attitudes of both courts to the primacy of the political in the handling of the financial crisis.

7.2 The President and the Court

The very structure of Schmitt's *The Guardian of the Constitution*, published in 1931, shows the author's two main aims[5]: first, in part one of the book, Schmitt wanted to demonstrate that the Court of Constitutional Justice foreseen in article 19 of the Weimar Constitution to adjudicate constitutional matters should not be considered as the guardian of the Constitution, as this would require it to act politically and so in violation of the limits of the judicial function; then, in part two, Schmitt claimed that the situation of the German state in the thirties was characterized by an extreme fragmentation of power, which ultimately demanded a strong intervention of the President of the Reich as the true guardian of the Constitution; this is Schmitt's proposal in part three of his book symptomatically presented in connection with Germany's financial crisis in the thirties.[6]

Schmitt concludes the book in a way that also summarizes the principal arguments of his legal and political works:

> [The Constitution] presupposes the whole German people as a unit which has an immediate capability for action, that is, it is not mediated by an organization of social groups. That is to say, it can give expression to its will and in the decisive moment it will be able to secure its wholeness and integrity in the face of the pluralistic divisions. The Constitution seeks in particular to give the President the potential to bind himself directly with the general political will of the German people and through that to act as protector and preserver of the constitutionally appropriate unity and wholeness of the German people. The continued and sustainable existence of the contemporary German state stands or falls on the process of this attempt.[7]

Contrarily to this strong intervention of the Reich's President, the Court of Constitutional Justice set up by article 19 of the Weimar Constitution only decided in cases of clear and manifest violations of the Constitution, which was precisely the opposite of what was expected from an institution called upon to settle doubts and uncertainties.[8]

Schmitt's book triggered a direct response by Kelsen on his text with the revealing title "Who Should Be the Guardian of the Constitution?"[9] Kelsen starts his essay by stating that the demand for guaranties of the Constitution, that is, of institutions able to control the constitutionality of certain acts of parliament and government, corresponds to the specific "rule of law" principle of the utmost legal conformity of state acts.[10]

---

[5]See Schmitt (1996). The book is composed of three parts: "Justice as the guardian of the Constitution"; "The concrete constitutional situation of the present time"; "The Reich's President as the guardian of the Constitution".

[6]See Dyzenhaus (1997: 76).

[7]See Schmitt (1996: 159) [I use the translation set in Dyzenhaus (1997: 77)].

[8]See Schmitt (1996: 52–53).

[9]See Kelsen (2008a, b: 58–105).

[10]See Kelsen (2008a, b: 58).

Having said that, Kelsen notes that

> When it is generally the case that an institution should be created which will control the constitutionality of certain acts of state that directly implicate the constitution, this control may not be allocated to one of those very organs whose acts are to be controlled. The political function of the Constitution is to set legal limits on the exercise of power. Constitutional guarantees ensure that these legal limits are not transgressed. And if there is anything that is immune to doubt it is that no other body is less suited to such a function than the one to which the Constitution allocates the exercise of power, whether this be in whole or in part, and which is therefore best placed in virtue of legal opportunity and the political process to harm the Constitution. For there is no other fundamental legal-technical proposition that attracts so much consensus as that no one should be judge in his own cause.[11]

Only a court would enjoy the institutional conditions to settle constitutional conflicts. And the main reason behind the option for a special constitutional court—instead of common courts in a diffused system—was a concern on the lack of uniformity permitted by the American model, in which "different law-applying organs may have different opinions with regard to the constitutionality of a statute".[12]

Kelsen, who acted himself as a judge between 1920 and 1929—in the Austrian Constitutional Court he helped to put up[13]—, introduced the modern concept of constitutional review in a parliamentary, pluralistic democracy. His proposal of a centralized constitutional court with competences of abstract constitutional review of legislation served as a model to all major European constitutional courts that emerged after the Second World War, from Germany to Portugal.

In one important study on the controversy between Schmitt and Kelsen, Oliver Lepsius sustains that the texts of both authors on the guardian of the Constitution conceal, as a subtext, a dispute over the theory of democracy.[14] This dispute was not to be conducted on an abstract level, needing a legal hook so to speak, which was provided by the problem of constitutional review. According to Lepsius it is even doubtful whether Kelsen and Schmitt were themselves completely aware that the main difference between them concerned the concepts of people and democracy. If their dispute is really about the theory of democracy, its unraveling using as a pretext the problem of constitutional review inevitable involved a disagreement on the relationship between justice and politics and on the compatibility between constitutional justice and the separation of powers.[15]

[11]See Kelsen (2008a, b: 58–59, 88).

[12]See Kelsen (1942: 185); idem (2008: 19); see also Paulson (2003: 235–236).

[13]See Öhlinger (2003: 211–214); Lagi (2012: 283).

[14]See Lepsius (2007: 109).

[15]See van Ooyen (2008: VIII–IX).

7.3 Pluralistic Democracy Versus Identitarian Democracy

If one wants to summarize as briefly as possible the opposition between Kelsen and Schmitt on the concept of democracy, the most expedient way to do it is to say that Schmitt is an identitarian thinker on democracy, whereas Kelsen is a constructive one.

Schmitt sees fundamental rights, as well as parliamentarianism, as opposed to democracy, which he understands as the affirmation of the collective unity of a concrete people. This is why the President of the Reich can act as the guardian of the Constitution: he can secure the unity of the people even in times of crisis. Schmitt understands the state and the Constitution as the sovereign political unity of a homogeneous people. According to Schmitt, democracy refers to a collective identity and not to the experience of balancing competing pluralistic interests.

Schmitt's identitarian and plebiscitary conception of democracy lies at the root of his opposition to the "ancient belief, liberal rather than democratic, (…) that Parliament is the place where the party's egoism can be transformed, by force of an artifice of the idea or the institution, in a means to create a supra-egoist and supra-partisan will, a political will of the state".[16] Even if this transformation was still possible in the times of the constitutional monarchy—in which Parliament imagined itself as a stage where society appeared in the face of the state[17]—it would surely be no longer possible, so Schmitt claimed, after the Weimar Constitution. Weimar inaugurates in Germany a new function of the Constitution, in the sense that it no longer serves primarily as a limit to executive power, but as the basis of all power.[18] This structural transformation of the function of the Constitution entailed two main consequences. First, the separation between state and society gave way to a "total state"; second, and closely connected with the former, the parliamentary state was succeeded by a pluralistic state of strongly organized political parties.

As democracy became the only legitimating basis of political power in the Weimar Constitution, Schmitt considered that there was no more space for the separation between state and society. On the contrary, the situation that characterized Weimar's Germany was one in which "society, turned into state, transforms itself in an economic state, a cultural state, a caring state, a welfare-state, a provisioning state; the state resulting from society's self-organization cannot really become apart from it and comprehends everything that is social, that is, everything that has any relationship with human sociability".[19] This is what Schmitt calls the "turn to the total state": a state in which the traditional lines between the sphere in which the private law society governs itself and the sphere of state action, or the public domain, have been suppressed.[20] According to Schmitt there is a dialectic

[16]See Schmitt (1996: 88).

[17]See Schmitt (1996: 74).

[18]See Lepsius (2007: 107).

[19]See Schmitt (1996: 79).

[20]See Schmitt (1994: 166 ff.).

development “from the absolute state of the seventeenth and eighteenth century, through the neutral state of the nineteenth century, to the total state of the identity between state and society”.[21]

In close connection with this development towards the “total state” Schmitt describes the transformation of the parliamentary state of the nineteenth century into the pluralist party state of the twentieth century. In a scenario in which the legislature has become a “stage and centre of the pluralist distribution of the state’s unity in a majority of strongly organized social complexes, it doesn’t help much to speak of ‘parliamentary sovereignty’, thus resorting to a formula coined for the situation of the nineteenth century constitutional monarchy, as an answer to the most difficult constitutional law’s problem of our time”.[22]

Schmitt’s conception of democracy is the result of the confluence of at least three streams: first of all there is his view of democracy, developed under the influence of Rousseau and therefore opposed to the concept of political representation, centering, instead, in the unity of a concrete people in its immediate presence[23]; secondly, we have his view of the parliamentary system as essentially adequate to constitutional monarchy but growingly dysfunctional before the constitutionalization of the executive power,[24] and the existence of strongly organized political parties; finally, there is Schmitt’s view of the “total state”, as above mentioned. All these streams flowed together in a plebiscitary view of democracy in which the head of the executive power was envisaged as the privileged interlocutor of the people’s will.

Kelsen’s view of democracy directly opposes all this. He considers Schmitt’s conception to be built on the fiction of a preexisting people: “the people that gives form to the state is a unitary homogeneous collective which has a unitary collective interest that expresses itself in a unitary collective will. Parliament is not able to produce this collective will that stands beyond all opposition of interests, and so beyond political parties; on the contrary, parliament is the arena of the opposition of interests, and of the fragmentation of—Carl Schmitt would say pluralistic—political parties”.[25]

According to Kelsen the “people” is not an entity existing prior to the state or the constitution; it is an organ of the state built for purposes of legitimation and conceivable only in normative terms.[26] Furthermore, democracy is released from the fictions and myths of identity politics and connects to parliamentarianism as the only form compatible with modern complex societies.[27] In fact Kelsen presents

[21]See Schmitt (1996: 79).

[22]See Schmitt (1996: 91).

[23]See de Brito (2000: 131 ff.).

[24]On this development, see Lepsius (2007: 104–109).

[25]See Kelsen (2008a, b: 93).

[26]See Lepsius (2007: 116–117); idem (2010: 150–151); see also Kelsen (1949: 293).

[27]See Kelsen (2006: 174 ff.).

parliamentarianism as "the necessary compromise between the primitive idea of political freedom and the principle of differentiated division of labor".[28]

This is not the place to develop Kelsen's conception of democracy, but it can be summed up in the following main aspects:

(i) Democracy is connected to a double concept of freedom, that is, individual and collective freedom, in a way that attempts to preserve both.
(ii) Democracy is attached to real social-cultural communities.
(iii) Democracy is understood in a pluralistic way, in the sense that it gives space to what Rawls would call the "fact of reasonable pluralism".
(iv) Democracy sees the strengths of social integration that are inherent to the majority principle as resting in parliamentarianism and social compromise.
(v) Democracy is attuned to the choosing of political representatives by means of free elections.
(vi) Democratic legitimacy is understood in procedural, not substantial terms.[29]

Considering Kelsen's conception of democracy, the place given to constitutional justice in the state and the non-opposition between judicial review and popular sovereignty are consequential. Contrarily, Schmitt considered that envisaging the courts as guardians of the Constitution would be "directly opposed to the democratic principle considered in its political consequences". According to him:

> Judicial review could be political successful in the nineteenth century, in France as well as in the German constitutional monarchies, in the face of the king's power to enact decrees. On the twentieth century judicial power is no longer directed against the king, but against parliament. This signifies a momentous transformation of judicial independence. The old separation between state and society has also been suppressed in this case and the formulas and arguments that were proper to the nineteenth century must not be simply transferred to the completely different political and social situation of the twentieth century. (…). The concentration of all constitutional disputes in a sole court composed by professional judges that are independent and immovable would amount to the creation of a second house of parliament whose members would be career civil servants. (…). From a democratic point of view it would be almost impossible for an aristocracy in robes to assume such a function.[30]

Before this, Kelsen asks: why is Schmitt assuming that the Constitutional Court must confront only the Parliament and not also the executive power? In fact, according to Kelsen, Schmitt's text is, all of it, permeated with "the tendency to ignore the possibility of a violation of the Constitution by the Chief of State or the Government".[31] Schmitt's answer to this question, we already know it, was that Parliament in the twentieth century was undermined by party pluralism. In the face of a Parliament that is unable to function, submerged by the disintegrating methods

[28]See Kelsen (2006: 178).

[29]See Jestaedt and Lepsius (2006: XXV–XXVI).

[30]See Schmitt (1996: 155–156).

[31]See Kelsen (2008a, b: 101).

of the pluralist state of political parties, "the job of the Chief of State is to 'rescue' the state".[32] For Schmitt, according to Kelsen, the norms that regulate the organs and the legislative procedure are not the 'Constitution'; the 'Constitution' is, instead, "a situation that corresponds to the unity of the German people. The meaning of this 'unity'—which has a substantial, and not merely formal, character —is something not more precisely determined".[33] For Schmitt the deadly sin of Parliament is pluralism, as opposed to the unity of the German people represented by the President of the Reich.[34]

Whereas for Schmitt democracy exists before the Constitution, in any case before constitutional law, for Kelsen democracy is a product of constitutional law; in fact, democracy is constituted by the law and its procedures. In this light the incompatibility between constitutional justice and democracy disappears. As Kelsen says in his *On the Essence and Value of Democracy*, "the destiny of democracy depends in great measure on a systematic organization of all control institutions. Democracy without control is on the long term impossible".[35]

Even if one believes Kelsen's conception of democracy to be (mostly) right and Schmitt's to be (mostly) wrong, as I do, the two conceptions cannot stand alone and completely apart from each other. Paraphrasing Kant, perhaps we could say that Kelsen's democratic procedures without democratic identity are empty just as Schmitt's democratic identity without democratic procedures is blind. But what is important to point out is that the tension between both conceptions is not something of the past. For a confirmation of this one has simply to consider Bruce Ackerman's book *The Decline and Fall of the American Republic*. He thinks that the death of the republic does not necessarily mean the end of democracy. Even if the American constitutional tradition is overwhelmed by presidential power Ackerman maintains that the presidency may well remain an elective office, and he even alludes to Schmitt in connection with this. The problems posed by "executive constitutionalism" are as alive today as they were in Schmitt's time.[36]

In the end there was one common point to both Schmitt and Kelsen's conceptions of democracy: neither of them had the experience of the Demos as an empirical and social magnitude, as in the legal orders originated in the American and French Revolutions. But whereas Schmitt sought to compensate this absence with an existential idea of the people, Kelsen proposed to construct the people as a normative reality.[37]

[32]See Kelsen (2008a, b: 103).

[33]See footnote 32.

[34]According to Schmitt's view of political representation this phenomenon amounts to a presentation of the people's invisible unity: cf. Schmitt (2010: 209).

[35]See Kelsen (2006: 209).

[36]See Ackerman (2010: 83–85).

[37]See Lepsius (2007: 123).

7.4 Judicial Review and the Proper Functions of a Court

In Carl Schmitt's view one must distinguish, first of all, between judicial control of a law on the basis of its conformity with the Constitution and the political protection of the Constitution. This distinction is a direct result of Schmitt's separation between the Constitution as the outcome of a collective decision on the political existence of a State, or as a substantial form of political unity, and constitutional law as its normative accomplishment.[38]

Judicial control is only possible, according to Schmitt, regarding norms with an uncontroversial determinable content which make possible a mere subsumption of the case: the judge applies the constitutional norm to the case at hand and refuses to apply the legal norm. However, when the constitutional norm has the nature of a principle this is no longer possible[39]: the judge must decide a conflict over the content of a wholly indeterminate norm. He must establish in an authoritative way a normative content that was previously in doubt. But when the judge decides over the content of an indeterminate constitutional norm he will be no longer acting as a judge but as a true legislator.[40] So, according to Schmitt, the judiciary has no legitimate role to play in such cases.

Schmitt admits that this had been precisely the case regarding the American Supreme Court resort to concepts such as property, liberty and equality. However, in that case, the Court had been legitimized by its appearance in front of the state as the protector of a natural social and economic order believed to be above discussion. In other words, in the American case, the separation between state and society still held, according to Schmitt, in the time of his writing. But that could not be adapted, in Schmitt's opinion, to a continental European state, given the diversity of its social and political situation.[41]

Schmitt's major premise appears then to be that there is a fundamental contradiction between the function of the judiciary and the political function: since the decision about constitutionality entails a political dimension, it can no longer be a judicial one. Kelsen, by contrast, held that there is a political element to every judicial decision, so that the political is always part of the judicial function.

According to Kelsen, if one sees a political dimension whenever one must decide a conflict—as Schmitt undoubtedly does—then there is a greater or lesser element of decision, that is, of exercise of power, in every judgment. The greater the degree of judicial discretion the stronger the political dimension of the decision, which may even approach legislation in character. As a consequence "there is only a quantitative, not a qualitative, difference between the political character of legislation and the one of the judicial function".[42] So Kelsen refuses the picture set by

[38]See Herrera (1994: 208).

[39]See Schmitt (1996: 15).

[40]See Schmitt (1996: 45).

[41]See Schmitt (1996: 12–14).

[42]See Kelsen (2008a, b: 67).

Montesquieu of the judge as automaton and claims that its adoption by Schmitt is strange given his own acceptance that there is in every judicial ruling an element of pure decision that cannot be derived from the norm.[43]

A second move of Kelsen against Schmitt concerns the claim made by the latter that no subsumption of the material facts under a norm is possible in a constitutional case.[44] This would be correct if one envisaged the subsumption of the facts of the case under a norm, but not with regard to the subsumption of the fact of the production of the norm under a (constitutional) norm that governs this fact and is therefore higher.[45]

Finally, Kelsen contends that although there are no natural law norms above the Constitution it is possible to positivize such norms in the Constitution, as in the case of liberty and equality. In this case it must be realized that such positivization is in fact a delegation of power to judges to decide the constitutionality of statutes in terms of concepts that have no determinate content.[46] But Kelsen strongly opposed such a wide delegation of discretion to a Constitutional Court, and said that could not be the meaning of the Constitution. In his own words (which inevitably bring to mind the arguments to be presented by Jeremy Waldron against judicial review[47]), with such a wide delegation of discretion,

> the Constitutional Court would be given an absolute power that in general must be felt as intolerable. What the majority of the justices see as just can be in complete disaccord to what stands as just for the majority of the population and certainly stands in opposition to what the majority in parliament, which has enacted the statute, holds as just. That this cannot be the meaning of the Constitution, that is, to make every law enacted by the parliament dependent upon the free discretion of a political council more or less arbitrarily assembled, like the Constitutional Court, only because of the use of so ambiguous words like 'justice' and others similar, is something self-evident.[48]

The remedy to this situation is not, however, as Kelsen candidly suggested, to avoid the use of vague terms in the Constitution, but to develop a theory of judicial review. It is not enough to assert, as Kelsen did, that the Constitutional Court only acts as a "negative legislator".[49] The idea of a "negative legislator" amounts to this: whereas civil, penal or administrative courts apply norms and generate more concrete norms that rule the cases brought before them, a Constitutional Court applies a constitutional norm and destroys a general legislative norm, that is, it enacts the *contrarius actus* to the one produced by the legislator.

As we know well enough, Schmitt's account of a quasi-legislative nature, and not only a negative one, of the Constitutional Court's development of constitutional

---

[43]See Kelsen (2008a, b: 67, 72).

[44]See Schmitt (1996: 31, 42).

[45]See Kelsen (2008a, b: 70–71); Dyzenhaus (1997: 113); La Torre (2013: 159–160).

[46]See Kelsen (2008a, b: 76).

[47]See Waldron (2006: 1348).

[48]See Kelsen (2008a, b: 40).

[49]See Kelsen (2008a, b: 78–79).

principles was right. No modern Constitution can avoid an extensive use of ambiguous concepts, in the words of Kelsen, and the restriction of that use is not surely a promising strategy if one wants to limit the activity of a Constitutional Court. It is not enough to affirm, as Kelsen did, that "if one wants to restrain the power of the courts, and therefore the political character of their function, (…) then one must limit as much as possible the space of free discretion conferred by laws to courts".[50] In a much more realistic way Schmitt praised the tendency of professional judges to exercise judicial self-restraint towards the executive and legislative powers, only striking down their acts when intrinsically unjustifiable in a manifest way. However he only extracted from that tendency a confirmation of his own thesis according to which the courts are not, given their mission, to solve doubts regarding the content of a constitutional norm.[51]

7.5 The Court and the Political Branches of Government

Schmitt's reason to condemn constitutional justice comes down to its consisting "not in a judicialization of politics, but in a politicization of justice".[52] Kelsen's defense of this indictment is well known: on the one hand there is an unavoidable political moment in every judicial decision; on the other hand, constitutional justice represents in fact a deepening of the principle of separation of powers, in the sense of a control of power by means of checks and balances.[53]

Once more we are confronted with the question of the political or judicial character of the defense of the Constitution. Schmitt's view is revealed by the place he assigns to the constitutional guardian in the structure of the constitutional state. According to Schmitt the search for a guardian of the Constitution is, in the majority of cases, a sign that something is wrong with the Constitution. This is in fact his main worry when discussing this issue: he aims at finding the institution—in his view the President of the Reich, to which article 48 of the Weimar Constitution conferred special powers of emergency—most fit to protect the Constitution in times of crisis.[54]

This is not of course Kelsen's point of view. His purpose is not to devise an institution specially attuned to times of crisis but an institution that can take part in the normal life of a constitutional democracy. Whereas Schmitt is after an institution able to protect his idea of the Constitution, if necessary against constitutional

[50]See Kelsen (2008a, b: 76).

[51]See Schmitt (1996: 22, see also pp. 50–52).

[52]See Schmitt (1996: 22, see also p. 35).

[53]See van Ooyen (2008: IX).

[54]See Schmitt (1996: 1).

law, Kelsen looks for an institution that can secure the normal enforcement of constitutional law.[55]

Kelsen was correct in the sense that there is no necessary incompatibility between constitutional review and democracy, from a political point of view. On the contrary, constitutional review is one of those controls that make democracy a real possibility. For Kelsen no such thing as the people in its concrete existence exists beyond the procedures that make its voice manifest in a constitutional democracy. But Schmitt was also correct in pointing out that, from a legal point of view, the development of constitutional principles by constitutional courts present a real danger of encroachment upon the proper dominion of the legislator.

Both authors acknowledged the presence of a decisionistic element in every judicial decision. How are we to deal with this inevitable presence? Surely not by simply saying, as Kelsen did, that the element of decisionism present in every judicial decision is merely the result of an element of discretion given to the judge by the norm. Nor is it acceptable to exclude courts from any effective role as guardians of the Constitution, as Schmitt did, only by saying that the application of a norm cannot be entirely controlled by another norm, even if the premise is true.

In the case of judicial decisions the type of normative indeterminacy that is inevitably present in constitutional norms is part of the judicial praxis itself and it is in this praxis that courts can produce their own legitimacy through coherence and transparence, securing the rule of law against singular case disappointments. Schmitt's earlier works admitted this reading,[56] but his mounting insistence on the importance of the exceptional case has left no place for the normal intervention of the judicial praxis.[57]

7.6 The Presence of Schmitt and Kelsen in the Current European Constitutionalism

It is now time to recover our initial question: why bother reading Schmitt and Kelsen today? What is their relevance to European constitutionalism? I'm afraid their relevance is rather admonitory: the weaknesses of their respective conceptions on the guardian of the Constitution are all too present in the present Euro crisis.

Kelsen admission of the presence of a political, decisionistic element, in all judicial decisions is no secure basis to construe a theory of constitutional review that respects the principle of separation of powers. And Kelsen's warning against a wide delegation of discretion to a Constitutional Court, by means of the use in

[55]See Lepsius (2007: 115, 121).

[56]See Schmitt (2009: 38–41). On this, see also Section III of Luís Pereira Coutinho's contribution to this volume.

[57]See Lembcke (2012: 76–77).

Constitutions of such concepts as "justice", "liberty" or "equality", is surely no promising way to construe such a theory.[58] In fact it amounts to no theory at all.

On the other hand, Schmitt's conception of the guardian of the Constitution, with its surrender of the Constitution before the executive power, is the main source of the "executive constitutionalism", as above mentioned. The executive power can, no doubt, enjoy democratic legitimacy. However, in this context, democracy will most probably assume a plebiscitary, not deliberative, nature.[59]

The weaknesses in the conceptions of the guardian of the Constitution of both Kelsen and Schmitt make it difficult for such a guardian to act as an "exemplar of public reason", in the words of Rawls.[60] More important, it can be argued that both weaknesses are presently at work in European constitutionalism, and particularly in the case of Portugal.

Damian Chalmers recently wrote an article putting the hypothesis of a Schmittian Europe in what regards the functioning of the European Stability Mechanism (ESM). According to him "the ESM and the government seeking support decide the measures necessary to restore stability, notably the level of financial support and the conditions to be attached. These are set out by a Memorandum of Understanding and not by any law".[61] As is shown by Chalmers the only substantive constraint imposed by the ESM Treaty on the Memorandum of Understanding—which governs a debtor state fiscal and welfare policy—is for its content to reflect "the severity of the weaknesses to be addressed and the financial assistance instrument chosen" (see article 13, paragraph 3 of ESM Treaty). The Memorandum of Understanding is a decision uncovered by the EU law and perhaps even by the internal law of the member state asking for financial assistance; yet it apparently generates law, as legal measures must be taken to implement it.[62]

---

[58]Curiously this warning is kept by modern positivists like Luigi Ferrajoli, when he says that "the only way that the legislator has to submit the judge to his will is to reduce as much as possible the discretionary powers and to execute well his own job, that is, to produce legal norms with the most univocal and precise meaning as possible". See Ferrajoli (2013: 54).

[59]See Posner and Vermeule (2010: 204–206).

[60]See Rawls (1996: 231).

[61]See Chalmers (2013: 26–27). It must not be forgotten at this point that Schmitt defended a development of an economic and financial state of exception beside an original military and police state of exception. According to Schmitt, each nucleus of the state has its own form of exception. The judicial state has its form of exception in the martial court, the executive power in the suspension of constitutional rights, and the legislative constitutional state in the executive decrees with force of law on matters of economy and finance: see Schmitt (1996: 131). This last one could perhaps be the ideal scenario for the development of a situation in which the guarding of the European constitution would increasingly belong to the political realm [this shift from a legalistic to a political constitution is the hypothesis suggested by Franz C. Mayer, although in a somewhat different, more institutional, context: see Mayer (2004: 411 ff.; 433–435)].

[62]See Chalmers (2013: 27). Chalmers also points out two other Schmittian features of Europe's response to the financial crisis, beside the power of decision viewed as a foundational power that precedes law and gives a prior power to the administration. On the one hand, the interests of the political order and of ensuring no threat to stability, rather than any broader justification, were assumed as the central aims of the ESM, as stated in Article 3 of the ESM Treaty; on the other

This is confirmed in the case of Portugal. On the 17th May of 2011, following Portugal's request of financial assistance to the European Commission, the IMF and the European Central Bank, a Memorandum of Understanding on Specific Economic Policy Conditionality and a Loan Agreement were signed, that including a joint financing package of €78 billion, covering the period from 2011 to mid-2014. Contrary to what happened in Greece and Ireland, these documents were not submitted to the Portuguese Parliament for approval—the Parliament was dissolved at the moment—and were only signed by the Government.[63]

The management of the crisis in Europe has taken place through a "primacy of the 'Political' in the Union sensu Schmitt". This statement is used to describe the attitude of the European Court of Justice, which has chosen not to question Europe's new modes of economic governance as embodied in the ESM.[64] In this respect, Portugal seems to be an exception: in a series of rulings from 2011 to 2014 the Portuguese Constitutional Court stroke down the pay and pension cuts for public employees introduced by the Government and approved by Parliament, grounding itself mainly on the violation of the principles of equality and reliance.

This is not the place to discuss these rulings,[65] but only to point out that the Court's approach is open to criticism with regard to the legitimacy of striking down decisions in matters of economic and financial policy democratically taken by the Parliament—and that on the ground of concepts as indeterminate as equality or reliance. In Kelsen's view the Court has certainly pushed to the limit the political dimension inherent in all judicial decisions. On the other hand, as noted by some commentators, the decisions of the Portuguese Court can be viewed precisely as the reaffirmation of the Portuguese "social sovereignty" by means of the law's judge and not the law's author.[66]

In the end Kelsen meets Schmitt: the political management of the crisis triggers a political management of the judicial activity. In this scenario it is not simply the case that politics has nothing to win while justice can lose it all, as the saying of François Guizot goes[67]; rather it may be the case that both justice and (deliberative) politics can lose it all.

(Footnote 62 continued)
hand, the crisis is presented as one of systemic risk whereby the whole European economy could collapse in a way that to refuse aid or to default can be viewed as an act of enmity not only towards the euro, but Europe itself.

[63]See Alexandrino (2014: 53).

[64]See Everson and Joerges (2013: 8, 22–24). See also the authors' analysis of the *Pringle* case, at pp. 19 ff.

[65]See Nogueira de Brito (2014: 73 ff.).

[66]See Cisotta and Gallo (2013: 480).

[67]Quoted in Schmitt (1996: 35).

References

ACKERMAN, Bruce. 2010. The Decline and Fall of the American Republic, Cambridge (Mass.): The Belknap Press of Harvard University Press.

ALEXANDRINO, José de Melo. 2014. Jurisprudência da Crise. Das Questões Prévias às Perplexidades. In O Tribunal Constitucional e a Crise: Ensaios Críticos. Eds. Gonçalo Almeida Ribeiro e Luís Pereira Coutinho. Coimbra: Almedina.

BRITO, Miguel Nogueira de. 2014. Putting Social Rights in Brackets? The Portuguese Experience with Welfare Challenges in Times of Crisis. In *Social Rights in Times of Crisis in the Eurozone: The Role of Fundamental Rights Challenges*. Ed. Claire Kilpratrick and Bruno De Witte. EUI Department of Law Research Paper No. 2014/05. Available at SSRN: http://ssrn.com/abstract=2428855 or http://dx.doi.org/10.2139/ssrn.2428855.

BRITO, Miguel Nogueira de. 2000. A Constituição Constituinte: Ensaio sobre o Poder de Revisão da Constituição. Coimbra: Coimbra Editora.

CHALMERS, Damian. 2013. European Restatements of Sovereignty. In *Law, Society and Economy Working Papers* 10/2013, London School of Economics and Political Science Law Department.

CISOTTA, Roberto and GALLO, Daniele. 2013. Il Tribunale Costituzionale portoghese, i risvolti sociale delle misuri di austerità ed il rispetto dei vincoli internazionali ed europei. *Diritti Umani e Diritto Internazionale*, vol. 7, n.º 2.

DYZENHAUS, David. 1997. Legality and Legitimacy: Carl Schmitt, Hans Kelsen and Hermann Heller in Weimar. Oxford: Clarendon Press.

EVERSON, Michelle and JOERGES, Christian. 2013. Who is the Guardian for Constitutionalism in Europe after the Financial Crisis? LEQS Paper No. 63/2013, June 2013.

FERRAJOLI, Luigi. 2013. Dei Diritti e delle Garanzie: Conversazione con Mauro Barberis. Bologna: Il Mulino.

HERRERA, Carlos Miguel 1994. La Polémica Schmitt-Kelsen sobre el Guardián de la Constitución. In *Revista de Estudios Políticos* (Nueva Época), Núm. 86. Octubre-Diciembre.

JESTAEDT, Matthias and LEPSIUS, O. 2006. Der Rechts- und der Demokratietheoretiker Hans Kelsen – Eine Einführung. In Hans Kelsen. 2006. Verteidigung der Demokratie. Ed. Matthias Jestaedt and Oliver Lepsius. Tübingen: Mohr Siebeck.

KELSEN, Hans. 1942. Judicial Review of Legislation: A Comparative Study of the Austrian and the American Constitution. *The Journal of Politics*, 4.

KELSEN, Hans. 1949. General Theory of Law and State, 3rd printing. Translated by Anders Wedberg. Cambridge (Mass.): Harvard University Press.

KELSEN, Hans. 2006. Vom Wesen und Wert der Demokratie (2. Auflage 1929). In Verteidigung der Demokratie. Ed. Matthias Jestaedt and Oliver Lepsius. Tübingen: Mohr Siebeck.

KELSEN, Hans. 2008a. Wesen und Entwicklung der Staatsgerichtsbarkeit. In *Wer soll der Hüter der Verfassung sein? Abhandlungen zur Theorie der Verfassungsgerichtsbarkeit in der pluralistischen, parlamentarischen Demokratie*. Ed. Robert Chr. van Ooyen. Tübingen: Mohr Siebeck.

KELSEN, Hans. 2008b. Wer soll der Hüter der Verfassung sein? In *Wer soll der Hüter der Verfassung sein? Abhandlungen zur Theorie der Verfassungsgerichtsbarkeit in der pluralistischen, parlamentarischen Demokratie*. Ed. Robert Chr. van Ooyen. Tübingen: Mohr Siebeck.

LA TORRE, Massimo. 2013. Chi Ha Paura del Giudice Costituzionale? Decisionismo e Positivismo Giuridico. In *Quaderni Fiorentini per la Storia del Pensiero Giuridico Moderno* Vol. 42.

LAGI, Sara. 2012. Hans Kelsen and the Austrian Constitutional Court (1918-1929). In *Revista Coherencia*, Vol. 9, n.º 16, Enero-Junio.

LEMBCKE, Oliver W. 2012. Urteilskraft in der Praxis des Bundesverfassungsgerichts. Eine Erinnerung an Hannah Arendt. In *Subsumtion: Schlüsselbegriff der Juristischen Methodenlehre*. Ed. Gottfried Gabriel and Rolf Gröschner. Tübingen: Mohr Siebeck.

LEPSIUS, Oliver. 2007. Der Hüter der Verfassung – demokratietheoretisch betrachtet. In La Controverse sur « le gardien de la Constitution » et la justice constitutionnelle. Kelsen contre Schmitt. Eds. Olivier Beaud and Pasquale Pasquino. Paris: Éditions Panthéon-Assas.

MAYER, Franz C. 2004. Wer soll Hüter der europäischen Verfassung sein? In *Archiv des öffentlichen Rechts*, 129, no. 3, pp. 411–435.

ÖHLINGER, Theo. 2003. The Genesis of the Austrian Model of Constitutional Review of Legislation. In *Ratio Juris*, Vol. 16, no. 2, June, pp. 211–214.

VAN OOYEN, Robert Chr. 2008. Die Funktion der Verfassungsgerichtsbarkeit in der pluralistischen Demokratie und die Kontroverse um den 'Hüter der Verfassung'. In Hans Kelsen, *Wer soll der Hüter der Verfassung sein? Abhandlungen zur Theorie der Verfassungsgerichtsbarkeit in der pluralistischen, parlamentarischen Demokratie*. Ed. Robert Chr. van Ooyen. Tübingen: Mohr Siebeck.

PAULSON, Stanley L. 2003. Constitutional Review in the United States and Austria: Notes on the Beginings. In *Ratio Juris*, Vol. 16, No. 2, June, pp. 235–236.

POSNER, Eric A. and VERMEULE, Adrian. 2010. The Executive Unbound: After the Madisonian Republic. New York: Oxford University Press.

RAWLS, John. 1996. Political Liberalism. New York: Columbia University Press.

RENAN, Ernest. 1996. Qu'est-ce que une nation? In *Qu'est-ce que une nation? et autres écrits politiques*. Ed. Raoul Girardet. Paris: Imprimerie Nationale Éditions.

SCHMITT, Carl. 1994. Die Wendung zum Totalen Staat. In *Positionen und Begriff im Kampf mit Weimar, Genf, Versailles 1923–1939*, 3rd ed., Berlin: Duncker & Humblot.

SCHMITT, Carl. 1996 (1931). Der Hütter der Verfassung, 4th ed. Berlin: Duncker & Humblot.

SCHMITT, Carl. 2009 (1912). Gesetz und Urteil. München: Verlag C. H. Beck.

SCHMITT, Carl. 2010 (1928). Verfassungslehre, 10th ed. Berlin: Duncker & Humblot.

WALDRON, Jeremy. 2006. The Core of the Case Against Judicial Review. *Yale Law Journal* 116, 1346.

Chapter 8
Theories of Judicial Behavior and the Law: Taking Stock and Looking Ahead

Tiago Fidalgo de Freitas

8.1 Introduction

Several theories have been put forward to try to make sense of how apex courts decide the cases that are brought before them and to measure judicial activism. They are strikingly different in scope and purpose, methodology and assumptions, but they all try to understand how the adjudication process unfolds and law is put into practice. As the analysis shall illustrate, not all of them are mutually incompatible. Quite the opposite: they serve as different lenses shedding light on distinct aspects of judicial decision-making, each engaging in a different enterprise.[1]

Amongts these, *positive (political) theories of judicial review*—more suggestively labelled *theories of judicial behaviour*—aim at suggesting a cognitive framework accounting for the ways in which rulings are delivered, focusing on how courts do it and why: what motivates and influences judges to decide, in concrete, each case.[2] They attempt to go beyond the reasons judges adduce in their opinions, claiming that the real explanations for judicial decisions are not necessarily the

---

[1]See Dyèvre (2008: 8–14).

[2]For an overview of the existing theories of judicial behaviour, see Baum (2008: 5–19), Burbank (2011: 41–60), Dyèvre (2008: 10–22, 2010: 300–312), Friedman and Martin (2011: 147–156), Magalhães (2003: 257–269), Magalhães and de Araújo (1998: 11–16), Posner (2008: 19–56), Robertson (2010a: 579–588), Segal and Spaeth (2002: 86–114), Segal (2011: 18–34). For an intellectual history of judicial behaviour theories, see Maveety (2002: 1–44).

T.F. de Freitas (✉)
European University Institute, Florence, Italy
e-mail: tiago.freitas@eui.eu

T.F. de Freitas
School of Law, University of Lisbon, Lisbon, Portugal

T.F. de Freitas
Lisbon Centre for Research in Public Law, Lisbon, Portugal

L.P. Coutinho et al. (eds.), *Judicial Activism*,
Ius Gentium: Comparative Perspectives on Law and Justice 44,
DOI 10.1007/978-3-319-18549-1_8

rationales that are stated in the majority's or in an individual judge's opinion. They would rather lie in other factors, pertaining to the individual judge or to the general context in which she moves. Indeed, as positive theories were born out of the legal realism movement[3] and dominated by political scientists, they typically give precedence to extra-legal explanations.[4] Being causal accounts of judicial decision-making—i.e., theories that assume, and argue, that judicial decisions are determined by factors which can be interpreted as causes—, they aim at enabling predictions.

Technically, the outcome of judicial decisions is taken as the dependent variable and the authors try to identify the independent variable that might determine it. To do so, they resort to *models*. These are representations of the reality that focus on the most explanatory variables of a certain behaviour, concentrating on the big picture and providing a framework that can be systematically used to understand a set of cases. They generally consider whether certain characteristics of the object relate to one another by systematising enormous amounts of data and extracting inferences about the existence of patterns. While doing so, they necessarily simplify the complexity of the reality they analyse and go beyond the idiosyncrasy of case-studies. At the same time that they illuminate past deeds, they aim at predicting future behaviours. This does not mean, however, that all models must be both explanatory and predictive: some only try to map and make sense of observed phenomena, while others focus on anticipating upcoming events. One essential characteristic is that models must be falsifiable or at least testable.[5]

In the following pages, the most relevant positive models will be discussed: the attitudinal and the strategic (internal and external) models. The so-called 'legal models'—i.e., those that are based on legal variables to explain judicial behaviour, such as the plain meaning of the law, the intent of the framers, precedent, and balancing—have been bracketed. The reason for this is that they are not real positive models, but rather normative: they do not analyse how the decision-making process actually takes place, but prescribe how it ought to.[6]

The objective of the subsequent sections is to state their purpose and briefly evaluating their potential for the current enterprise: that of measuring and understanding when and why judicial activism occurs. The positive accounts of judicial

---

[3]For an overview of the legal realism movement, see Leiter (2010).

[4]See Segal and Spaeth (2002: 97–103).

[5]See Segal and Spaeth (2002: 44–48), Spaeth (2008: 754–755), Friedman and Martin (2011: 148–150).

[6]In addition, political scientists do not really engage with the legal literature and picture it as no more than a caricature, dubbing it as "meaningless" and not even hesitating in admitting that they rely on anecdotal evidence for their claims regarding the legal model—see Segal and Spaeth (1993: 62). It is therefore not surprising that they claim that the legal model "serves only to rationalise the Court's decisions and to cloak the reality of the Court's decision-making process"—see Segal and Spaeth (1993: 34); see also Segal and Spaeth (2002: 48–85). Similarly, considering that positive theories "attack a model of the law that simply does not exist" and that their "descriptions of the legal model do not correspond to the conceptions of the law held by lawyers, judges, and law professors", see Gerhardt (2005: 912). For a different account of a legalist model of judicial review, see the chapter by Almeida Ribeiro in this volume.

law-making that will be surveyed are general theories about judicial behaviour, and not theories that are focused on specific types or categories of issues adjudicated by courts.

As it will be seen, all of them are insufficient—either alone or altogether—and no 'size fits all'. What is more: certain theoretical approaches are strongly conditioned by the institutional environment of origin, and cannot persuasively suggest any universalist claims. In fact, most of this work has been written by US scholars, generally on US courts, with an emphasis on federal courts and particularly on the Supreme Court.[7] When it is not written by US scholars and about US courts, it is still heavily influenced by the US model and its assumptions; its transferability is, therefore, doubtful.[8]

8.2 The Attitudinal Model

The attitudinal model was the first positive model proposed by political scientists to analyse judicial behaviour.[9]

According to this theory, judges would come to the bench with a crystallised set of ideological predispositions and would systematically apply them in their adjudication of the cases at hand. It would be their raw preferences and attitudes to policy that would determine the content of their rulings. Essentially political in nature, those principles and values would be shaped by their personalities, background, and presuppositions. The consequence is therefore that the primary determinant of judicial decision-making would be the judge's own values.[10] As such, the legal arguments that judges use in their opinions would be simple post hoc justifications and not true causes of judicial behaviour. Put bluntly yet simplistically, this means that conservative judges would vote for conservative decisions, whereas liberal judges would vote for liberal ones.

To measure their preferences, the proponents of the attitudinal model submit a number of possible proxies: the judges' background or personal attributes, region of birth, judicial experience, past voting records, the political preferences of the

[7]Spaeth (2008: 763). Explaining the reasons for this, see Robertson (2010b: 21–22). The author adduces one main factor for the prevalence (and influence) of the US scholarship: the fact that US (positive) political science scholarship seems to technically have the lead in the subject. See also Magalhães and de Araújo (1998: 16–18, 40–42).

[8]Robertson (2010b: 24), even states that "no one, to [his] knowledge, has ever convincingly applied such an attitudinal model to, for example, a European court". Examples of solid work regarding its applicability to European and Asian jurisdictions include de Araújo (1997), Volcansek (2000), Magalhães (2003), Ginsburg (2003), and Vanberg (2004).

[9]The landmark work on this model is that of Segal and Spaeth (1993, 2002). For earlier versions, see, e.g., Rohde and Spaeth (1975).

[10]Although this model might work for all courts, it works particularly well for apex courts, which cannot be overruled by other courts—see Segal (2008: 25).

appointing authority, as well as their published work or interviews.[11] The choice of the 'measure of judicial ideology' is a very important step in these accounts.

This is the dominant model to analyse the US Supreme Court. The fact that US Supreme Court justices have life tenure (and therefore no incentives to seek higher offices), no electoral accountability, and complete control over their docket make it a particularly adequate model.[12] It is because Supreme Court justices are so completely unconstrained that they can freely implement political policy preferences.[13]

The implication of this model is that changes in judicial personnel are likely to bring about changes in judicial politics.[14] This theory comes with the corollary that promotions or demotions of judicial personnel are bound to tamper with the delicate balance of judicial politics.

From another perspective, this means that judicial decisions can only be moulded by external actors through the appointment process: the initial selection of a liberal or of a conservative judge. And the selection of politically dependable judges, from this standpoint, is a victory of the attitudinal school.[15] Drawing a parallel with game theory, it resembles the adverse selection game, in which the only relevant fact is the a priori type of the appointed actor.[16]

Interestingly, by defending that judges decide cases only in accordance with their pre-existing political preferences, attitudinalists claim that no other institutions constrain judges. By way of doing this, they assert that the latter decide their cases completely insulated from the political context.[17]

---

[11]Segal and Spaeth (1993: 221–234) most rely on past voting record and content analysis (i.e., press editorials that characterise the US Supreme Court nominees before their confirmation), but set aside the social background. For a different perspective, focusing on how judges gain their preferences, see Baum (2011: 79).

[12]Not all apex courts share these features. The term of Portuguese constitutional justices, for example, lasts for 9 years and it is not renewable [see Article 222(3) of the Portuguese Constitution]; at the same time, the court has virtually no control over its docket. For other relevant data, see de Araújo (1997: 55–64, 69), as well as Magalhães and de Araújo (1998: 21–26).

[13]See Segal and Spaeth (1993: 69–72, 358), recognising that the full application of the model may be limited to the US Supreme Court on civil rights and liberties matters. On the same point, see Friedman and Martin (2011: 166), hinting at selection bias.

[14]On the factors that affect the presidential nomination (partisanship and ideology; political environment; prior experience; region; religion, race, and sex; and friendship and patronage), see Segal and Spaeth (2002: 179–186, 1993: 126–131).

[15]See Burbank (2011: 60), Posner (2008: 169). On the topic, see Epstein and Segal (2007: 119–145).

[16]See Landau (2005: 697).

[17]See Friedman (2006: 274).

8.3 The Strategic Model

Proponents of the strategic model do concede that the judges' preferences and values play a role in judicial decision-making. However, significantly influenced by the rational choice theory axiom that human behaviour is inherently interactive,[18] they add a supplementary caveat: that their influence is significantly conditioned and constrained by the institutional setting in which judges operate.[19]

This model's claim is that judges would defect from their ideological ideal point so as to effectively weigh on the court's final decision or, at least, its long term policies. In other words: judges would be led to rationally deviate from their brute preferences by the presence of other relevant actors within the systems. Each player would behave strategically on the basis of her preferences, of her perceptions, and in anticipation of the other players' preferences and strategies. It would be a game of mutual calculation in which judges would not wait for the other actors to act and see what happens, but would think ahead and modify their positions, even if that would mean going for the second-best outcome. The consequence of this would be that at times courts would not get away with their most preferred result, but would instead meet halfway between theirs and those of other institutions. It would therefore be a matter of anticipated reaction. And "the implication of anticipated reaction is that institutions may be responding to constraint, even if this is unobservable".[20]

This theory, along with the attitudinal model, acknowledges that all institutions have preferences regarding policy outcomes.[21] The difference is that it also sustains that, in acting, they must take into account the preferences of other actors that play a role in the ultimate policy choice.[22]

It rests, then, on a sharp dichotomy between sincere behaviour, whereby a judge would not take account of the other judges' or political actors' preferences but would rely solely on his own views and preferences, and strategic behaviour, whereby a judge is driven by his determination to ensure a final outcome which is the closest possible to his preferences. This does not mean, though, that sincere (attitudinal) and strategic judges will always behave differently: "strategic considerations may require only occasional and limited departures from judges' most preferred positions".[23] The fundamental difference is, then, one of motivation to act.

The strategic model has two different versions, depending on whom the relevant other actors are considered to be: the remaining judges in the court (for the internal strategic model) or the broader political environment (for the external strategic model).

---

[18]See Segal (2011: 30).

[19]The seminal work on the strategic theory belongs to Epstein and Knight (1997).

[20]See Friedman (2006: 312).

[21]Claiming that both attitudinal and strategic models are in practice one wherein actors are assumed to have preferences and to act strategically to maximise them, see Landau (2005: 696).

[22]See Epstein (2008: 496–497).

[23]See Baum (2011: 73–74).

Regardless of which of the two is chosen, the result is always "an account of how individual judicial policy preferences lead to group decisions".[24]

8.3.1 The Internal Strategic Model

The internal strategic model emphasises the collegial structure of judicial bodies and the dynamics of the deliberation process.[25] In a sentence, the theories based on this model predict that judges will vote on the basis of what they expect their colleagues will do.

A number of institutional elements constrain the unfolding collegial game in procedural terms. In particular, the court's statute and rules shape the room for internal dynamics, as well as determine both where the power rests in the court and more crucially how that power is exercised.[26] All procedural stages might be pertinent: from the admissibility moment to the preliminary vote, from the assignment of the task of writing the majority opinion to the decision to join, concur, or dissent.[27] Several factors are relevant: the rules concerning the quorum for decisions, the majority required to strike down laws, the size of the court, who assigns the writing of opinions for the court,[28] whether the court has the power to set its own agenda by controlling its own docket (e.g., the US Supreme Court's certiorari practice).[29]

There are two limitations to research done within this model. On the one hand, it presupposes, at the empirical level, that there is open access to data on opinion assignment and to the minutes of conference meetings and internal documents. In the US, it is possible to resort to, and empirically substantiate, this type of analysis because US Supreme Court data is available; the same cannot be said, though, of many other countries. On the other hand, this model requires a deliberative court, i.e., one in which judges debate the available normative directions and interact in ways that lead them to consider one another's views, or at least one in which (explicit or implicit) bargaining takes place.[30] The truth, however, seems to be that, at most, what occurs is a certain degree of accommodation among opinions.

---

[24]See Robertson (2010b: 22).

[25]Emphasising the role of collegiality and the contribution of the economic analysis of law for its understanding, see Kornhauser (2008: 705–708), with further references.

[26]See Friedman (2005: 291).

[27]See Spiller and Gely (2008: 41).

[28]See Friedman (2006: 291).

[29]On case selection and the US Supreme Court's caseload, see Segal and Spaeth (2002: 240–252, 1993: 179–185), as well as Rohde and Spaeth (1975: 118–133).

[30]Arguing that internal procedural rules and customary practices are extremely relevant variables in assessing the deliberative performance of a court, see Afonso da Silva (2013).

This corresponds to the exchange of suggestions after draft versions of documents are circulated, so as to "'improve' the meaning of the text by eliminating uncertainty, dodging thorny problems, and offering greater clarity".[31]

8.3.2 The External Strategic Model

The external strategic model, instead of focusing on the court's collegial dynamics, highlights the broader political setting in which courts and judges operate. In seeking to maximise their preferences, judges would be, to a large extent, constrained by their political and institutional environment. Judges would anticipate the reactions of other actors to their rulings, just as other actors may anticipate the judicial decisions. These actors would range from presidents, legislatures, the executive branch, through a number of interest groups and lobbies, to lower courts.

This trend of the strategic theory assumes that the court will construe the constitutional provisions as close to its ideal preferred outcome as possible without running the risk of being trumped by any other political branch. The result of the judicial decision-making process would therefore be a function of the interactions between the court and its political and institutional environments.

The general assumption underlying this theory is that the potential risk of a preference, as incorporated in a ruling, being overturned would be the main variable that would determine the degree of judicial activism. Consequently, the high probability of non-compliance with a ruling by the legislative and executive branches would diminish the room for an active court. Conversely, the high probability of the proper implementation of the judicial decision would afford the Court ample margin of discretion and activism.

This theory departs from the presupposition that the court has a vested interest in actively preserving its authority, legitimacy and institutional integrity. This supposes, in turn, that it entails having its decisions implemented by the other branches and thus attain a high level of compliance with its decisions.[32]

Several institutional variables may account for variations in judicial policy-making. In specific, the rigidity of the constitutional amending process, the existence of veto powers, the policy preferences of the legislature and the executive, the distance between the policy preferences of the disputants, or the normative chasm between the preferences of the legislative majority and the opposition, public opinion and public support for the court, and precedents do explicate judicial policy making to varying degrees.

---

[31]See Friedman (2005: 287).

[32]Several reasons might explain non-compliance: the lack of coercive capacity, the lack of clarity in the court's opinion, or the fact that decisions only bind the parties to litigation—see Segal and Spaeth (1993: 337–345, 348–353), analysing several case-studies.

It is easy to understand why constitutional rigidity, for example, might play a role in judicial law-making. If the legislature can easily reverse the rulings of the constitutional court by amending the constitution, it will be more likely that the court will defer to the policy preferences of the legislature. Otherwise, the court would be overturned and that might harm the court's institutional standing. Conversely, if the amendment procedure is lengthy and costly, the court will be more at ease with confronting the legislator.[33]

Constitutional rigidity alone, however, could only explain the variations among countries with different constitutional arrangements. Differently, it cannot explain variations among countries where constitutions are equally rigid. Nor can it explain variations in judicial activism throughout time with the same constitutional framework.[34]

In this game, the political branches have another set of weapons available: judges may be impeached, jurisdiction may be stripped, courts may be packed, and judicial budgets may be cut. Even if these tools do exist, the doctrine of anticipated reaction claims that the political branches need not use them and still keep the judiciary in check.

Without denying the impact of the appointment process, the strategic model suggests that external actors can also influence judicial behaviour after this point in time through the use of incentives such as denials of promotions, reputational losses, impeachment, and reversals.[35]

8.4 Limitations of the Positive Model(s)

Even if the empirical work of positive scholars has shown that ideology is, amidst other variables, a statistically relevant factor for determining judicial outcomes, its effects have been overstated.[36] Several trends of criticism to this school of research can be presented, some of which are internal, whereas some others are external.[37]

The main internal negative points lie on its methodological issues. Indeed, the empirical scholars' findings are only as good as their measures,[38] i.e., what variable

---

[33]See Lijphart (1999: 216–231).

[34]See Dyèvre (2008: 16–18).

[35]Landau (2005: 697) considers that this model resembles the game known as 'moral hazard'. It is doubtful that it is so, nevertheless, because there is no transfer of any risks that would allow courts to be unusually chanceful.

[36]See Cross (2011: 92, 99–104).

[37]For an overview, see Gerhardt (2005: 912–920).

[38]An example of how research tailoring may adversely impact the results is that of Amaral-Garcia et al. (2009). The authors assessed a total of 270 rulings of the Portuguese Constitutional Court over a period of 23 years (1985–2007) and concluded that "constitutional judges in Portugal are quite sensitive to their political affiliations and their political party's presence in government when voting"—see Amaral-Garcia et al. (2009: 381, 402). While doing so, they focused only on *ex ante* review of constitutionality "because this method is more related to party politics and usually

is chosen to determine their quantifiability across groups of cases.[39] One of the assumptions of virtually all positive models is that law's role as a constraint has been downplayed. However, it is very likely that this movement might have developed among positive scholars in a path-dependent fashion, much due to the dominant intra- (rather than inter-) disciplinary trends.[40] In effect, positive scholarship is self-referential, with only glancing citation to what legal scholars say.[41] As an example, one can take the fact that positive scholars do not distinguish among branches of law. This omission potentially has far-reaching consequences, because different methods of interpretation might apply.[42]

Among several methodological problems,[43] the issue of behavioural equivalence (or that of collinear variables) is self-evident: can one really say that the vote of a judge is a function of her ideology rather than her best understanding of the law? When the effects of two possible causes are the same, one cannot ascertain which of those two possible causes is the prevailing one.[44]

However, its external failures are perhaps the ones that are the most relevant for the purpose of this chapter. Even though there are several revelations of these, they can all be summarised as follows: the positive model fails to take the judicial argument seriously as a determinant of judicial decision-making, ignoring it altogether.

To begin with, it assumes that there is nothing substantial that distinguishes courts from (other) policy-making institutions (be it from the legislative or from the executive branch). "Courts are assumed to have and pursue collective interests in wielding influence and protecting their status and power. This assumption leads to studies of court decisions in terms of the court's strategic concerns". The

(Footnote 38 continued)
receives a lot of media attention", even though it was acknowledged that "the vast majority of the work by the Constitutional Court is on concrete judicial review" (Amaral-Garcia et al. 2009: 387). The problem is precisely that over that period of time, the Court decided a total of 18.936 cases (see http://www.tribunalconstitucional.pt/tc/tribunal-estatisticas.html Accessed 21 Nov 2014). This means that, although the paper makes universal claims about the behaviour of Portuguese constitutional justices, the authors only went through less than 1, 5 % of the Court's caseload. Magalhães (2003: 269–325) has, however, reached parallel conclusions. For more nuanced results, see de Araújo (1997: 85–182), as well as Magalhães and de Araújo (1998: 21–40). From a legal perspective, see Blanco de Morais (2011: 121–144, 481–497, 548–555, 968–980). For an overview, of the Court's profile, see Santos (2011: 71–208).

[39]On this topic, referring to the importance of the concept of 'construct validity', aimed at determining how well measures of particular variables capture phenomena of interest, see Braman and Pickerill (2011: 121).

[40]This argument is put forward (with evidence) by Braman and Pickerill (2011: 120–126). For a critical analysis, see Gerhardt (2005).

[41]See Friedman (2006: 263).

[42]See Friedman and Martin (2011: 157–158).

[43]Burbank (2011: 46), enumerates the following methodological faults: behavioural equivalence, the inability to accommodate cases presenting multiple issues, selection bias, coding bias, and systematic coding errors.

[44]See Baum (2011: 76), Burbank (2011: 49–50).

consequence is that judges are regarded as being free to decide cases any way they wish and that they use this freedom to try to further their own ideological or policy preferences.[45]

Furthermore, the political scientists' obsession with quantifiability and falsification cannot be easily squared with the law. Judicial law-making, even from a behavioural approach, cannot be explained in a single dimension.[46] Judges are humans and that entails the pursuit of a broader range of goals rather than policy maximising alone. Rational choice theory, however clear and structured, leaves out too many of the factors that drive judges.[47] By focusing only on policy objectives, without even considering the possibility that other factors might influence, to a greater or lesser extent, their behaviour, it leaves a considerable span of human behaviour motivations out of the picture.[48] Consequently, this conception is also narrow. Indeed, it is at the very least plausible that judges also care for non-ideological considerations factors, such as the integrity of the law, their own reputation, popularity or prestige, career considerations, the public interest, and the avoidance of reversal. It is very likely that judges maximise the same things everyone else does[49]—and that cannot be fully grasped by "empiricists interested in measurement and operationalisation".[50] This methodological bias leads political scientists to overstate their claim and become simplistic, neglecting other important forces that also bear upon and influence judges.

In third place, by merely focusing on outcomes, it completely disregards the legal opinion—the centre of all judicial activities—itself. There is "something deeply unsettling about the work of positive scholars: the fact that it confines the efforts of all judicial actors to mere 'window dressing'".[51] The most important part in a judicial decision is the legal opinion itself and not (only) the outcome. In common law systems, the reason for this is clear: apart from awarding a judgement and argumentatively explain how one such result can be reached, an opinion also contains the rules that regulate a certain area of the law. And this latter aspect is independent of whether the justification does a good job of squaring the case with the existing body of law. But in civil law systems as well, at least for the inherently and ontological argumentative nature of legal reasoning.[52] Judges must not only explain how they reach the outcome in that particular case, but also how that result squares with the rules of other cases. Attention to outcomes only can be misleading. And "in law, however, what courts say often spells out what it is they have actually

[45]See Robertson (2010b: 22).

[46]See Burbank (2011: 50–51), Gerhardt (2005: 914–916).

[47]For an appraisal of the use of rational choice theory in judicial politics, see Spaeth (2008: 761–763, 768).

[48]See Baum (2008: 11–14), Baum (2011: 80–83).

[49]See Posner (2008: Chap. 3).

[50]See Braman and Pickerill (2011: 127).

[51]See Burbank (2011: 48), Robertson (2010b: 21).

[52]See Alexy (1989: Chap. C).

done".[53] Examples of this are comical, but apparent at the same time: positive scholars "would have treated the most famous case in American history as simply 'Marbury loses', without any concern for what John Marshall actually said in reaching that result".[54] Additionally, by focusing on votes rather than on opinions, real differences in judicial ideology are obscured. This means that, at the end of the day, these models do not model the law. "At best they are predicting the *outcome* of a certain set of cases or a *vote* by a justice on the merits, without controlling for law in any way".[55]

8.5 Concluding Remarks

None of the limitations presented above should, in any circumstance, be read as discarding judicial behaviour theories. On the contrary: their contribution to make sense and to measure judicial activism has been critical.

The positive models have made it clear, and have proved it with statistical data, that judges, when adjudicating constitutional cases, are not constrained by the law in the way normative theories—and particularly separation of powers theories—seem to require and have us believe.[56] In other words: differently from what normative theories prescribe, in some circumstances some judges do vote in patterns that reflect their ideology and aim at maximising their preferred policy outcomes. Judicial behaviour analyses have shed light on what *can* and what *cannot* be expected from normative theories of judicial review, thereby posing a standing challenge for lawyers and political philosophers to fine-tune their theories so as to more precisely demarcate what ought to be the exact province of the judiciary.

At the end of the day, positive theories do not deny the influence of law; they rather consider it as a mere influence among others. And that can be said to be, for lawyers, both its greatest relevance and challenge.

Acknowledgments I would like to thank Luís Pereira Coutinho for having invited me to participate in the Lisbon conference on judicial activism that was at the root of this article. I am indebted to Ruth Rubio-Marín, Miguel Nogueira de Brito, Mariana Melo Egídio, and Afonso Brás for their comments on earlier versions of this paper; the usual disclaimer applies, though.

[53]See Friedman (2006: 266); Friedman and Martin (2011: 165–166).

[54]See Friedman (2006: 266), referring to Marbury v. Madison, 5 U.S. 137 (1803). The same could be done with other cases, such as Planned Parenthood v. Casey, 505 U.S. 833 (1992) or affirmative action cases—see Cross (2011: 92, 99–104). For further examples of how positive theories would misrepresent the role and the opinions drafted by Chief Justice John Marshall, see Gerhardt (2005: 917–919).

[55]See Friedman and Martin (2011: 157).

[56]See Friedman (2006: 279).

References

Alexy, Robert. 1989. A theory of legal argumentation. The theory of rational discourse as theory of legal justification. Oxford and New York: Oxford University Press.

Amaral-Garcia, Sofia, Nuno Garoupa and Veronica Grembi. 2009. Judicial independence and party politics in the Kelsenian Constitutional Courts: The case of Portugal. *Journal of Empirical Legal Studies*, 6:2.

Baum, Lawrence. 2008. Judges and their audiences. A perspective on judicial behavior. Princeton and Oxford: Princeton University Press.

Baum, Lawrence. 2011. Law and policy: More and less than a dichotomy. In *What's law got to do with it? What judges do, why they do it, what's at stake*, ed. Charles Gardner Geyh. Stanford: Stanford University Press.

Braman, Eileen and J. Mitchell Pickerill. 2011. Path dependence in studies of legal decision-making. In *What's law got to do with it? What judges do, why they do it, what's at stake*, ed. Charles Gardner Geyh. Stanford: Stanford University Press.

Burbank, Stephen B. 2011. On the study of judicial behaviors: Of law, politics, science, and humility. In *What's law got to do with it? What judges do, why they do it, what's at stake*, ed. Charles Gardner Geyh. Stanford: Stanford University Press.

Cross, Frank B. 2011. Law *is* politics. In *What's law got to do with it? What judges do, why they do it, what's at stake*, ed. Charles Gardner Geyh. Stanford: Stanford University Press.

de Araújo, António. 1997. O Tribunal Constitucional (1989–1997). Um estudo de comportamento judicial. Coimbra: Coimbra Editora.

Dyèvre, Arthur. 2008. Making sense of judicial lawmaking: A theory of theories of adjudication. EUI Working Papers 2008/09. Florence: European University Institute. Available via http://cadmus.eui.eu/bitstream/handle/1814/8510/MWP_2008_09.pdf?sequence=1. Accessed 19 Nov 2014.

Dyèvre, Arthur. 2010. Unifying the field of comparative judicial politics: Towards a general theory of judicial behaviour. *European Political Science Review*, 2:2.

Epstein, Lee. 2008. The U.S. Supreme Court. In *The Oxford handbook of law and politics*, eds. Keith E. Whittington, R. Daniel Kelemen and Gregory A. Caldeira. Oxford and New York: Oxford University Press.

Epstein, Lee and Jack Knight. 1997. The choices justices make. Washington DC: CQ Press.

Epstein, Lee and Jeffrey A. Segal. 2007. Advice and consent. The politics of judicial appointments. Oxford and New York: Oxford University Press.

Friedman, Barry. 2005. The politics of judicial review. *Texas Law Review*, 84:2.

Friedman, Barry. 2006. Taking law seriously. *Perspectives on Politics*, 4:2.

Friedman, Barry and Andrew D. Martin. 2011. Looking for law in all the wrong places: Some suggestions for modelling legal decision-making. In *What's law got to do with it? What judges do, why they do it, what's at stake*, ed. Charles Gardner Geyh. Stanford: Stanford University Press.

Gerhardt, Michael J. 2005. The limited path dependency of precedent. *University of Pennsylvania Journal of Constitutional Law*, 7.

Ginsburg, Tom. 2003. Judicial review in new democracies: Constitutional Courts in Asian cases. New York: Cambridge University Press.

Kornhauser, Lewis A. 2008. The analysis of courts in the economic analysis of law. In *The Oxford handbook of law and politics*, eds. Keith E. Whittington, R. Daniel Kelemen and Gregory A. Caldeira. Oxford and New York: Oxford University Press.

Landau, David. 2005. The two discourses in Colombian constitutional jurisprudence: A new approach to modelling judicial behavior in Latin America. *George Washington International Law Review*, 37.

Leiter, Brian. 2010. Americal legal realism. In *A companion to philosophy of law and legal theory*, 2nd edn, ed. Dennis Patterson. West Sussex: Blackwell Publishing.

Lijphart, Arend. 1999. Patterns of democracy. Government forms and performance in thirty-six countries. New Haven: Yale University Press.

Magalhães, Pedro Coutinho. 2003. The limits to judicialization: Legislative politics and constitutional review in the Iberian democracies. Dissertation, The Ohio State University. Available via https://etd.ohiolink.edu/ap/10?0::NO:10:P10_ACCESSION_NUM:osu1046117531. Accessed 19 Nov 2014.

Magalhães, Pedro Coutinho and António de Araújo. 1998. A justiça constitucional entre o direito e a política: o comportamento judicial no Tribunal Constitucional português. *Análise social*, 33: 1.

Maveety, Nancy. 2002. The study of judicial behavior and the discipline of Political Science. In *The pioneers of judicial behavior*, ed. Nancy Maveety. Ann Harbor: The University of Michigan Press.

Morais, Carlos Blanco de. 2011. Justiça constitucional, vol 2, 2nd edn. Coimbra: Coimbra Editora.

Posner, Richard A. 2008. How judges think. Cambridge: Harvard University Press.

Robertson, David. 2010a. Apellate courts. In *The Oxford handbook of empirical legal research*, eds. Peter Cane and Herbert M. Kritzer. Oxford and New York: Oxford University Press.

Robertson, David. 2010b. The judge as political theorist. Contemporary constitutional review. Princeton and Oxford: Princeton University Press.

Rohde, David W. and Harold J. Spaeth. 1975. Supreme Court decision making. San Francisco: W H Freeman & Co.

Santos, Ana Catarina. 2011. Papel politico do Tribunal Constitucional. O Tribunal Constitucional (1983-2008): Contributos para o estudo do TC, seu papel político e politização do comportamento judicial em Portugal. Coimbra: Coimbra Editora.

Segal, Jeffrey A. 2008. Judicial behavior. In *The Oxford handbook of law and politics*, eds. Keith E. Whittington, R. Daniel Kelemen and Gregory A. Caldeira. Oxford and New York: Oxford University Press.

Segal, Jeffrey A. 2011. What's law got to do with it: Thoughts from « the realm of political science » . In *What's law got to do with it? What judges do, why they do it, what's at stake*, ed. Charles Gardner Geyh. Stanford: Stanford University Press.

Segal, Jeffrey A. and Harold J. Spaeth. 1993. The Supreme Court and the attitudinal model. Cambridge: Cambridge University Press.

Segal, Jeffrey A. and Harold J. Spaeth. 2002. The Supreme Court and the attitudinal model revisited. Cambridge: Cambridge University Press.

Silva, Virgílio Afonso da. 2013. Deciding without deliberating. *International Journal of Constitutional Law*, 11:3.

Spaeth, Harold J. 2008. Reflections about judicial politics. In *The Oxford handbook of law and politics*, eds. Keith E. Whittington, R. Daniel Kelemen and Gregory A. Caldeira. Oxford and New York: Oxford University Press.

Spiller, Pablo T. and Rafael Gely. 2008. Strategic judicial decision-making. In *The Oxford handbook of law and politics*, eds. Keith E. Whittington, R. Daniel Kelemen and Gregory A. Caldeira. Oxford and New York: Oxford University Press.

Vanberg, Georg. 2004. The politics of constitutional review in Germany. Cambridge: Cambridge University Press.

Volcansek, Mary L. 2000. Constitutional politics in Italy. The Constitutional Court. New York: St. Martin's Press.

Chapter 9
The Passive Sovereignty of the Constitutional Judge a State Theory Approach

Luís Pereira Coutinho

9.1 Introduction

In a book dedicated to judicial activism, the following paper explores its apparent opposite: I put forward the hypothesis of *judicial passivity* as a virtue of courts charged with the task of judicial review of legislation. In a preliminary notion, *judicial passivity* (not to be confused with passivity as a necessary institutional posture of the judicial branch, prevented by definition from acting at its own initiative[1]), means the resistance of courts to act on principle, enforcing constitutional norms and invalidating legal solutions. That, taking into account a prudential assessment of exceptional circumstances at the security, economic, financial or public health levels.

This paper was initially inspired by the situation of the Portuguese Constitutional Court when called to scrutinize budget laws adopted during the Euro crisis. In case those laws were unconstitutional, but still effectively necessary to face an economic and financial emergency, could the Court remain passive? Although those circumstances motivated the inquiry, the same doesn't address them specifically—first of all since the unconstitutionality of the said budget laws is not certain, even though many of the corresponding norms ended up being declared so.[2]

Above and beyond, the scope of the paper concerns the general problem of constitutionality in times of emergency, a problem placed in other circumstances, such as those surrounding the Emergency Banking Act, adopted in 1933 before the

[1]On the exclusion of passivity, see the contribution by Massimo La Torre in this volume.
[2]On this, see Ribeiro (2013) and the collection of essays published in Ribeiro and Coutinho (2014).

L.P. Coutinho (✉)
Faculdade de Direito da, Universidade de Lisboa,
Alameda da Universidade, 1649-014 Lisbon, Portugal
e-mail: lpcoutinho@fd.ulisboa.pt

L.P. Coutinho et al. (eds.), *Judicial Activism*,
Ius Gentium: Comparative Perspectives on Law and Justice 44,
DOI 10.1007/978-3-319-18549-1_9

imminent failure of the American banking system, or the USA PATRIOT Act, adopted six weeks after the terrorist attacks of September 11th. I believe that, in the powers of constitutional jurisdictions called to scrutinize emergency legislation, one finds the most important contemporary expression of that general problem. That, also considering that advanced democracies tend to deal with emergencies precisely through ordinary legislation reviewable by courts. The tendency towards a "legislative model" of dealing with emergencies,[3] is aggravated by the unsuitability of express constitutional provisions for emergencies—when existent, often constructed to deal with problems of disorder or war—to address typical contemporary emergencies such as terrorism and financial crises.

The acceptance of judicial passivity—which this paper doesn't aim at, but only at considering preliminarily its defensibility—would admittedly be unconventional, running counter the idea of judicial review as a crowning institution of the rule of law. In this volume, Alexander and La Torre exclude in an outright manner what they believe to be unacceptable forms of "judicial abdication". But even if one accepts from the start that judicial passivity means a challenge to the rule of law—involving the acceptance of breaches to constitutionality avowed by the very institution designed to enforce it—one still believes the discussion is not over. That since the absolutist claims in favor of the rule of law present in dominant conceptions developed within legal theory must still be assessed within state theory. That is the purpose of this essay.

9.2 The Sovereignty of Constitutional Courts

When considering the said hypothesis, one should start by asking whether constitutional courts, as reviewers and nullifiers of laws, are holders of sovereignty. In a Hobbesian sense, they may be considered so. As explained in Chapter 26 of the *Leviathan*, to set forth a judge of the sovereign "is to make a new Sovereign". Sovereignty in this sense is thus an ultimate power, either to make or to reject laws, corresponding to the last word of the state.

It may be said that, in identifying the judicial reviewer of legislation as sovereign, one is incurring in a categorical error. That since a constitutional state with judicial review means, in its own definitional structure, the eradication of sovereignty in the Hobbesian sense.[4] In this line of reasoning, sovereignty in a constitutional state only exists at the constituent level and therefore, neither the legislator nor the courts charged with judicial review, are sovereign, being instead mere constituted powers under the Constitution.

[3]On the contemporary tendency to adopt a "legislative model" to handle emergencies, see Ferejohn and Pasquino (2004: 215).

[4]In the words of Martin Kriele (1994: 122–123), "the existence of a sovereign in [the Hobbesian] sense, on the one side, and of the constitutional state, on the other, are opposed and mutually excluding situations".

Moreover, in the same line of reasoning, the lessening of the powers of the state to mere constituted powers means, not only the eradication of sovereignty as a continuous supreme power, but also a definitive challenge to sovereignty as a doctrine of *political right*[5]: the doctrine according to which the pursuit of *salus publica* implies the "capacity" for prudentially facing the changing ways of *Fortuna*, eventually in spite of moral and legal norms or commitments. From that perspective, the emergence of the constitutional state, and the inherent empire of constitutional law—of a law uncompromisingly pronounced by courts against the active legislator—would have precisely taken the place of a *political right* centered on sovereignty as "capacity".

In a normativist articulation, the definitional structure of the constitutional state implies indeed a fundamental aspiration to fully convert state action into normative action.[6] In that logic, *Fortuna*, if represented at all, is to be tamed by powers within norms, the "capacity" of which is not really called into question. Constitutional courts are there precisely to enforce norms *without exception*—except of course for the exceptions foreseen by norms themselves—, remaining blind to problems of "capacity".

The persisting doubt, however, is whether this structure is solid enough to resist all circumstances. In a way, the constitutional state inarticulately presupposes a thoroughly planed off ground of uncircumstantial peace, of unquestioned *normalcy*: a ground within which questions of "capacity" for insuring it remain unproblematic. It might thus be said that the constitutional state, in its utmost coherence, is a post-historical state within which the strict empire of norms cannot be challenged—*is* not challenged—by the ways of *Fortuna*.

But is it possible for a worldly state to be an Augustinean city? And if that is not the case, isn't it necessary for the ultimate enforcers of its norms—courts charged with judicial review of legislation—to remain aware of that impossibility, thus placing problems of "capacity" as well as problems of normativity, being consequently open in some circumstances to remain passive before active agencies of the state charged with facing *Fortuna*?

These questions must be placed if one wishes to seriously address the possibility of constitutional courts as sovereigns—as *passive* sovereigns, capable of holding off the last word of the state in due acknowledgment of the needs inherent to the pursuit of *salus publica* by the legislator. A positive answer to the same questions admittedly means that the constitutional state cannot be a strictly regular construction, i.e., that *political right* may in specific circumstances breach the normativity of positive constitutional law, that being acknowledged by its very enforcers.

[5]In the definition of Martin Loughlin (2003: 69), *political right* is that "set of [prudential] precepts and maxims enabling the state to maintain itself and flourish", centered around a concept of sovereignty "as much concerned with capacity as with competence, with power not just authority".

[6]See below, Sect. 9.3.

9.3 Political Right and the Rule of Law

1. As said above, *judicial passivity* as a virtue may possibly be justified within a conception of sovereignty as a doctrine of *political right*, then silently avowed by constitutional jurisdictions as holders of the last word of states—even if this means a breach to the rule of law aspiration basically involved in their conversion into constitutional states.

Indeed, the tradition of the rule of law, underlying the constitutional state, is theoretically opposed to the tradition of *political right*. It may even be said that its fundamental aim, in its "constitutionalist" articulation, is precisely to eradicate the *reason of state*, fully replacing it by law as a criterion of state action. It is in this horizon—the discursive horizon of the rule of law and not of *political right*—that constitutional courts were instituted.

In a Kelsenian framework, law is not only an unchallengeable criterion of state action, but a criterion of statehood itself. And even if this construction was formulated by Kelsen as an epistemological hypothesis, the corresponding normativism can be taken implicitly as a normative claim towards a substantial "depoliticization" of the state.[7] Moreover it was precisely with the same implication that the Kelsenian framework was later received by European post-war constitutionalism when instituting constitutional courts.[8]

It's the normative claim implicit in the Kelsenian framework, and afterwards made explicit, that Carl Schmitt more vigorously contested—I'm referring to "the first Carl Schmitt", the Carl Schmitt of *Der Wert des Staates und die Bedeutung des Einzelnen* and of *Politische Theologie*, who can undoubtedly be taken as the most important defender of *political right* in the twentieth century.[9]

Indeed, when resoundingly stating that "Sovereign is he who decides on the exception",[10] Schmitt was precisely putting into question, in an emphatic way, the Kelsenian pretension to fully eradicate the *political* doctrine of sovereignty. For Schmitt, the intended reduction of the state to the rule of law—its full taming within

[7]See Dyzenhaus (1997: 179).

[8]Even if that may have involved something Kelsen himself would never consider admissible: a wide delegation of discretion in constitutional courts. On this latter aspect, see the contribution of Nogueira de Brito in this volume.

[9]I distinguish a "first" and "second Schmitt", taking into account the presuppositions of the concept of state. For the first Carl Schmitt, the presupposition of the concept of state is the concept of law (the concept of the state is conceived by presupposing a principle of validity corresponding to law, being the purpose of the state the worldly realization of law: it is the very realization of law in the phenomenal world that demands an entity, the state, that is not reducible to normativity, confronting itself with law in order to realize it). Inversely, in the "second Schmitt"—the Schmitt of *Der Begriff des Politischen*—, the concept of the state finds its presupposition in a concept of the political centered on a friend-enemy distinction. For further developments, see Coutinho (2013).

[10]See Schmitt (1985: 5) [I use the George Schwab translation of *Politische Theologie*, as identified in the references].

the boundaries of legal norms interpreted by courts—implied in reality the disregard of those circumstances in which it becomes imperative for the state to act according to political criteria, in the sense of criteria distinct from legal criteria and even opposed to the same.

In Schmitt's mind were the extreme circumstances of *Fortuna* such as an existential threat to the state. Indeed, if circumstances such as these are conceivable before "the actual truth of things", the entity with power to decide on the same—the state—cannot possibly be conceived as purely normative. On the contrary: it must be conceived as sovereign in a *politically rightful* sense and, therefore, as the one who decides on the exception with the "unlimited authority" that is necessary to tame *Fortuna*.

If that wasn't the case, in Schmitt's logic, the state itself, as the ultimate guardian of order, would be compromised. Inherently, the very possibility of worldly realization of law would be damaged without repair: a *Rechtstaat*, a state under the rule of law, must be also a *Staat*.

It should be stressed that, for Schmitt, the intentionality of the sovereign when deciding on the exception is far from arbitrary. If the sovereign may act autonomously in terms that are irreducible to legal norms, it is because it is for him to guarantee something that encompasses the very possibility of norms: it is for him to guarantee normalcy, "the effective normal situation". In fact, normalcy must be guaranteed for the norm to be in force. In Schmitt's words:

> This effective normal situation is not a mere 'superficial presupposition' that the jurist can ignore; that situation belongs precisely to its immanent validity. There exists no norm that is applicable to chaos. For a legal order to make sense, a normal situation must exist.[11]

To suppose that "the effective normal situation" exists by itself, thus independently of the political means reserved to the sovereign, is a metaphysical conviction. It is precisely such conviction that Schmitt attributes to Kelsen, stating that:

> Kelsen solved the [political] problem of the concept of sovereignty by negating it. The result of his deduction is that 'the concept of sovereignty must be radically repressed'. This is in fact the old liberal negation of the state vis-à-vis law and the disregard of the independent problem of the realization of law.[12]

When briefly recovering here the discussion between Schmitt and Kelsen—which amounts essentially to the discussion between two great traditions: the tradition of *political right* and the tradition of the rule of law—I do not intend to take sides, but only to stress once again that the tradition of the rule of law, which finds an utmost expression in a normativist articulation of the constitutional state and in the inherent institution of constitutional courts, fundamentally opposes sovereignty as a political doctrine. That by silencing the problem it historically faced.

In fact, in a Kelsenian logic—the logic of the rule of law in its utmost coherence —, no state agency, least of all constitutional courts, can be sovereign, thus acting

[11]See Schmitt (1985: 13).

[12]See Schmitt (1985: 21).

in an autonomously political way. Constitutional courts are there precisely to guarantee that no state powers remain capable of referring their action to sovereignty as a political concept (or to sovereign as a doctrine of *political right*).

In that logic, constitutional courts may, notwithstanding, acknowledge "freedom of conformation" (*Gestaltungsgfreiheit*) to other state powers. There is however a radical difference between the doctrine of "freedom of conformation" and the political doctrine of sovereignty. Indeed, the first doesn't involve, by no means, a positive acknowledgment of the political autonomy of the latter. On the contrary: "freedom of conformation" is only that margin that is left to state agencies *after* their complete fulfillment of the legal criteria that bind them. The admission of "freedom of conformation" of other state agencies by a constitutional court is then a merely negative acknowledgment, fully coherent with the rule of law, considering its material extension as determined by itself. It is not, as in the case of the political doctrine of sovereignty, a *positive* acknowledgement of the *necessity* of political action beyond legal criteria.

2. As said, in a Kelsenian logic, neither constitutional courts nor other state powers can be truly sovereign in a *politically rightful* sense. The question that remains to be asked however is whether that result can be admitted, i.e., whether the problem of preservation of an "effective normal situation"—and inherently "the independent problem of the realization of law", in Schmitt's terms—can be disregarded.

When placing the question in these terms I do not intend to endorse Schmitt's thesis, but only to state the pertinence of the underlying problem, which is mainly ignored, eventually at risk, within a prevailing "Business as Usual model" of dealing with emergencies: a model always based implicitly or explicitly on "notions of constitutional absolutism and perfection",[13] eventually overlooking the fact that constitutions are "constructed to deal with a range of more or less normal circumstances and may produce bad results if applied outside of those conditions".[14]

I don't intend to deny that at stake is a hazardous problem, to be treated in avoidance of any radicalization resulting in the overwhelming of the rule of law by the political logic of sovereignty. That was admittedly Schmitt's path. Thus, when placing the problem others disregarded, Schmitt may have disregarded, on his turn, the essential problem faced by the rule of law which essentially amounts to the taming of arbitrariness.

The resulting question then can be putten as follows: is it possible, in due acknowledgment of the problem placed by Schmitt, to equate solutions that don't simply obliterate the rule of law? Is it possible to find some sort of balance between the tradition of the rule of law and the tradition of *political right*?

To answer this question involves an extended investigation program. My modest aim in this paper is only to put under discussion a preliminary hypothesis necessarily attached to a non-normativist logic of the constitutional state: the hypothesis

[13]See Gross (2003: 1043).

[14]See Ferejohn and Pasquino (2004: 220).

of constitutional courts as holders of the balance between the said traditions, i.e., as ultimate regulators able to switch between the rule of law and *political right*, that eventually resulting in the deferral of their normal function and corresponding passivity before unconstitutional laws.

In that hypothesis, one may say *mutatis mutandis*, constitutional courts will play a role similar to the hetero-investiture function once performed by the Roman Senate in the exercise of its latent *imperium*: before emergencies, it was for the Senate to play the vital epistemic role of acknowledging the exception but not the active role of facing it.

9.4 The Political Question Doctrine

1. I have been considering the possibility of constitutional courts as *passive* sovereigns that, as such, hold back the last word of the state before the active taming of *Fortuna* by active state powers, then acknowledging that political criteria—*autonomously* political criteria, thus possibly lawbreaking—may exceptionally preside over state action.

In that case, constitutional courts emerge as the holders of the balance between the tradition of the rule of law, on the one side, and the tradition of *political right*, on the other—i.e., as crown institutions of the rule of law in circumstances of normalcy, but also as evaluators of those exceptional circumstances in which it becomes necessary for the state to act according to political criteria, and then, possibly, as avowers of the reemergence of sovereignty as "capacity".

In the institution of constitutional courts as holders of the balance in this sense lies a guarantee that the reemergence of political sovereignty will not be arbitrary, in here lying an essential safeguard against a mere annulment of the rule of law.

As said above, this hypothesis involves a breach of the Kelsenian logic underlying the institution of European constitutional courts. The same hypothesis will not be strange, however, to the American tradition of judicial review. Indeed, in this latter context, the said hypothesis can be articulated through the "political question doctrine" in its prudential variant.[15] In that variant, the doctrine found its utmost articulation in Alexander Bickel.

It is worth considering previously the theoretical context in which that doctrine was articulated by Bickel. Acknowledging that the American Supreme Court is at first charged with the "function of enunciating principle", Bickel also acknowledged the difficulties the same "function", when taken to its extreme logic, could involve in difficult circumstances. Indeed, in these circumstances, the Supreme

[15]The "political question doctrine" has a "functional" and a "prudential" variant. The first can be understood within separation of powers even in times of normalcy. It is the second , which eventually allows the Supreme Court to hold back the application of principles in difficult political circumstances, that concerns us in this paper. On the distinction between a "prudential" and a "functional" approach to the political question doctrine, see Tribe (2000: 366 ff.).

Court would find it hard to escape the inexorable logic of principle and thus to reach the necessary compromises.

Bickel enunciated the conundrum in the following terms:

> Principle as such permits no principled flexibility (...). But at the same time, it cannot in our society constitute [always] a hard and fast rule of action (...). This is nothing to be proud of. It is a disagreeable fact, and it cannot be wished away. It is no service to any worthy objective simply to close one's eyes to it. Yet the question persists, how does the Court charged with the function of enunciating principle, produce or permit the necessary compromises?[16]

After exemplary placing the question—and portraying with striking clarity the "disagreeable" nature of political matters—Bickel provides a solution based an "essentially important fact, so often missed". The fact "that the Court wields a threefold power":

> It may strike down legislation as inconsistent with principle. It may validate (...) legislation as consistent with principle. *Or it may do neither.* It may do neither, and therein lies the secret of its ability to maintain itself in the tension between principle and expediency[17]

Hence, when before sensitive political issues, the Court *should resist issuing decisions on the merits*, i.e., it should decline the exercise of jurisdiction. According to Bickel, the Court could do so through the exercise of "passive virtues", these being "mediating techniques" by which it allows itself *not* to decide, holding back its last word. Through those techniques judges would thus refrain from doing "the most important thing they do".[18]

Doctrines such as "ripeness" and "the political question" would be "mediating techniques" of that sort, wise devises through which judges prudently abandoned the "apocalyptic frame of mind" their function could lead them to—in Bickel's interesting portrayal[19]—thus avoiding the issuing of inexorably principled decisions.

The most interesting amongst the "mediating techniques" suggested by Bickel—revealing an acute awareness of the particular nature of political matters—is "the political question doctrine". According to it, constitutional courts should decline jurisdiction when sensing a "lack of capacity" to address the issue at hand—with the same being left to other branches of government—taking into account, namely,

---

[16]See Bickel (1986: 69).

[17]See footnote 16.

[18]See Bickel (1986: 112). Bickel resorts to the words originally used by judge Brandeis, for whom «the mediating techniques of "not doing" were "the most important thing we [judges] do"».

[19]Bickel uses this description when addressing an "absolutist position" that found its utmost representative in judge Black, who never refrained from "propagating his absolutes", raising "a grave question of process—a question, some might say, of candor". According to Bickel, "there would be fewer occasions for differences in result if cases coming before the Court were viewed more closely, more narrowly, in a less apocalyptic frame of mind. On the immediate merits of many cases, more discord strikes the ear than is necessarily involved. The Court has been entering upon more argument than it needs to resolve".

"the strangeness of the issue and its intractability to principled resolution" or "the sheer momentousness of it".[20]

The "Court's sense of lack of capacity" is founded "*in both intellect and instinct*". These words, in which the echo of Machiavelli is clearly present, accurately reveal the *autonomously* political nature of the judgment involved in declaring a question a "political question"—and thus the political sovereignty of the Court. In here, in the *passive political sovereignty* of the American Supreme Court, lies the crux of the paradox Bickel starts by articulating: "the least dangerous branch of the American government is the most extraordinarily powerful court of law the world has ever known".[21]

2. As said above, the idea of *passive* sovereignty of Courts—articulated through the political question doctrine or through another medium—is more congenial to the American constitutional tradition than to the Kelsenian normativist logic followed in Europe.

For in the American tradition, the Constitution is not—at least, was not originally—a merely legalistic document exclusively destined at taming power at all costs in all circumstances. First and foremost, the constitution *creates* the power corresponding to the state. In Martin Loughlin's words, in the tradition assumed by American constitutionalism:

> A constitution is not essentially an act of authorization; it is a mode of generating and orchestrating the public power of a state. The constitution is not a segment of being but a process of becoming. (…) Constituent power cannot be absorbed into some basic norm, for this would be to deny the continuity of the political dynamic that provides the state with its most basic energy. (…). Constituent power cannot be entirely absorbed into norms (…). [It] is the power that gives constitutions their open, provisional, and dynamic qualities, keeping them responsive to social change and reminding us that the norm rests ultimately on the exception [i.e. on the guarantee of the "effective normal situation"]. Constituent power expresses a belief that the interdependence of democracy and constitutionalism is a paradox and not a contradiction, and recognizes the need for agencies of the state to work actively.[22]

The American constitutionalism logic is not, therefore, primarily one of negation or even of minimization of state power. "In framing a government", James Madison stated, "you must *first* enable the government to control the governed; and in the *next place* oblige it to control itself".[23] Inherently, to reduce the constitution to a merely legalistic document, deaf to the necessities of power at all costs in all circumstances, would be self-defeating. In other words, it was never assumed, in the

---

[20]In Bickel's words, the "Court's sense of lack of capacity is "compounded in unequal parts of (a) the strangeness of the issue and its intractability to principled resolution; (b) the sheer momentousness of it, which tends to unbalance judicial judgment; (c) the anxiety, not so much that the judicial judgment will be ignored, as that perhaps it should but will not be; (d) finally ('in a mature democracy'), the inner vulnerability, the self-doubt of an institution which is electorally irresponsible and has no earth to draw strength from", see Bickel (1986: 184).

[21]See Bickel (1986: 1).

[22]See Loughlin (2003: 113).

[23]See Madison (1999: 295).

American tradition, "that legalism can altogether abolish politics" even if in these last decades an increasingly dominant American constitutional theory could erroneously lead to that conclusion.[24]

The said logic was most notably pursued by Abraham Lincoln, presiding over his preparedness to adopt in exceptional circumstances those measures that, "whether strictly legal or not, were ventured upon what appeared to be a public necessity". And it was also notably articulated by the same when asking: "Must a government, of necessity, be too *strong* for the liberties of its own people, or too *weak* to maintain its own existence?".[25]

It may be inferred that Lincoln, when maintaining the existence of government and its capacity to face exceptional circumstances, thought of his own action as fundamentally defensive of a constitutional framework which is *simultaneously an enabling framework of power and a limitative framework of principle, neither of which can break or dissolve the other*. Moreover, in Lincoln's logic, such constitutional framework would have a fundamentally moral quality in it. Indeed, a necessary attentiveness to actual forces—and inherently to "public necessity"—has a teleological logic of its own, given man's worldly condition.

It may be said that it is precisely that constitutional framework that is immanently present in a prudential construction of the "political question doctrine" as a "passive virtue" of the Supreme Court. Correspondingly, when resorting to the same doctrine, and acting as a passive sovereign, the Court is not betraying the Constitution it must defend. On the contrary: it is acknowledging its "open, provisional, and dynamic qualities"[26]—the inherent lack of an absolute separation between the constituent and constituted moments—and recognizing the need for the agencies of the state to work actively in a "responsive" manner.

9.5 Black Holes?

Considering the above, judicial passivity—and inherently the passive sovereignty of constitutional jurisdictions—will be considered differently, as to its defensibility, in two different traditions.

In the American tradition, as originally articulated by Madison, judicial passivity will be coherent with constitutionalism: if a passive judicial practice expresses a tension between necessity and principle, that tension corresponds to the paradoxical nature of constitutionalism itself, its simultaneously *enabling* and *limiting* character. Inversely, in the Kelsenian tradition underlying the creation of European constitutional courts—a tradition in which a continuous sovereignty is "radically

[24]See Loughlin (2010: 297).

[25]Lincoln's words before the American Congress in July 1861, quoted in Kelly, Harbison and Belz (1991: 293).

[26]See Loughlin (2003: 113).

repressed" and thus a strict separation between constituent and constituted powers is implied—judicial passivity will breach the logic of constitutionalism: a passive judicial practice, therefore, can only be accepted if constitutionalism is taken to be fundamentally incoherent and not just inherently paradoxical.

The question that must be raised is whether the incoherence that a Kelsenian logic necessarily attaches to the possibility of judicial passivity as a virtue reveals a primary deficiency of the same logic. That deficiency, if asserted, will have essentially to do with the untenable character of the underlying aspiration to fully turn worldly power into normative power, repressing its openness and dynamicity before public necessity.

Openness and dynamicity of public power, it should be stressed, mustn't and shouldn't be equated with "black holes", even if it may entail the possibility of violating otherwise accepted constitutional principles. That will not be the case if at stake are demonstrable public necessities evaluated *in a deliberative way* by sovereign courts, considering the values at stake and eventually *deciding* as a result to remain passive in name of the state and ultimately of the "rule of law project" it guarantees.[27] In this sense, one may say somewhat paradoxically that judicial passivity is a form of judicial activism, its apparent opposite, at least if one equates judicial activism with the active exercise of practical reasoning by the judges.[28]

The possibility of courts deliberatively deciding on the exception, but not on how to respond to it—to be determined by active state powers—, is enough not to consider the latter as sovereigns in a Schmittian sense. Indeed in this latter sense, the sovereign decides both on the existence of the exception and on the measures capable of facing it.[29] There will be no guarantee, therefore, that the exception isn't a mere pretext to produce a permanent "juridical void"[30] or that an "overreaction" is

[27]The expression "rule of law project" is taken from Dyzenhaus (2006: 3) who, when reflecting on legality in a time of emergency, seeks "to find a way of coordinating the roles of the judiciary and the other branches of government, when the latter are productively engaged in the rule-of-law project". Apparently there is nothing arguable in those words. However, the difficulty with Dyzenhaus's thesis concerns his endorsement of Kelsen's "identity thesis", i.e., the identification of the state with law (with a substantive concept of law in Dyzenhaus's case, see p. 199). Within that thesis the "rule of law project" is abstracted from its political condition, which is the state, taken in itself as the guarantee of that project. Dyzenhaus doesn't seem to accept then that an element of confrontation with law may be in extreme circumstances inherent to the realization of law in the phenomenal world. I don't know whether one can be so assertive.

Surprisingly though, Dyzenhaus states that it does not follow from his thesis "that all possible acts by public officials should be subject to the rule of law" and seems to endorse the Israeli Supreme Court position on ticking bomb situations. So it seems that, even for him, there are situations in which public officials may act extra-legally, but only as long as they "expect to be criminally charged (…); at trial they may try a defence of necessity". So for Dyzenhaus, there can be after all an element of confrontation with law inherent to the realization of law, that element not concerning the state itself but its officials…

[28]See the contributions of La Torre, Alexander and Ribeiro in this volume.

[29]See Dyzenhaus (2006: 39).

[30]See Agamben (2003: 41–42).

not taking place.[31] And we do know from experience that the active branches of the state tend not to be sensitive to fundamental rights and other limiting legal principles in times of emergency.

Contrariwise, the passive sovereignty of courts, if considered necessary for the re-emergence of the active sovereignty of other state powers, virtually means in itself a guarantee against "juridical void" and "overreaction" scenarios, correcting the possible excesses of the "legislative model" of dealing with emergencies—excesses resulting from the typical accumulation by the legislatures of the roles both to recognize an emergency and to create the measures to deal with it.[32] That, as long as the acknowledgment of the exception remains a truly independent and deliberative moment, involving the adoption of a true political decision by a constitutional court, something Schmitt would never consider admissible.[33]

Moreover, there is something to be gained, also from a rule of law perspective, by clarifying that judges are actually exercising passive sovereignty and deciding on the exception: they will be bound to assess explicitly the values at stake and to offer reasons for the solution of passivity they adopt. Conversely, they won't be given the opportunity to disguise their reasoning through some form of "lip service" to the rule of law, perversely maintaining it as a façade.

This latter path was many times taken by judges, thus pretending to maintain a strictly legalistic conception of their job, while serving an inverse logic dictated by necessity, which then passed without being argumentatively assessed.[34] On a side note, it may be said that this was the path taken by Portuguese Constitutional Court before budget laws approved during the Euro crisis, with that being aggravated by its calling unto itself the role of assessing and even defining the measures to face an exception that went explicitly unacknowledged.[35] One may say that, in that case, the result was a worst possible scenario: neither the rule of law nor *political right* ended up being served…

Regardless of this last note, what is being stressed is that the endorsement of judicial passivity may be a better solution also from a rule of law perspective. That, not only to insure the explicitly reasoned nature of the decisions on the exception, but also to insure that normal situations are better dealt with, not being confused with exceptional situations. This last aspect has a decisive relevance. As pointed out in a different context by David Dyzenhaus:

---

[31]On the high risks of overreaction in times of emergency, see Gross (2003: 1038).

[32]See Ferejohn and Pasquino (2004: 217).

[33]As Nogueira de Brito explores in this volume, Schmitt's aversion to any sort of political element in judicial decisions led him to dismiss the possibility of a constitutional court as a guardian of the constitution and the same logic would surely lead him to dismiss the possibility of a constitutional court as a guardian of state sovereignty.

[34]As David Dyzenhaus (2006: 35 ff.) thoroughly reports, when faced with exceptions, judges in fact have the tendency to "defer" to other branches of government while paying the said "lip service" to the rule of law.

[35]See references on note 2.

> Judicial lip service to the rule of law in exceptional situations has consequences for the way judges deal with ordinary situations. One finds that judges begin to be content with less substance in the rule of law in situations which are not part of any emergency regime, all the while claiming that the rule of law is well maintained. Second, the law that addresses the emergency situation starts to look less exceptional as judges interpret statutes that deal with ordinary situations in the same fashion. As a package, these concerns seem to show that once the exceptional or emergency situation is normalized, that is, addressed by ordinary statutes and treated by judges as part of a 'business as usual', rule-of-law regime, so the exception starts to seep into other parts of the law.[36]

The same point is swiftly made by Oren Gross in a context closer to one's own:

> [The] statement that the Constitution is the same in times of war as in times of peace is in danger of being reversed, so that the Constitution will be the same in times of peace as in times of war.[37]

Before the undesirability of legal "black holes", it should be mentioned finally that the passivity of constitutional jurisdictions before emergency doesn't bar modes of assessment of the measures taken by active officials (at this latter level, an "Extra-Legal measures model", such as the one proposed by Oren Gross,[38] is worth considering). Indeed, judicial passivity means exclusively a decision *on* the exception and doesn't exclude mechanisms, namely of ratification, regarding the implementing measures taken by active officials when facing it, insuring they remain duly aware of a responsibility that is ultimately personal.

9.6 Concluding Remarks: The Method of Political Right

As said, the fundamental problem to be faced when addressing the possibility of judicial passivity regards the worldly possibility (or impossibility) to repress the openness and dynamicity of public power before public necessity. It is still a form of repression in this sense, the pretension to fully anticipate in normative terms, through constitutional provisions for exception, the degree in which openness and dynamicity remains a possibility in all future circumstances.

Regardless of the solution one finally adopts, what may be said is that an endorsement of judicial passivity will necessarily involve an endorsement of *political right* as an element that is present in constitutionalism, be it in a breaching, incoherent manner, be it in a paradoxical manner, according to the theoretical framework one adopts. And it will be for the sovereign court to passively act within the corresponding method of political right.

---

[36]See Dyzenhaus (2006: 27).

[37]See Gross (2003: 1046). That point is made by Gross even if the Author ultimately rejects a "normalcy-emergency" dichotomy (p. 1089).

[38]See Gross (2003).

The same method will not, of course, be referred to positive constitutional law. It will be referred to the discursive tradition that conceived the concepts of state and sovereignty, concepts that a passive court will take as personified in itself and not denied by positive constitutional law.[39] In such context, judicial passivity—namely through the acknowledgment of a question as a "political question"—mustn't be referred necessarily to a specific constitutional provision for exceptional circumstances or for exceptional powers. If admitted, that passivity will be referred to the theoretical construction of the constitutional state as still a state.

References

AGAMBEN, Giorgio. 2003. State of Exception. Trans. Kevin Attell. Chicago and London: University of Chicago Press.

BEAUD, Olivier. 1994. La Puissance de l'État. Paris: Presses Universitaires de France.

BICKEL, Alexander M. 1986. The Least Dangerous Branch – The Supreme Court at the Bar of Politics. New Haven and London: Yale University Press.

COUTINHO, Luís Pereira / RIBEIRO, Gonçalo Almeida. 2014. O Tribunal Constitucional e a Crise: Ensaios Críticos. Coimbra: Almedina.

COUTINHO, Luís Pereira. 2013. Os Pressupostos do Conceito de Estado em Carl Schmitt: Do Direito ao Político. In *Carl Schmitt Revisitado*. Eds. Carlos Blanco de Morais and Luís Pereira Coutinho, Lisboa: Instituto de Ciências Jurídico-Políticas.

DYZENHAUS, David. 1997. Legality and Legitimacy: Carl Schmitt, Hans Kelsen and Hermann Heller in Weimar. New York: Oxford University Press.

DYZENHAUS, David. 2006. The Constitution of Law: Legality in a Time of Emergency. Cambridge: Cambridge University Press.

FEREJOHN, John / PASQUINO, Pasquale. 2004. The Law of the Exception: A Typology of Emergency Powers. International Journal of Constitutional Law, 2/2, p. 210–239.

GROSS, Oren. 2003. Chaos and Rule: Should Responses to Violent Crises Always be Constitutional. *Yale Law Journal*, 112/4, p. 1011–34.

KELLY, Alfred H. / HARBINSON, Winfried A. / BELZ, Herman. 1991. The American Constitutionalism: Its Origins and Development, 7th ed., New York: W.W. Norton & Company.

KRIELE, Martin. 1994. Einfuhrung in die Staatslehre: Die Geschichtlichen Legitimitätsgrundlagen des Demokratischen Verfassungstaates, 5th ed., Opladen: Westedeuscher Verlag.

MADISON, James. 1999. The Federalist no. 51. In *James Madison Writings*. Ed. Jack N. Rakove. New York: Literary Classics of the United States.

LOUGHLIN, Martin. 2003. The Idea of Public Law, Oxford: Oxford University Press.

LOUGHLIN, Martin. 2010. Foundations of Public Law, Oxford: Oxford University Press.

RIBEIRO, G.A. 2013., Judicial Activism Against Austerity in Portugal, *I-CONnect — Blog of the International Journal of Constitutional Law*. URL -http://www.iconnectblog.com/2013/12/judicial-activism-against-austerity-in-portugal/.

[39]In the twentieth century, the pertinence of such methodological approach was notably defended, not only by Carl Schmitt, but by Charles Eisenmann—who referred to sovereignty as a "*concept issued by doctrine*" in opposition to "*concepts issued by positive law*"—or more recently by Olivier Beaud (1994: 12). See also Loughlin (2003).

SCHMITT, Carl. 1985. Political Theology: Four Chapters on the Concept of Sovereignty. Trans. George Schwab, Chicago and London: University of Chicago Press.
TRIBE, Laurence. 2000. American Constitutional Law, 3rd. edition. New York: The Foundation Press.

Part III
Judicial Activism in Context

Chapter 10
The Contextual Nature of Proportionality and Its Relation with the Intensity of Judicial Review

Jorge Silva Sampaio

10.1 Introduction

The principle of proportionality is perhaps the most successful constitutional principle, given the unanimity of its use.[1] It is even designated as the "key and method of Constitutional Law dogma".[2] All this is reflected today in the existence of a "firm consensus" about its "indispensable role in constitutional rights reasoning".[3]

Besides being a structuring principle of law, it is a "methodological tool" of undeniable importance.[4] Moreover, it has established itself as a reference in the case law of the higher courts and, as the main structuring method of balancing, one can say that it is, nowadays, the most important judicial instrument, placing itself at the "centre of the modern Court's work".[5] Proportionality is so important that, often, the very use of other principles such as *equality*[6] or *legitimate expectations*[7] even requires its assistance.

---

[1]For a global overview about the use of the principle, among many others see Sweet and Mathews (2008: 73 ff).
[2]See Ossenbühl (1996: 40).
[3]See Klatt and Moritz (2012a, b: 1).
[4]See Barak (2012: 131).
[5]See Klatt and Meister (2012a, b: 2).
[6]The principle of equality has been often used in conjunction with the principle of proportionality, in which it is intended to gauge the disproportionality of a measure's inequality. Regarding this topic, among others, see Michael (2011: 153 ff).
[7]About the links between these two principles, among others, see Novais (2011: 182 ff).

J.S. Sampaio (✉)
Faculdade de Direito da Universidade de Lisboa,
Alameda da Universidade, 1649-014 Lisbon, Portugal
e-mail: jsilvasampaio@gmail.com

L.P. Coutinho et al. (eds.), *Judicial Activism*,
Ius Gentium: Comparative Perspectives on Law and Justice 44,
DOI 10.1007/978-3-319-18549-1_10

This principle "serves different and varied functions", and its meaning may "vary depending on the role that it intends to fulfil". Thus, this concept varies depending on the area of law in which it is used (Criminal, Constitutional, Administrative, or International Law).[8] This massive use obviously means that proportionality is at the centre of *judicial activism*,[9] and it is therefore important to understand how it relates with judicial review and whether its use can be a cause for judicial activism.[10]

Notwithstanding all this, even today there are many questions related to it. In addition to many other criticisms,[11] the very *legitimacy* of the principle has been called into question, with the same being still accepted by some authors with caution. For example, some consider that the *expansive force* of fundamental rights has gone too far, advocating that one should invest in another interpretative model in which the principle of proportionality and, consequently, the Constitutional Court itself would lose some importance.[12,13]

From another perspective, even if many uphold the principle of proportionality and often claim that its "structured approach is the most suitable", providing "concrete content" and allowing for "adequate protection" to constitutional rights,[14] and also playing a "disciplining and rationalising effect on judicial decision-making",[15] some authors such as Tsakyrakis have more recently argued that by

[8]See Barak (2012: 146).

[9]About this concept, on the present book, see for example the chapters of Massimo La Torre, Lawrence Alexander, Steven D. Smith, Gonçalo de Almeida Ribeiro, Miguel Nogueira de Brito, Luís Pereira Coutinho or Maria Benedita Urbano. Besides these studies, see also, for example, Kmiec (2004: 1463 ff), Dickson (2007).

[10]In this paper I will generally refer to the concept of judicial activism in situations in which courts *illegitimately* enter the political 'powers' functions (i.e., I will use a merely *formal* concept). The main issue here is precisely to know in which situations this activism actually happens. If one considers that some activism is admissible, then the question is to define the limit between admissible and non-admissible judicial activism. However this question will not be addressed in this paper.

[11]Specifically, in the first place, although there is huge consensus on the principle of proportionality, the truth is that even the terminology to use is still debated—"principle of proportionality", "principle of prohibition of the excess", etc.—and, moreover, its scope does not stop growing. See Lerche (2001: 351).

[12]Among others, see Böckenförde (2003: 165 ff), Papier (2005: 81 ff). For a list of several criticisms of the principle, see Barak (2012: 481 ff).

[13]In any case, even the biggest critics of proportionality do not intend to discontinue the principle's use, but only to decrease its impact by reducing its practical use. See Ossenbühl (1986: 34).

[14]See Barak (2012: 131–132).

[15]See Klatt and Moritz (2012a, b: 8).

allowing restrictions on fundamental rights in the light of public interests, proportionality has allowed a real "assault on fundamental rights".[16, 17]

However not everyone is so sceptical and critical of the concept. Given its universal use, authors like Beatty consider proportionality to be a constitutional principle that deserves universal acceptance, which is demonstrable by its adoption by a large number of jurisdictions. The author considers the generalization of the principle as proof of its universalist potential as a "neutral principle", undervaluing its possible political effects.[18] Although I agree with the advantages and inevitability of the principle, I would not go that far. Taking note of the positions defending a *universal* role and structure of proportionality,[19] I will argue instead that the structure and content of the principle is *influenced* on the one hand, by the *cultural context* (cultural, social and historical background) and, on the other hand, by the *legal context* (i.e., one cannot try to (re)construct this principle without taking into account its respective sources of law).

10.2 The Contextual Nature of Proportionality

10.2.1 General Aspects

First of all, it is important to note that jurisprudence and legal literature usually present proportionality's basic content as containing the following three tests: (i) rational connection (is the adopted governmental means rationally related to stated policy objectives?); (ii) necessity (is the adopted governmental means the least-restrictive one?); and (iii) proportionality in its strict sense (are the benefits of the adopted governmental means superior to the costs incurred by the infringement of the fundamental right?).[20,21]

---

[16]See Tsakyrakys (2012: 468 ff).

[17]The biggest problem of these theses is that they seem to forget the discussion about the *narrow* and *wide* thesis of fundamental rights' scope. About this theories, see Alexy (2010: 196 ff), Müller (1990: 40 ff). Answering some of the criticisms made of the principle, see Möller (2012: 709 ff), Klatt and Meister (2012a, b: 687 ff).

[18]See Beatty (2004: 159 ff).

[19]See, for example, Möller (2014: 31 ff).

[20]In general, see for example Schlink (2012: 722 ff), Clérico (2009: 39 ff), Bernal Pulido (2007: 692 ff). Sometimes authors also include in proportionality's content a previous test called "proper purpose" or "legitimate ends". See Barak (2012: 245 ff), Schlink (2012: 722), Klatt and Moritz (2012a, b: 8 ff). However this test seems to fit better when integrating a more general framework for the control of limitations on fundamental rights, in order to be also used in combination with other principles such as equality or human dignity.

[21]Regarding the American case, balancing is a three-tiered scrutiny framework with variable intensity of review: (i) strict scrutiny test (which requires "compelling state interests"); (ii) intermediate scrutiny test (which requires "important state interests"); and (iii) rational basis scrutiny test (which merely requires "legitimate state interests"). About American balancing see for

In second place, assuming its importance, one must ask why isn't proportionality used by everyone and why is it used in different ways in similar situations. For example, why is proportionality truly essential to judicial review in the majority of European countries, such as Germany, Portugal, Italy, Spain, while in other countries, such as the United States or Australia, the principle is barely used?

This question can be connected to the problem of *legitimacy* of constitutional review. Some believe this is a tired out discussion, not worth revisiting.[22] Others, perhaps wishing to evade it, consider that the answer simply depends on circumstances (constitutional, political, social, etc.) that are specific to each country; accordingly, it will be for each Constitution to outline its role and ultimately its legitimacy, nothing further being necessary or even possible.[23] More recently, though, the *counter-majoritarian difficulty* has been reiterated—the present book is proof of that—with new and violent ways to challenge it flourishing.[24,25] But is this difficulty similar everywhere?

Assuming the existence of this controversy in the USA and in Europe, the truth is that the "American constitutional adjudication has been attacked much more vehemently for being unduly political than the European counterpart"; the "expansive judicial interpretation of the constitution has fostered far greater criticism in the United States than in Europe, as evinced by the famed 'countermajoritarian' difficulty".[26]

This may be largely explained by the fact that "the selection of a particular model of judicial review often reflects a society's specific political, historical, and social heritage". Additionally, from the moment "a legal system has opted to recognise judicial review, and such review is [especially] exercised in accordance with the rules of proportionality, the contours of that institution can no longer be shaped by arguments relating to the preliminary issue of whether judicial review should be recognised by that system in the first place", because that entails a "reflection of the people's will".[27,28]

(Footnote 21 continued)
example Cohen-Eliya and Porat (2013), Bomhoff (2013). It is important to note that European courts sometimes use a similar three-tiered scrutiny framework for *each* proportionality test according to the different cases. See for example Clérico (2009: 31). That said, one can argue that the American balancing is very similar to the European rational connection test, just varying the scrutiny's intensity depending on the concrete case. Finally, recently arguing that the American balancing, as used by the jurisprudence, can be constructed to involve a kind of proportionality test, although using another terminology, see Yowell (2014: 87 ff).

[22] See Canotilho (2003: 84).

[23] See Schlink (1998: 378).

[24] See Bayón (2006: 214).

[25] In this sense, with important criticisms of the legitimacy of judicial review and even proposing its removal, see Waldron (2006: 1346 ff) and (1999).

[26] See Rosenfeld (2005: 199).

[27] See Barak (2012: 382–383).

[28] However, this does not necessarily mean that the "initial question" cannot be asked again, just as has been happening recently [for example, see the several studies discussing possible changes to

As Möller stresses, "[t]he question of which specific conception of test [of proportionality] is preferable is largely unexplored and only rarely even identified as a problem; it is therefore unresolved and there exists a considerable diversity in the approaches of the courts".[29] Not diminishing the importance of this issue, I believe however there is a previous question to be asked: as the specific content of the proportionality principle influences the court's margin of judicial review, is it really possible and desirable to defend a universal model of the principle, potentially applicable in every legal system?

Moreover, even if the principle of proportionality is not expressly referred to in all legal systems, as previously mentioned, the principle is used in almost all those legal systems. For example, in the Portuguese Constitution there are several particular references to the principle[30]: among other, article 18(2) states that restrictions to fundamental rights must be "*necessary*". This could mean that in Portugal the control of fundamental rights restrictions concerning proportionality is performed only with recourse to the rule of necessity. However, proportionality is predominantly understood in legal literature and jurisprudence as a three-prong principle (involving commands of suitability, necessity and proportionality in its narrow sense).[31] The question concerns then the basic content of the principle of proportionality, considering that in most cases there are no legal references to it; in other cases there are only references to specific rules of proportionality; and there are even cases where Constitutions do refer to the principle but they do not explain what its content is.

The answer to these questions, in my opinion, must rely on the cultural and legal context surrounding the principle.[32] In this regard, I will argue that the proportionality rules can differ from one legal system to another. More specifically, firstly, I understand that the *cultural context* is decisive to explain the degree in which the legitimacy of judicial review is discussed, the same being true about the use of

(Footnote 28 continued)
the Portuguese and Brazilian Constitutional Justice in Morais and Ramos (2012)]. The reopening of supposedly resolved issues has to do with the proper functioning of democracy.

[29]See Möller (2014: 33).

[30]See Articles 18(2), 19(4) and (8), 28(2), 30(5), 65(4), 168(2) and (3), 189(5), 266(2), 267(3), 270, 272, 272(2), and 282(4), all from the Portuguese Constitution.

[31]See, among others, Canas (1994: 591 ff), Canotilho (2007: 266 ff). However, one may ask if the constitutional legislator wanted to establish some differences in the content and structure of the principle depending on the situations in which it is applied—i.e., wanted to create different principles of proportionality for different cases. More recently, Novais (2003: 765 ff) talks about a fourth test of proportionality called *reasonability* which is different from proportionality in its strict sense, and according to which one must evaluate the reasonability of a measure's consequences for the affected people (and, contrary to what happens with proportionality in its strict sense, in this case one does not consider the proportionality of the measure itself).

[32]More generally, the importance of context can be found immediately in terms of language: without a proper contextual framework sometimes one cannot even understand what others mean.

proportionality. Secondly, I believe that the *legal context* is also crucial for the justification of a typical European proportionality content allowing for a strong judicial review.

10.2.2 Cultural Context

To make my point, I will start with the comparison between the cultural contexts standing behind European proportionality,[33] on the one side, and American balancing, on the other.[34]

First of all, it is important to note that "despite important analytical similarities, legal, political and philosophical culture in America and [Europe] bring about quite a different understanding and role for balancing and proportionality within their respective cultures". One first significant difference concerns the fact that German proportionality emerged in *administrative law* (and not in private law) and, as part of an attempt to control "executive power", it was "considered as a limit imposed on the administrative restrictions of individual freedoms"[35]; whereas balancing appeared in *private law* and "was developed to serve the exact opposite purpose: as a check on what was considered the Supreme Court's overzealous rights protection during Lochner era". Furthermore, "proportionality evolved in the framework of the formalistic and doctrinal jurisprudence of the Prussian administrative courts (…), unlike balancing which was a prominent aspect of the Progressivists' anti formalism revolution".[36]

In Germany,[37] an ambitious project is laid down in its constitution: "to bring about a profound transformation of German consciousness and attitudes so that the values upon which human rights are founded would become acknowledged and internalised in German society"; and "[t]his goal could only be realised by according the state a non-neutral stance in society".[38] It is precisely within this context that the German theories of *objective* and *positive* dimensions of fundamental rights emerged, the same involving public duties of protection, guarantee and promotion of fundamental rights.[39] Regarding the specific duty of protection, and differently from the USA, according to the German Constitutional Court—with the same happening generally in other European countries—"the individual whose

[33]Especially in countries of continental Europe such as Germany, Portugal, Spain, Italy or even France.

[34]In this section I will follow some of the main ideas of Cohen-Eliya and Porat (2013)

[35]See Canotilho (2007: 266).

[36]See Cohen-Eliya and Porat (2013: 4–6).

[37]But also in other European countries affected by dictatorships in the last century, such as Portugal, Spain or Italy.

[38]See Cohen-Eliya and Porat (2013: 45).

[39]See, for example, Sampaio (2015: 246 ff).

constitutionally protected interest may be infringed upon by third parties has a claim against the state if the existing laws do not protect him or her sufficiently". Therefore, if the legislature does not act to protect the individual right, it "not only violates objective constitutional law but an individual right of the citizen as well".[40,41] This obviously presents a problem of *separation of powers*; however separation of powers alone cannot justify a lack of respect for constitutional directives.[42] On his side, Michelman argues that "American constitutional law does not deny or exclude the state's protective function or duty", and the differences lie in the fact "that the professional constitutional cultures entertain somewhat different ideas regarding limits on the appropriate role of the judiciary, and of adjudication, in the implementation of a political principle that both cultures nurture".[43]

In addition, European "political theory emphasises that a person is embedded in a community with shared values that expresses solidarity towards all of its members and holds an "organic" conception of the state and its relationship with the individual". The European countries are more or less "'democratic social' version[s] of the interventionist state", which partially explains their enormous interest in the concept of *human dignity*.[44,45] In the USA a vision of essentially *negative freedom* dominates. As in a typical liberal state, "American governments have largely abandoned the project of redistributing wealth, showing little commitment to social welfare states of the European type".[46] Furthermore, unlike what happened in most European countries, "American political culture did not have to adjust or change its course following the Second World War". The American aversion to government intervention and emphasis on popular democracy were even reinforced after the war. Additionally, "[t]he American political culture is founded on the values of liberty, personal responsibility", and "[t]hese values shaped the system of

---

[40]See Grimm (2005: 153).

[41]The state is not only prohibited to violate fundamental rights with its actions (*Übermassverbot*—principle of excess prohibition), but it is also prohibited to protect and promote insufficiently fundamental rights (*Untermassverbot*—principle of deficit prohibition). About the *Untermassverbot*, see for example Störring (2009), Alexy (2010: 278 ff), Novais (2010: 307 ff). And this aspect is extremely important: as Grimm (2005: 138) argues, it reveals the existence of a different institutional relationship between the legislature and the judiciary.

[42]See Grimm (2005: 153).

[43]See Michelman (2005: 127).

[44]See Bognetti (2005: 92).

[45]For example, the German Constitution expressly establishes the existence of a social state—see Article 20(1), and Article 28(1)—and the Portuguese Constitution, although not expressly referring to a social state, in addition to establishing an extensive catalogue of social rights, states in Article 2 that the Portuguese Republic is a democratic state based on the rule of law with a view "to achieving economic, social and cultural democracy and deepening participatory democracy", and establishes several economic, social and cultural state tasks [see Article 9(d) and Article 81(a) and (b)]. About the Social State in Germany, see, amongst others, Heinig (2011: 1887 ff), and in Portugal, see Novais (2011: 291 ff), Sampaio (2015: 145 ff).

[46]See Whitman (2005: 108).

government in the USA as based on strong faith in the potential of the individual and a deep-rooted wariness of government".[47]

In Europe, the Constitutional Court "is viewed as a political organ that is an integral part of the state and shares in the task of elaborating and shaping social values and norms". Therefore, in this context, as Grimm says, "there is no pre-established difference between courts and legislatures regarding the particular contribution of each and that which an interpreter has to enforce, regardless of what the constitution says". And for this reason "constitutional courts inevitably cross the line between law and politics".[48,49] Consequently, in Europe there is a "flexible conception of the majority of European Constitutional Courts as operating between the lines of politics and law"[50]; in consequence, a flexible conception of separation of powers prevails.[51] On the contrary, "American constitutionalism seeks to set limits on judicial power" and to stress the differences between the judicial role and the political role.[52]

After the Second World War, the German Constitution was designed by assigning a key role to fundamental rights, with the state being given the lead role to "give effect to the "new" humanistic values enshrined therein".[53] Meanwhile, in America, "the preference for state neutrality and a minimal role for the state shaped a narrowly construed Constitution, one that is generally hostile to the realisation of 'values' by the government". The noted "difference in constitutional design has implications regarding the centrality or marginality of proportionality and balancing in their constitutional systems"[54] and also on the judicial review system it should be added. The above-mentioned protective function derived from fundamental rights is

[47]See Cohen-Eliya and Porat (2013: 46 and 53).

[48]See Grimm apud Kommers (1997: 44).

[49]Of course this idea can be rather exaggerated. However, the truth is that Constitutional Courts are clearly established in constitutions as different institutions with different functions (even if these functions intersect and their boundaries are blurred) but at the same level of importance of the legislatures. One can disagree, but this is what is enshrined in the constitutions.

[50]Even if it was essential, it does not seem to be possible to separate completely these two concepts, given that "law is politics and politics is (Constitutional) law". As Zamboni (2008: 5–6) puts it, this happens "because the political organisational form of the nations state is characterised, in part, by the fact that the law (…) is a tool available to Parliaments and Governments (…) in order to effectuate programs within a certain community".

[51]It is important to note that there is an aspect that escapes the initial setup of this principle by Montesquieu: the constitutional legislator included in the constitution the existence of a Constitutional Court, which is responsible, in particular, for the review of normative acts' constitutionality. I.e., the constitutional justice was tasked with policing compliance with the constitution by other branches of the state, and is thus "a proper and specific power of the state, yet it has not been endowed with coercive means to give effect to their sentences, but one must trust in respect of it by the legislator and by other courts". See Hohmann-Dennhardt (2011: 3–4).

[52]See Cohen-Eliya and Porat (2013: 47–55).

[53]The same happened in other European countries such as Portugal, Spain and Italy after the end of their dictatorial regimes. In Portugal, see for example Miranda and Cortês (2010: 83).

[54]See Cohen-Eliya and Porat (2013: 55).

common in countries that experienced authoritarian regimes or dictatorships, and they share some constitutional characteristics with Germany that do not exist in the American system.[55]

Furthermore, in European countries, "the expansive nature of constitutional rights created a structural need for proportionality in its intrinsic sense; in the USA, the narrower scope of constitutional rights allows for a bounded type of balancing".[56] It is important to note here that under what some have named *new constitutionalism* (or *neo-constitutionalism*)[57] it is possible to identify a general European trend towards the use of the theory of fundamental *rights as principles.*[58] This theory means that constitutional rights have a large scope and therefore clash more often, contrarily to what happens in the USA, where fundamental rights have a restricted scope and are much more rigid, rule-like norms (such as the "rights as shields" of Schauer). Apparently, this may suggest that in Europe one can find more judicial activism compared with the USA or, at least, more *judicial activity.*[59]

As seen here, there are great differences between the typical European constitutional system and the American one. And it appears that proportionality as a judicial tool used to supervise the state's activity is a doctrine that fits better the European context of a social democratic state (allowing the control of violations on both negative and positive rights), than the American type of liberal state.[60] In short, a correct understanding of judicial review, separation of powers and proportionality are strongly influenced by the cultural context or, in other words, by the "constitutional tradition" of each country.[61] This explains why European countries, which were affected by dictatorships, look at constitutional justice as an essential component of separation of powers, even though the necessity of protecting fundamental rights may lead to clashes amongst them.

[55]See Grimm (2005: 154).

[56]See Cohen-Eliya and Porat (2013: 60). Alexy (2010: 66 ff) even argues that the foundation of proportionality is the nature of fundamental rights.

[57]For a general approach to neo-constitutionalism, among many others, see Sampaio (2015: 313 ff), Prieto Sanchís (2013: 23 ff), García Figueroa (2009), Carbonell (2007).

[58]This does not mean that there are no criticisms to this theory. Criticizing the so called *principle's theory*, among others, see Schlink (1976), Habermas (1998), Poscher (2003), Šušnjar (2010).

[59]Nevertheless, the problem is not as different in each system as it might seem, because American courts will have to previously define interpretively what the protected scope of fundamental rights is, and this interpretative task can also entail judicial activism (or at least a dubious increase in judicial activity), due to its subjectivity.

[60]In a similar way, although with different arguments, see Evans and Stone (2007), Mullender (2000: 503).

[61]Referring only to separation of powers, see Saunders (2001: 132).

10.2.3 Legal Context

10.2.3.1 General Aspects

The different cultural context between America and continental Europe is a decisive reason explaining the differences between the use of proportionality in Europe and the use of balancing in the USA as well as the different understanding about judicial activism.

However, in my opinion, the difference in the construction of the principle of proportionality is somewhat also explained by different cultural contexts, but its foundation is the respective *legal context*, which is the key element. One can also say that the cultural context is the basis of the main architecture of each legal system. But once a legal system is created, its *concretisation* will also be influenced by the main features of that legal architecture.

First of all, as I previously mentioned, the basic content of proportionality lies in the tests of (i) rational connection, (ii) necessity, and (iii) proportionality in its strict sense. And this specific configuration of the principle allows for a detailed and really strict judicial review by constitutional courts. As already stressed, the first issue here is to determine why the use of proportionality as a strong judicial review parameter causes much less intense discussion in Europe, although it is also criticised, than in America where the anti-majoritarian nature of the judicial review has been strongly debated.[62] The answer seems to be both the different cultural and legal context.

A second question arises: how do we know what the basic content of the principle of proportionality is when, in most cases, Constitutions do not even mention it explicitly? Within this context, the first problem to address is the discussion around the use of principles unspecified by Constitutions as judicial review parameters. This problem can be solved, I believe, by using the concept of *implicit principles*[63]—principles by definition "non-explicitly formulated in some constitutional or legal provision" and thus created or "constructed" by interpreters".[64] No problem derives from the inclusion in the "constitutionality block" of implicit principles, provided that they are concretised or revealed from other explicitly enshrined constitutional principles. And this is a work to be pursued by jurisprudence and legal literature.[65,66]

---

[62]More recently, influenced by scholars as Waldron, authors have again discussed the role of constitutional courts, although in less extreme ways. See for example Linares (2008).

[63]Concerning the subject of implicit principles, among others, see Barak (2012: 53 ff), Reimer (2001: 205 ff, and 397 ff).

[64]See Guastini (2001: 138).

[65]In conclusion, the Constitution, like any other text, is not only explicit language but also "the spaces which structures fill and whose patterns structures define" (Tribe)—the "*visible Constitution*" is always accompanied by the "*invisible Constitution*". See Barak (2012: 55).

[66]For example, in the German constitutional system, the principle of proportionality is not explicitly enshrined in the Constitution, but jurisprudence and doctrine usually find the principle in the wider Rule of Law principle (*Rechtstaat*). See, among others, Hesse (1999: 148 ff). In Portugal,

Notwithstanding the aforementioned, there is still an unresolved issue: how are such implicit rules to be "created"? Are there any limits to their construction? First of all, it is important to mention that implicit principles are not created by interpretation (in its narrow sense), but through "integration into Law by the interpreters", which can be done in different ways: sometimes legal practitioners obtain them from single rules, others from more or less large groups of rules and still others from the legal system as a whole.[67] In any case, this is a "rhetorical-persuasive process, with a degree of persuasiveness dependent once again on initial legal data (the principles to be implemented, their possible formulation, the possible existence of precedents, etc.), on cultural factors and on material valuations—involving in particular an adequacy judgement that is 'instrumental' to the implicit principle with a certain configuration, serving that judgement as an adequate implementation and development of the initial principle".[68]

The principle of proportionality is usually inferred from the principle of the Rule of Law.[69] Even when the principle is explicitly mentioned in Constitutions, the truth is that the construction of its content still reflects the idea of the Rule of Law. This process of construction of rules is of course *discretionary* in high degree—, especially when rules are inferred from very general principles or from the legal system as a whole—, that leading some to argue that the court is acting as legislator and thus violating the principle of separation of powers. However, one can argue that is not the case, since the judge is only assuming "the principle as implicit in the language of corresponding sources".[70] Nevertheless, it is clear that this admittedly discretionary process must have limits and some of them correspond precisely to the *legal characteristics* of each legal system.

It thus becomes clear why the principle of proportionality is also determined by the *legal context*: even if its construction involves some discretion, limits are to be found in the structure of corresponding legal systems. And this not only explains the differences between European proportionality and American balancing, but can even *require* the existence of some differences. Regarding the legal context, the most important features are related to: (i) the type of Constitution; and (ii) the judicial review system. That said, let us analyse the main features of the European constitutional system (here mainly represented by the German and Portuguese cases) and the American constitutional system.

(Footnote 66 continued)
there is no explicit constitutional reference to the principle of protection of legitimate expectations, but the Portuguese jurisprudence and doctrine also find this principle in the wider Rule of Law principle. See, for example, Novais (2011: 261 ff).

[67]See Guastini (2001: 138).

[68]See Pino (2010: 71).

[69]Amongst others, see Bernal Pulido (2007: 606 ff), Barak (2012: 226 ff). For other foundations of the principle, see Bernal Pulido (2007: 599 ff), Barak (2012: 211 ff).

[70]See Guastini (2001: 138).

10.2.3.2 Differences Between European and American Rule of Law

Regarding the European constitutional legal system, one must begin by stressing that the importance given to Constitutions was such that it created a significant phenomenon of "*constitutionalisation of the legal system*",[71] which is the process and result of the transformation of the law caused by the Constitution.[72] Therefore, the "supremacy of the Constitution" is a decisive characteristic of the European material *Rechtstaat* and means that the legislature is bound and subordinate to the Constitution.[73]

In this context, because it is so impressive, it is relevant to mention the seven main features of typical European Rule of Law[74,75]: (i) the existence of an entrenched written Constitution, resistant to ordinary legislation and difficult to amend; (ii) the existence of a judicial guarantee of the Constitution with inherent review of legislation[76]; (iii) the endowment of the Constitution with a special binding force, with the same being considered as true law and not as a mere programmatic statement; (iv) the *over-interpretation* of the Constitution, in which courts and doctrine widely use logical arguments, analogy and constitutional principles—requiring the use of balancing[77]—, therefore extending and intensifying the presence of the Constitution in the legal system, to the point of encompassing the whole law,[78] and interfering in the solution of all controversies[79]; (v) the *direct application* of constitutional norms—the Constitution regulates not only the relations between the powers of state and between state and citizens, but all

---

[71]About this concept, see Favoreu (1998: 184 ff).

[72]Constitucionalization is a "process", not an "all or nothing" quality. Therefore, it is possible to talk about different degrees or intensities according to each constitution. There are examples of merely nominal and semantic constitutions, of constitutions without judicial guarantees (or merely with political guarantees), and the post-war (and dictatorships) constitutions that seem to be the cases with the most complete processes of constitutionalisation. See Prieto-Sanchís (2009: 115).

[73]See Heun (2011: 39).

[74]It is clear that the American and British concept of *Rule of Law* is materially different of the German concept of *Rechtstaat*.

[75]See Guastini (2006: 49 ff).

[76]With several possibilities existing at this level. On this, see Sweet (2013: 823 ff).

[77]Among many others, see Prieto Sanchís (2009: 175 ff). It is however important to stress that this specific balancing in the sense of principle theory is different from more general types of balancing, such as the American one that was already mentioned. See Šušnjar (2010: 69–70).

[78]The constitution radiates throughout the legal system, and includes all its branches. See Jarass (2006: 649).

[79]See for example Guastini (2006: 50). Due to its particular structure, constitutional principles allow an enormous expansion of the constitution's scope of influence—Alexy even speaks of the "constitution's omnipresence" (*Allgegenwart der Verfassung*). And the greater the scope of the constitution, the smaller the margin for discretion for the legislator [see Prieto Sanchís (2013: 33)]. Additionally, there is also an "extension of protection" of fundamental rights, since the expansion of its scope of protection, due to its principled nature, involves "the extension of the courts' decision powers". See Sieckmann (2011: 58).

social relations,[80] with a phenomenon of "*elimination of constitutional barriers*" occurring[81]; (vi) interpretation in accordance with the Constitution, that involving in the limit for the Constitutional Court to step outside its role as a *negative legislator*, issuing *interpretative rulings* or *manipulative rulings*; and (vii) the influence of the Constitution on political relations—constitutional principles, strongly moralised and politicised, intervene in political argumentation, regulating relations between the branches of government and also allowing courts to supervise political argumentation by establishing legal standards according to the Constitution.

Moreover, it must be stressed that the *supremacy* of the Constitution is assisted by the guarantee of a special body—the Constitutional Court (called the "guardian of the Constitution"). Any statute that violates the Constitution is unconstitutional and void, and "the unconstitutionality is enforceable by the Constitutional Court which has comprehensive competences to declare a statute unconstitutional".[82] This court appears as a constitutional body that "aims to guarantee the 'constitutional functioning of the State', i.e. the correct and normal development of the 'political process'".[83,84]

Consequently, it can be concluded that the role of this special court and its authority can be explained precisely "by legal reasons such as its constitutional position and the scope of its jurisdiction", and by cultural reasons (such as historical ones) like "the emphasis on the rule of law" "and the self-evident acceptance of judicial guardianship of it shows some distrust of the political process and a corresponding faith in the work of courts" (which can be explained by the previous authoritarian regimes).[85] Additionally, it is important to point out that, given all the Constitutional Court's functions and especially its judicial review function, this

---

[80]Today, there is little doubt about this direct application. What is being discussed is the extent of this application, especially with regard to the regulation of relations between private individuals. See Prieto Sanchís (2013: 27).

[81]It becomes possible to access the Constitution, regardless the mediation of the legislator, *directly* and *permanently*, as it is difficult to find a legal problem that lacks at least some constitutional relevance, see Prieto Sanchís (2009: 114).

[82]See Heun (2011: 39).

[83]See Costa (2007: 98). The existence of a constitutionalised legal system, as mentioned, involves major consequences for the "balance of forces between the state powers", namely the shift of the role of the legislature to the judiciary, especially the Constitutional Court. See García Figueroa (2003: 167). And due to this Alexy also talks of an "omnipotence of Courts" (*Omnipotenz der Gerichte*).

[84]In addition, the jurisdiction of Constitutional Courts also extends to electoral disputes, banning of undemocratic political parties, impeachment cases of elected officials, and so on. Therefore, as Sweet notes, Constitutional Courts "are given functions that would be viewed as too 'political', or constitutionally important to confer to ordinary courts". And "[p]artly for this reason, CCs are loath to develop formal deference doctrines, such as the 'political question' doctrine of the US Supreme Court, which would signal abdication of their duties". See Sweet (2013: 822–823).

[85]See Koopmans (2003: 69).

organ also "contributes, at its level and in its way, to the formation of the state's "political will" and participates in its upper management".[86]

In summary, in continental Europe, the Rule of Law can be characterised by the binding and *radiant* strength of a material and axiological Constitution that seeps into the entire legal system. And the Constitution is protected by a special court that can assess laws made by political entities. In other words, the European Rule of Law presupposes (very) *strong courts* and *strong rights.*[87]

Let us compare this strong Rule of Law with the American case.[88] First of all, it must be stressed that the United States also has a formal and material Constitution serving as a constraint to the power of Congress and enshrining a considerable group of fundamental rights, more specifically of civil liberties. But there are at least three relevant differences. Firstly, it is possible to find "a much broader consensus regarding the contours of fundamental rights" in continental Europe than in the United States. A good example is the attitude towards the death penalty. In Europe there is solid consensus against the death penalty (its abolition was often initiated 'from above' and, in several cases, was a pre-condition for admission into entities such as the Council of Europe or the European Union).[89] Contrarily, "the death penalty remains a highly divisive issue within the United States and within the Supreme Court".[90] Secondly, the American Constitution does not enshrine *social rights* (as the Portuguese does) and does not mention the existence of a *social state* (as the German does).[91] Thirdly, related to the latter aspect, unlike the European case in which extensive positive duties of *protection* and *promotion* falling on the state stem from fundamental rights[92,93]—that involve the possibility of violation of

---

[86]See Costa (2007: 103).

[87]For the concepts of "weak" and "strong courts" and "weak" and "strong rights", see Tushnet (2008).

[88]In the British case the differences are even bigger due to its parliamentary model. In fact, "[t]he British doctrine of the sovereignty of Parliament embodied" the rule according to which "by issuing a statute, an Act of Parliament, the legislative bodies had the final say. No court was entitled to question the legality of a statute; and every law-making body in the country was subject to it". See Koopmans (2003: 15). And due to this, the legal context is much more decisive when comparing the British case with the typical European one. In addition to the United Kingdom, the legal context is also more important to sustain differences in the use of proportionality in other cases such as Canada and New Zealand, in which the respective legal system establishes weak judicial review systems. See Tushnet (2011: 321 ff).

[89]For example, the death penalty was abolished in Portugal in 1867.

[90]See Rosenfeld (2005: 237).

[91]And it seems clear that a "different degree of commitment to social-democratic norms among different political systems" can be found, as for example in the American and the European systems. See Krieger (2005: 192), Michelman (2005: 170), Tushnet (2003: 88).

[92]About the concept of positive duties, among others, see Fredman (2008: 65 ff).

[93]And even if the social rights involve amazingly "policentric questions" [about this concept, see King (2012: 189 ff)], one can find several decisions of the Portuguese and German Constitutional Courts related to social rights. Among others, see Portuguese Constitutional Court's rulings nos. 353/2012, 5th July; 187/2013, 5th April; 413/2014, 30th May. And for the German Constitutional

the Constitution also when the state fails to act—, in the American case the relevance assigned to these duties is diminished if not null (that being explained by the emphasis given by the Constitution to the extent of negative liberties[94]), the judicial review of these duties being inadmissible in any case.[95]

It is important to mention that in the United States judicial review also exists, and its creation seems to be related to the "scepticism against uncontrolled parliamentary supremacy as known from the British constitutional system".[96] Paradoxically, one may add, "[w]hile constitutional review has been entrenched longer in the United States, it is more firmly grounded in" continental Europe.[97] There are several reasons for that. Firstly, as mentioned, in continental Europe judicial review is performed by a *special body*—the Constitutional Court—whereas in the American case judicial review is pursued by the Supreme Court. Institutional differences between the two kinds of institutions should be pointed out, such as the specialization of a Constitutional Court in constitutional matters[98] and those concerning the appointment of judges.[99]

Beyond these aspects, there is a great difference in comparison with the European systems: the American Constitution does not specify in detail the role and the jurisdiction of the Supreme Court.[100] Therefore, there is "no clear textual basis holding that the Supreme Court is invested with a power of judicial review as the ultimate authority over constitutionality of federal and state law". And "this vagueness has led to an ongoing debate over judicial review".[101] Conversely, in the European case the role and jurisdiction of the Constitutional Court is clear and widely described in the Constitution: usually, it is the Constitution that designates Constitutional Courts as authoritative interpreters of the higher law, that establishes enforceable rights, and that explains how will function the interaction between that courts and the other branches of government and the citizenry.[102] In sum, it is the

(Footnote 93 continued)
Court see, for example, the rulings BVerfG, 1 BvL 1/09 (2010); BVerfGE 103, 242 (*Pflegeversicherung* III) (2001).

[94]See Rosenfeld (2005: 212).

[95]See Michelman (2005: 177), Grimm (2005: 137 ff).

[96]See Pirker (2013: 138).

[97]See Rosenfeld (2005: 202).

[98]See Heun (2011: 170). Regarding the argument of *expertise*, see for example Ferreres Comella (2001: 269–270).

[99]For example in Germany and Portugal, appointments require a two-thirds majority vote in parliament, which obviously "cannot be achieved without a consensus among the major political parties". In contrast, in the American case the "appointment of a president's nominee requires a simple majority vote in the Senate". See Rosenfeld (2005: 235).

[100]Alex Stone Sweet (2013: 822) refers precisely that "[c]ompared with the major alternative, however, the specialised CC has a powerful advantage, in that the framers can more easily tailor the details of jurisdiction to specific purposes".

[101]See Pirker (2013: 138).

[102]As Sweet mentions, "[t]he legitimacy resources that flow from explicit constitutional arrangements are enormously important". See Sweet (2013: 828).

lack of a clear constitutional mandate as the authoritative constitutional adjudicator that leads critics to attack the US Supreme Court as being essentially political.[103]

But these are not the only existing differences. In fact, in the American case, judicial review is limited to concrete review (and thus a posteriori). On the contrary, in the European case the possibilities of judicial review are broad: for example in the Portuguese case there is abstract and concrete review, there is prior and a posteriori review, and there is also the possibility of a state omissions review; in the German case there is the possibility of concrete and abstract review and of constitutional complaints. This short description immediately reveals a huge difference regarding the scope of jurisdiction and powers between the American and the European cases. But if we recall the concept of *abstract review* as well as some decisions constitutionally assigned to European Constitutional Courts, we notice that the magnitude of the differences between both systems is even greater.[104] All these differences explain the fact that the legitimacy of the American constitutional adjudicator is much more fragile and contested than that of the European constitutional judges.[105]

In conclusion, it can be said that "[i]n the context of a broad consensus regarding an expanded constitutional sphere, the increased scope of constitutional adjudication may become widely accepted as legitimate".[106] And due to all the above, it is now clear that there are important institutional differences between the American constitutional system and the European one, i.e., the legal context between these two systems is very different, that having a decisive influence in the construction of the proportionality principle in each constitutional system.

---

[103]See Rosenfeld (2005: 203).

[104]Abstract review can be defined as a "constitutional process for review and decision with generally binding force (with force of law) of the formal and material validity of a legal rule" [see Canotilho (2007: 1005)]. This means that Constitutional Courts may declare the unconstitutionality of a legal rule in abstract, regardless of a concrete case. In addition to all these types of review, the Constitution, either explicitly or implicitly, permits also several types of "manipulative sentences" which evidence its power.

In a merely descriptive way, even if these decisions may pose some problems, European Constitutional Courts have been using the following decisions: (i) decisions with limiting effects in the strict sense, in which there is a limitation (reduction or mere manipulation) of the normal effects of unconstitutionality that the decision should contain; (ii) decisions with appealing effect, in which the court appeals the government to amend or abolish the rules that will be unconstitutional in the future; (iii) decisions with limiting temporal effects, in which the sanctioning effects of the declaration of unconstitutionality are limited; (iv) interpretive decisions, in which the court will interpret a legal rule according to the constitution, to save it from unconstitutionality; and (v) decisions with additive effects, which consist of positive decisions of unconstitutionality that can result in either a judgment of invalidity or the statement of a rule or a principle, in order to ensure the creation of conditions to guarantee that the violated right achieves compatibility with the constitution. With a comparative analysis of use of these decisions in several countries, see Brewer Carias (2013).

[105]Referring only to the German constitutional judge, see Rosenfeld (2005: 219).

[106]See Rosenfeld (2005: 206).

10.2.3.3 Consequences of the Different Rule of Law's Characteristics on the Structure of Proportionality

The latter conclusion can be clarified by an example. As already mentioned, most authors argue that proportionality requires at least three tests: rational connection, necessity, and proportionality in its narrow sense. Other authors, though, consider that the test of proportionality in the strict sense assigns an excessive margin of judicial review to courts.[107] Thus, this test should be eliminated given its political nature, with the balancing being left to "society".

However, and considering the above, one can't really argue in an *overall way* that the use of proportionality in its narrow sense inevitably leads to a violation of the separation of powers principle and, therefore, to judicial activism: the admissible *intensity* of judicial review will vary according to the cultural and legal context and the particularities of each case. And as a result of the differences between the European and the American Constitutions—and also between the European Constitutional Courts and the American Supreme Court—, the construction and contents of the principle will necessarily vary, in particular in light of the characteristics of the Rule of Law involved. In this sense, the characteristics of the European context, or contexts, will justify a principle of proportionality applied in all its tests, even if that involves strict scrutiny of legislative activity. Contrarily, the different characteristics of the American context will involve a principle of proportionality (or a simple balancing test as it already exists) that is less intrusive, stopping short for example (and at least) of proportionality in its strict sense.[108]

10.3 The Influence of the Proportionality's Content on the Intensity of Judicial Review

As I stated, the cultural and legal contexts have a decisive impact on the structure and content of proportionality and, consequently, also in the admissible *margin of judicial review*.[109] Nevertheless, while the connection between the principle of proportionality and the margin of judicial review is clear, one should not confuse these concepts. It is true that the cultural and legal contexts influence both the

---

[107]Nevertheless one must stress that the margin of judicial review also depends a lot on the concrete intensity of review used in each proportionality test. This means for example that if a court uses a strict scrutiny on the necessity test and a mere evidence scrutiny on the proportionality in its strict sense test, this court will probably be more *intrusive* in the first case.

[108]This does not mean that in theory it is not possible to construct a principle of proportionality in both cases with the traditional three tests, but the specific scrutiny allowed in each case will obviously have to be different. For example Clérico (2009: 38) argues that the principle of proportionality structure is always the same; it is the intensity of scrutiny that changes.

[109]Also connecting the principle of proportionality and the level of intensity of review, see Rivers (2006: 174 ff).

content of proportionality and the margin of judicial review in each legal system, but one cannot forget that the same margin is decisively affected by the contours of each case.[110]

Accepting that in typical European systems, the Constitutional Court has always the power to supervise state action or inaction, two different moments will still be relevant to determine the specific margin of judicial review that is admissible: (i) the first concerning the specific legal and cultural context, (ii) the second—also important—concerning all the particularities of the specific case (which also influences the proportionality's intensity of judicial scrutiny).[111] For example, the margin of judicial review will be wide when the case concerns the negative dimension of fundamental rights or specific negative rights. Inversely, that margin will be extremely small when the case concerns the positive dimension of fundamental rights and the inherent duties of protection and promotion. In the latter, at issue will be the "reservation of material and financial possibilities" (*Vorbehalt des Moglichen*), the political choice of the goods to protect and to promote (obviously related to the *scarcity of goods*), the intensity of restrictions on fundamental rights, the relevance of the public interest being pursued, and so forth.[112,113,114]

That said, the main conclusion to be reached is that, even between legal systems such as the American and the European ones, which have some similarities (due to

---

[110]Even if, just as Pirker, I understand that the institutional and cultural context have some influence over the margin of judicial review, I am arguing a different idea. Pirker maintains "that there is a pre-balancing exercise (previous to the proportionality balancing itself) undertaken by an adjudicator to assess whether he or she will engage in a full-scale proportionality analysis or rather refrain from it". See Pirker (2013: 71). I am stating that the cultural and legal context influence the *creation* of the principle of proportionality with a certain content.

[111]Therefore, it is not the proportionality *itself* that sets the margin of judicial review as Rivers seems to argue, but both the legal and cultural contexts, firstly, and the particularities of each case, secondly, that set the concrete margin of review that courts have in each case (and also set the intensity of the proportionality's scrutiny). Nevertheless, Rivers' conclusion is not so different from mine: he argues that depending on the specific case there is also a principle of judicial restraint that clashes with the principle of proportionality. And the result of the practical concordance (*praktische Konkordanz*) between these two principles (preserving as much as possible of each of them) will show the specific margin of judicial review. See Rivers (2006: 202 ff). It is not possible to address this question here but, in addition to other issues, even the existence of this *principle of deference* is really problematic if one considers the *normative force* of fundamental rights.

[112]Similarly, see Young (2012: 167 ff), and Sampaio (2015: 427 ff). Stressing the differences between the proportionality analysis regarding positive and negative rights, see Klatt and Moritz (2012a, b: 84 ff).

[113]And as Katharine Young argues this will involve the existence of different types of judicial review with different intensities, namely: (i) "deferential review"; (ii) "conversational review"; (iii) "experimentalist review"; (iv) "managerial review"; and (v) "peremptory review" (in this context, the court may, for example, use different types of manipulative decisions admissible in each legal system). See Young (2012: 385 ff).

[114]One must also remember that proportionality is only one of the judicial review tools that can be used by courts. In fact, there are other tools—other "limits to the limits" on fundamental rights—such as the principles of human dignity, equality or protection of legitimate expectations.

the existence of material and formal Constitutions and the possibility of judicial review), cultural and legal differences will lead to different constructions of proportionality. The same conclusion can, of course, be extended to other legal systems.[115] In continental Europe it will make sense to construct the principle of proportionality with the traditional three-prong structure (and more often with an intense scrutiny on each specific test), while in the United States, due to its specific context, it will make sense to use a more permissive balancing principle or a principle of proportionality without at least the test of proportionality in its narrow sense (and more often with a mere evidence scrutiny on the respective tests). However, this does not mean that courts will always have the same margin of judicial review: in fact they will not. But even in legal systems where it makes sense to have strong courts, the margin of judicial review will be ultimately influenced by the particularities of each case, therefore varying greatly—judicial review is not a static reality. And consequently, a strong *justification* (reasoning) of decisions (more or less intrusive ones) will also be decisive to support the actual positions taken.[116]

10.4 Final Remarks

As a good summary to explain the stressed differences between continental Europe and America's cultural and legal context, one can argue that the use of balancing in the context of proportionality in European's constitutional jurisprudence "was possible thanks to, not in spite of, a continued faith in legal formality, simply because balancing was seen as law, not politics or policy", that evidencing the relevance of cultural and legal contexts. Furthermore, the dominant understanding is not only that balancing is acceptable within this constitutional jurisprudence, but that "in fact [it plays] a central role in sustaining a distinctively legalist brand of constitutionalism, helping to garner commitment to and belief in the constitutional legal order". Differently, in the American case, "because of the background scepticism that tends to pervade them, and because of their association of the 'rise of balancing' with a paradigm shift from 'formalism' to 'realism', they often have trouble even seeing the European way of balancing" ("and they certainly have difficulty in believing it"). To the traditional American view, "the substantive has to be policy, legal formality can only realistically exist in the form of doctrinal rules

[115]Regarding the British case, this may explain and even support the reason why British courts normally remove the final stage of proportionality review. However, Rivers (2006: 203) criticises the British courts for being "excessively restrained".

[116]Constitutional judges cannot decide arbitrarily, especially when they intend to oppose to decisions taken by political powers. Therefore, they have to use "rational, constitutionally supported legal reasoning capable of justifying the result of a certain decision based on a balancing". See Novais (2003: 894). Concerning the necessary elements to a judicial decision be justified, among others, see Martínez Zorrilla (2007: 38 ff).

and categories, and any combination between the two can only ever be a pragmatic and unstable paradox".[117]

At this point, the connection between what is being argued and judicial activism becomes clear. The cultural and legal context means that the situations of judicial activism (such as, for example, those involving a violation of separation of powers) can similarly vary from one legal system to another. In other words, the "degree" to which the courts are 'activist' depends a lot on the respective constitutional and institutional context and cultural context.[118]

To conclude: in European countries that have 'strong constitutions' and '(very) strong courts', it is admissible, on the one hand, for the principle of proportionality to be used with its tripartite structure (and more often with an intense scrutiny on each specific test), even if that entails an overall large margin of judicial review—this does not means, however, that there cannot be *concrete* situations of judicial activism regarding the use of proportionality to review legislative measures. Nevertheless, in *general* the use of a strong proportionality principle by courts cannot be equated as judicial activism in the case of European Constitutional Courts, who thus have a much larger margin of judicial review than the American Supreme Court.[119] And this also means the threshold that distinguishes a non-activist judicial action from an activist one is therefore different in continental Europe in comparison to the United States.

Acknowledgments I would like to thank Luís Pereira Coutinho and Miguel Nogueira de Brito for their comments on earlier versions of this paper.

References

ALEXY, Robert. 2010. A Theory of Constitutional Rights. Oxford: OUP.

BARAK, Aharon. 2012. Proportionality – Constitutional rights and their limitations. New York: CUP.

BAYÓN, Juan Carlos. 2006. Derechos, Democracia y Constituición. In CARBONELL, Miguel. Org. 2006. Neoconstitucionalismo(s). 3ª Ed. Madrid: Trotta.

BEATTY, David. 2004. The ultimate rule of law. Oxford: OUP.

---

[117]See Bomhoff (2013: 235).

[118]Talking only about the constitutional and institutional context in the case of Common Law Supreme Courts, see Dickson (2007: 11–12). With a similar conclusion, Goldsworthy states that the reasons why "judges adopt different approaches to the adjudicative role on constitutional issues include the nature of the legal culture within which judges receive their education, the method for appointing judges, the pool from which they are drawn, the prevailing political culture in the country (and in particular the extent to which that has been affected by the 'rights revolution'), the nature and age of the Constitution and, lastly, the fact that judges somehow manage to find ways of adjusting their constitutions to 'the felt necessities of the time'". See Goldsworthy (2006: 343).

[119]In the American case the situation is reversed, which seems to justify the existence of strong judicial deference and weak judicial review.

BERNAL PULIDO, Carlos. 2003. El princípio de proporcionalidad y los derechos fundamentales. Madrid: CEC.

BREWER-CARÍAS, Allan. 2013. Constitutional Courts as Positive Legislators: A Comparative Law Study. Cambridge: CUP.

BÖCKENFÖRDE, Ernst-Wolfgang. 2003. Schutzbereich, Eingriff, verfassungsimmanente Schranken: Zur Kritik gegenwärtiger Grundrechtsdogmatik. In Der Staat

BOGNETTI, Giovanni. 2005. The concept of human dignity in European and US constitutionalism. In NOLTE, Georg. Ed. European and US Constitutionalism. Cambridge: CUP.

BOMHOFF, Jacco. 2013. Balancing constitutional rights - the origins and meanings of postwar legal discourse. Cambridge: CUP.

CANAS, Vitalino. 1994. Proporcionalidade (princípio). In DJAP. VII. Lisboa.

CANOTILHO, Gomes. 2007. Direito Constitucional e Teoria da Constituição. 7ª Ed. Coimbra: Almedina.

CANOTILHO, Gomes. 2003. Tribunal Constitucional, jurisprudências e políticas públicas. In APDC. Vol. II. Coimbra: Coimbra Editora.

CARBONELL, Miguel. Ed. 2007. Teoría del Neoconstitucionalismo(s). Madrid: Trotta.

CLÉRICO, Laura. 2009. Examen de Proporcionalidad en El Derecho Constitucional. Buenos Aires: Eudeba.

COHEN-ELIYA, Moshe / PORAT, Iddo. 2013. Proportionality and Constitutional Culture. Cambridge: CUP.

COSTA, Cardoso da. 2007. A Jurisdição Constitucional em Portugal. 3ª ed. Coimbra: Almedina.

DICKSON, Bruce. 2007. Judicial Activism in Common Law Supreme Courts. Oxford: OUP.

EVANS, Simon/STONE, Adrienne. 2007. Balancing and Proportionality: A Distinctive Ethic? Draft for discussion at the VII World Congress of the International Association of Constitutional Law. Athens.

FAVOREU, Louis. 1998. La Constitutionnalisation du Droit. In MATHIEU, Bertrand / VERPEAUX, Michel. 1998. La constitutionnalisation des branches du droit. Paris: Economica.

FERRERES COMELLA, Victor. 2011. The rise of specialized constitutional courts. In GINSBURG, Tom / DIXON, Rosalind. Comparative Constitutional Law. Cheltenham: Edward Elgar.

FREDMAN, Sandra. 2008. Human rights transformed — positive rights and positive duties. Oxford: OUP.

GARCÍA FIGUEROA, Alfonso. 2009. Criaturas de la Moralidade – Una aproximación neoconstitucionalista al Derecho a través de los derechos. Madrid: Trotta.

GARCÍA FIGUEROA, Alfonso. 2003. La teoría del Derecho en tiempos del constitucionalismo. In CARBONELL, Miguel. Org. Neoconstitucionalismo(s). Madrid: Trotta.

GOLDSWORTHY, Jeffrey. 2006. Interpreting Constitutions: A Comparative Study. Oxford: OUP.

GRIMM, Dieter. 2005. The protective function of the state. In NOLTE, Georg. Ed. European and US Constitutionalism. Cambridge: CUP.

GUASTINI, Riccardo. 2006. La « constitucionalización » del Ordenamiento Jurídico: el caso italiano. In CARBONELL, Miguel. Org. Neoconstitucionalismo(s). 3ª Ed. Madrid: Trotta.

GUASTINI, Riccardo. 2001. Estudios de Teoría Constitucional. México: Fontanamara.

HABERMAS, Jürgen. 1998. Faktizität und Geltung. Frankfurt: Suhrkamp.

HEINIG, Hans. 2011. The political and the Basic Law's Sozialstaat Principle — Perspectives from Constitutional Law and Theory. In German Law Journal. Vol. II. Issue no. 11.

HESSE, Konrad. 1999. Grundzüge des Verfassungsrechts der Bundesrepublik Deutschland. C.F. Heidelberg: Müller

HEUN, Werner. 2011. The Constitution of Germany — A Contextual Analysis. Oxford: Hart

HOHMANN-DENNHARDT, Christine. 2011. División de poderes, independencia de la justicia y la función del Tribunal Constitucional. In: HOHMANN-DENNHARDT, Christine / SCHOLZ, Rupert/ CRUZ VILLALÓN, Pedro. Orgs. Las Constituciones alemana y española en su aniversario. Madrid: CEPC.

JARASS, Jans. 2006. Funktionen un Dimensionen der Grundrecht. In MERTEN, Detlef/PAPIER, Hans-Jürgen. Hrsg. Handbuch der Grundrechte. Band II. Heidelberg: Müller.

KING, Jeff. 2012. Judging Social Rights. Cambridge: CUP.

KLATT, Matthias / MORITZ, Meister. 2012a. The Constitutional Structure of Proportionality. Oxford: OUP.

KLATT, Matthias / MORITZ, Meister. 2012b. Proportionality — a benefit to human rights? Remarks on the I•CON controversy. In I•Con. Vol. 10. n.º 3.

KMIEC, Keenan. 2004. The Origin and Current Meanings of Judicial Activism. In California Law Review. 92. Oct.

KOOPMANS, Tim. 2003. Courts and Political Institutions. Cambridge: CUP.

KOMMERS, Donald. 1997. The Constitutional Jurisprudence of the Republic of Germany. 2nd Ed. USA: Duke University Press.

LERCHE, Peter. 2001. Das Bundesverfassungsgericht im Streit und Methode. In BADURA, Peter / DREIER, Horst. Hrsg. Festschrift 50 Jahre Bundesverfassungsgericht. Erster Band. Tübingen: Mohr Siebeck.

LINARES, Sebastián. 2008. La (i)legitimidad democrática del control judicial de las leyes. Madrid: Marcial Pons.

MARTÍNEZ ZORRILLA, David. 2007. Conflictos constitucionales, ponderación e indeterminación normativa. Madrid: Marcial Pons.

MICHAEL, Lothar. 2011. Los derechos de igualdad como princípios iusfundamentales. In SIECKMANN, Jan-Reinhard. Ed. La teoría principialista de los derechos fundamentales — Estudios sobre la teoría de los derechos fundamentales de Robert Alexy. Madrid: Marcial Pons.

MICHELMAN, Frank. 2005. The protective function of the state in the United States and Europe: the constitutional question. In NOLTE Georg. Ed. European and US Constitutionalism. Cambridge: CUP.

MIRANDA, Jorge / CORTÊS, António. 2010. Anotação ao Artigo 1.º. MIRANDA, Jorge / MEDEIROS, Rui. Eds. Constituição Portuguesa Anotada. 2nd ed. Tomo I. Coimbra: Wolters Kluwer/Coimbra Editora.

MÖLLER, Kai. 2014. Constructing the Proportionality Test: An Emerging Global Conversation. In LAZARUS, Liora / MCCRUDDEN, Christopher /BOWLES, Nigel. Eds. 2014. Reasoning Rights - Comparative Judicial Engagement. Oxford: Hart.

MÖLLER, Kai. 2012. Proportionality: Challenging the Critics. In I•Con. Vol. 10. n.º 3.

MORAIS, Carlos Blanco de / RAMOS, Elival da Silva. Coords. 2012. Perspectivas de Reforma da Justiça Constitucional em Portugal e no Brasil. Coimbra: Almedina.

MULLENDER, Richard. 2000. Theorizing the Third Way: Qualified Consequentialism, the Proportionality Principle, and the New Social Democracy. In Journal of Law and Society. 27.

MÜLLER, Friedrich. 1990. Die Positivität der Grundrechte. Fragen einer praktischen Grundrechtsdogmatik. Berlin: Duncker & Humblot.

NOVAIS, Jorge Reis. 2011. Os Princípios Constitucionais Estruturantes da República Portuguesa. 2ª ed. Coimbra: Coimbra Editora.

NOVAIS, Jorge Reis. 2010. Direitos Sociais — Teoria Jurídica dos Direitos Sociais enquanto Direitos Fundamentais. Coimbra: Coimbra Editora.

NOVAIS, Jorge Reis. 2003. As restrições aos direitos fundamentais não expressamente autorizadas pela Constituição. Coimbra: Coimbra Editora.

OSSENBÜHL, Fritz. 1996. Abwägung im Verfassungsrecht. In ERBGUTH, Wilfried. Hrsg. Abwägung im Recht. Köln: Carl Heymanns.

PAPIER, Hans-Jürgen. 2005. Aktuelle grundrechtsdogmatische Entwicklungen in der Rechtsprechung des Bundesverfassungsgerichts. In GRUPP, Klaus / HUFELD, Ulrich. Hrsg. Recht, Kultur, Finanzen. Festschrift für Reinhard Mußgnug zum 70. Geburtstag am 26. Oktober 2005. Heidelberg: C. F. Müller.

PINO, Giorgio. 2010. Diritti e interpretazione — Il ragionamento giuridicio nello Stato costituzionale. Il Mulino, Bologna

PIRKER, Benedikt. 2013. Proportionality Analysis and Models of Judicial Review. Groningen: Europa Law Publishing.

POSCHER, Ralf. 2003. Grundrechte als Abwehrrechte. Tubingen: Mohr Siebeck.

PRIETO SANCHÍS, Luís. 2013. El constitucionalismo de los derechos: Ensayos de filosofía juridical. Madrid: Trotta.

PRIETO SANCHÍS, Luís. 2009. Justicia Constitucional y Derechos Fundamentales. Madrid: Trotta.

RIVERS, Julian. 2006. Proportionality and Variable Intensity of Review. In Cambridge Law Journal. 65(1). March.

ROSENFELD, Michel. 2005. Constitutional adjudication in Europe and the United States: paradoxes and contrasts. In NOLTE, Georg. Ed. European and US Constitutionalism. Cambridge: CUP.

SAMPAIO, Jorge Silva. 2015. O controlo jurisdicional das políticas públicas de direitos sociais. Coimbra: Coimbra Editora.

SAUNDERS, Cheryl. 2001. Dividing powers in the contemporary world. In: APDC. Vol. 1, Coimbra: Coimbra Editora.

SCHLINK, Bernhard. 2012. Proportionality (1). In ROSENFELD, Michel /SAJÓ, András. Eds. The Oxford Handbook of Comparative Constitutional Law. Oxford: OUP.

SCHLINK, Bernhard. 1998. The Dynamics of Constitutional Adjudication. In ROSENFELD, Michel /ARATO, Andrew. Eds. Habermas on Law and Democracy. Berkeley: University of California Press.

SCHLINK, Bernhard. 1976. Abwagung im Verfassungsrecht. Berlin: Duncker & Humblot.

SIECKMANN, Jans-Reinhard. 2011. Problemas de la teoría principialista de los derechos fundamentales. In CLÉRICO, Laura / SIECKMANN, Jans-Reinhard / Oliver-Lalana, Daniel. Coords. Derechos Fundamentales, principios y argumentación — Estudios sobre la teoría jurídica de Robert Alexy. Granada: Comares.

ŠUŠNJAR, D. 2010. Proportionality, Fundamental Rights and Balance of Powers. Leiden: Martinus Nijhoff.

SWEET, Alec Stone. 2013. Constitutional Courts. In ROSENFELD, Michel / SAJÓ, András. Eds. The Oxford Handbook of Comparative Constitutional Law. OUP, Oxford.

SWEET, Alec Stone / MATHEWS, Jud. 2008. Proportionality Balancing and Global Constitutionalism. In Columbia Journal of Transnational Law. n.º 47.

STÖRRING, Lars Peter. 2009. Das Untermaßverbot in der Diskussion: Untersuchung einer umstrittenen Rechtsfigur. Berlin: Duncker & Humblot.

REIMER, Franz. 2001. Verfassungsprinzipien: Ein Normtyp im Grundgesetz. Berlin: Duncker & Humblot.

TSAKYRAKIS, Stavros. 2012. Proportionality: An Assault on Human Rights? In I•Con. Vol. 7. n.º 3.

TUSHNET, Mark. 2003. The Issue of State Action/Horizontal Effect in Comparative Constitutional Law. International Journal of Constitutional Law. 1.

TUSHNET, Mark. 2008. Weak Courts, Strong Rights. Judical Review and Social Welfare Rights incomparative Constitutional Law. Princeton: PUP.

TUSHNET, Mark. 2011. The rise of weak-form judicial review. In GINSBURG, Tom / DIXON, Rosalind. Comparative Constitutional Law. Cheltenham: Edward Elgar.

WALDRON, Jeremy. 2006. The Core of the Case Against Judicial Review. In YJIL. Vol. 115. No. 6.

WALDRON, Jeremy. 1999. Law and Disagreement. OUP, Oxford.

WHITMAN, James. 2005. 'Human dignity' in Europe and the United States: the social foundations. In NOLTE, Georg. Ed. European and US Constitutionalism. Cambridge: CUP.

YOUNG, Katharine. 2012. Constituting Economic and Social Rights. Oxford: OUP.

YOWELL, Paul. 2014. Proportionality in the United States Constitutional Law. In LAZARUS, Liora / MCCRUDDEN, Christopher / BOWLES, Nigel. Eds. 2014. Reasoning Rights — Comparative Judicial Engagement. Oxford: Hart.

ZAMBONI, Mauro. 2008. Law and Politics — A Dilemma for Contemporary Legal Theory. Berlin: Springer.

Chapter 11
Politics and the Judiciary: A Naïve Step Towards the End of Judicial Policy-Making

Maria Benedita Urbano

11.1 Introduction

In the last decades state powers have significantly thrieven and expanded as a result of the development of the interventionist and regulatory State. As regards the judiciary, that expansion posed relevant problems of rationalization, both at the levels of judicial administration (i.e., of courts' structure and work organization) and judicial activity. In this paper, we are mostly interested in this later dimension, more precisely, in the phenomenon of judicial policy-making, also known under the name of judicial activism.

We believe that judicial policy-making constitutes a dangerous challenge for the basic and universal principle of the separation of powers and thus for the rule of law. Indeed, we believe that the empowerment of courts with political decision-making causes great harm, not only to the other branches of government, but also to the independence, impartiality and integrity of the judiciary itself. In that sense, the relation between judicial policy-making and the rationalization of judicial activity becomes self-evident. To put it briefly, rationalizing the judiciary might fight off that phenomenon.

11.2 Judicial Policy-Making

Our first priority will be to define 'judicial policy-making'. Additionally we will examine the conditions that favor this phenomenon.

M.B. Urbano (✉)
Universidade de Coimbra, Pátio da Universidade, 3004-545 Coimbra, Portugal
e-mail: mburbano@fd.uc.pt

L.P. Coutinho et al. (eds.), *Judicial Activism*,
Ius Gentium: Comparative Perspectives on Law and Justice 44,
DOI 10.1007/978-3-319-18549-1_11

11.2.1 Defining Judicial Policy-Making

Broadly speaking, by 'judicial policy-making' we mean the active political involvement of judges. To be more specific, the term 'judicial policy-making' is employed to describe the judiciary acting as a political branch, playing an active role in the political process, intervening in the political decision-making at the expense of the policy-making prerogatives of both the legislature and the executive, the majoritarian political institutions.

This inroad into political activity usually occurs via constitutional review. In truth, when controlling the constitutionality of legislative and executive acts, constitutional judges are increasingly interfering in policy matters, undermining majoritarian decisions.

In what concerns 'judicial policy-making', we believe that a feasible and useful distinction can be made between, on the one hand, the phenomenon per se (i.e., the practice in itself), and, on the other hand, the judges' behavior, guided by their own attitudes, orientations or philosophy. The practice in itself could be named, precisely, as 'judicial policy-making' or 'government by the judiciary'.[1] The judges' behavior could be named as 'activism' or 'judicial activism'. However, for convenience and brevity's sake, we will generally refer to both phenomena as judicial activism, in spite of the difficulties involved in defining the term "judicial activism"—even Schlesinger[2] offered no clear definition of it.[3]

The judicial interference in politics usually takes the form of lawmaking. It follows that the activist judge tends to be a judge who legislates. We don't intend to deny, of course, that on modern judicial practice, judging implies inevitably some kind of judicial creativity. But, as Cappelletti once pointed out, the problem with judicial activism lies not merely in the creation of law by judges, but rather in the degree of that creation.[4,5] So, the crucial question is how much and how far judges are legitimate to accomplish such judicial lawmaking. It is safe to say that judges go way too far on lawmaking when they shape and set new legal dispositions, both actively, i.e., intentionally—upholding social, economic and political regulation against the political branches' will or in the absence of that will—or passively.

Active direct lawmaking consists in creating new legal statutes (*innovative activism*) or in amending or rewriting already existing legal statutes (*corrective*

---

[1]'Government by the judiciary' (Boudin) or 'Government by judges' (Chief Justice M. Walter Clark). See Boudin (1911).

[2]The term 'judicial activism' was coined by Arthur Schlesinger Jr, in a 1947 article in Fortune magazine.

[3]Various authors highlight the difficulties in defining 'judicial activism'. See, e.g., Kmiec (2004: 1451), Young (2002: 1143–1144), Sowell (1989: 1), Sunstein (2005: 41–43). In any case, judicial activism might be consider both a normative and political phenomenon. Surely not the mere disagreement with particular judicial outcomes. See Young (2002: 1142).

[4]See Cappelletti (1990: 25, 28).

[5]And then, there are different degrees of judicial activism, from a shy or reluctant activism to an "overactivism" (term used by Vipin Kumar). See Kumar (2014: 23).

activism). This type of judicial activism mostly reflects political ambition or even political arrogance. This doesn't necessarily mean that constitutional judges wish to become professional politicians, but only that they willingly see themselves as political actors. Whatever their (un)declared intentions are, the point is that constitutional judges are interfering in public policies, acting against or at least in competition with the legislature and the executive.

Active undirect lawmaking occurs when a court's decision "leads to a legislative reaction of the Parliament". As underlined by Tate and Vallinder, legislators "alter desired policies in response to or in anticipation of the pronouncements of constitutional courts".[6] Actually, the mere presence of the court would seem to inhibit certain kinds of legislative activity and frequently legislators shape their bills to anticipate court decisions.[7]

Aside from active lawmaking, we may refer the existence of passive lawmaking. In fact, occasionally the creation of law by the judiciary is not fully intended: this is particularly the case for the declaration of partial nullity of a norm with expansive legal effects. Consequently, in these situations, constitutional judges usually don't have an hidden political agenda.

As we've said above, in treating the concept of judicial activism it is important to underline the lack of strict coincidence between judicial activism and judicial lawmaking. In fact, judges might do politics by merely nullifying norms or by finding rights contained within the penumbra of specific guarantees as demonstrated, for example, in the practice of the Warren Court.

11.2.2 Conditions for Judicial Activism

Even if the conditions for judicial activism differ from country to country, some of them can explain the increasingly expansion of the policy role of constitutional courts and alike. What is more, they can explain judicial activism. Some are objective conditions, other are rather subjective. Some correspond to a consensus view, whereas other might be accused of oversimplification. They may be described as follows:

1. **Objective conditions**

(a) Public confidence in the judiciary. Nowadays, in many countries, the judiciary has a better reputation than the majoritarian political institutions. Indeed, in some countries courts are famous for their pro-human rights, and especially pro-social rights stance. In contrast, people widely distrust the power of political branches. In many countries, a significant part of the population has

[6]See Tate and Vallinder (1995: 4).

[7]The German experience offers a clear example of that phenomenon. See Landfried (1995: 313).

negative perceptions of elected representatives' ability to wield a good and effective governance. This is due, among other things, to the fact that representatives are often viewed as ineffective, self-involved and corrupt.

(b) The growth of the Welfare State with the concomitant implementation of an extensive social security system and the strengthening of social rights (such as food, health care, housing, and social security). Most social rights are not self-enforcing and depend on social policies and on corresponding executive actions to become effective. In some cases constitutional judges, when reviewing social policies, claim that the legislator and/or the executive failed to meet their obligations towards the attainment of social rights and therefore commit themselves to enforce these rights.[8,9]

(c) The inability of the majoritarian political institutions to protect minority rights. According to a traditional view, they don't provide adequate protection for the rights and interests of minorities. Once that the minorities failed to obtain the protection of their rights and interests through the ordinary political process, they turn themselves to the judiciary, which very often commits itself with the task of protecting the rights and interests of minorities against the (tyranny of the) majority.

(d) The inefficiency of the majoritarian political institutions, usually due, according to some scholars, to party fragmentation and weak parties, leading to weak and unstable governmental solutions and therefore to poor and unsatisfactory governance. Allegedly, there is an inverse relation between a vigorous party system and judicial activism. Whether this thesis should be regarded as accurate or not is beside the point of this paper.

(e) The open-texture of constitutional norms and its incompleteness, namely of those related to principles and human rights. In truth, low normative density and incompleteness allow judges ample opportunity for legislative creativity and policy-making.[10] A few decades ago, Benjamin Cardozo stated that courts could legislate only interstitially. Unfortunately, that is not very consoling when the interstices of constitutions are far too wide.

2. **Subjective conditions**

Turning now to the subjective conditions, let us assume that the expansion of judicial policy-making is not just the product of objective facilitating conditions, but also the product of subjective states of mind.

In the first place, states of mind related to judges. According to Tate "It seems highly unlikely that judicialization could proceed very far in the absence of these [objective] conditions".[11] And yet, even in the presence of very favorable

[8]For a discussion of the social rights enforcement by the judiciary, see, generally, Landau (2012).

[9]See Urbano (2010: 626, 627).

[10]See Urbano (2010: 628, 629).

[11]See Tate (1995: 33).

facilitating conditions, the actual development of the judicialization of politics ultimately depends on personal attitudes of judges. Indeed, even under a very favorable set of facilitating conditions, restraintist judges should be expected to resist participating in policy-making, silencing their own political values. By contrast, activist judges are more likely to take every opportunity to use their decision-making to expand their own political values, unless, of course, they conform to the ones dominating majoritarian institutions.

Secondly, states of mind related to the majoritarian institutions, i.e., the traditional policymakers. Allegations have been made that frequently majoritarian institutions implicitly delegate or leave basic political and policy choices to the judiciary. This occurs especially regarding the resolution of highly sensitive issues, such as social rights, abortion, gay marriage and gay adoption, surrogate mothers and so forth.

The reason for that is eventually to be found in political and electoral calculations. In fact, very often the reason appears to be that the political/electoral costs of dealing with politically sensitive issues are too great to risk to rule them.[12] In that sense, the attractiveness of implicitly allowing the judiciary to settle such issues is very strong.

Delegating political and policy choices to the judiciary may also indicate the ineffectiveness of majoritarian institutions regarding the resolution of delicate and divisive issues. Undeniably, these issues usually paralyze the majoritarian bodies, making it difficult for them to decide and to ensure any policy effectiveness.[13]

An 'implicit delegation of powers', however, does not provide a valid justification for the judiciary to overstep its constitutional role.

11.3 The Judiciary and the Legislative Function

This leads to my next point.

11.3.1 Judicial Activism and the Separation of Powers

In the past decades the division and balance of powers has shifted notoriously. The legislative branch is no longer the dominant branch of national government. The most prominent example of this political-institutional rearrangement is the displacement of lawmaking power from the legislature to the executive. In fact, it has for some time been acknowledged that the executive branch is taking part to the exercise of legislative power. A question which then may arise is why do not

[12]See Tate (1995: 32).

[13]See Tate (1995: 32, 33).

formally to bestow the judiciary with a share of lawmaking function, reflecting the allocation of different responsibilities in new fields within a revised or reconceived theory of separation of powers.

Arguably because empowering the judiciary, or at least constitutional judges, to partake in the exercise of legislative power has proven to be a far more problematic idea.[14] The debate has been cast in terms of legitimacy (i.e., on the unelected judges' lack of democratic legitimacy), in terms of capacity (i.e., on the judges' inability or unsuitability to rule the country) and in terms of checks and balances (i.e., on the proper scope of the principle of separation of powers). We will focus on this latter issue.

The question of judicial activism must be addressed within the context of the doctrine of separation of powers.

The decision of the judiciary to intervene in the political decision-making process has consequences for the role of the third branch of government. Actually, it has consequences for the entire system of government. From the viewpoint of state stability, it's quite an evidence that the development of a stable governing structure requires that any exercise of political power should be submitted to control by other bodies. However, this leaves us with two problems to face.

Firstly, despite parliamentary and governmental democratic legitimacy and political accountability, the validity of legislative and executive actions also depends on a strong, focused and independent judiciary. According to the traditional tripartite separation of powers, the judiciary is empowered with significant responsibility for providing an effective check on the actions of the legislative and the executive branches of government. Its guardianship role is crucial to moderate the exercise of power at all levels of government. The functional separation of powers reflects somehow a division of labor according to expertise. And the judiciary, for its independency, neutrality and impartiality is especially suited to perform that task.

Well, the direct or even indirect involvement of the constitutional judges in policy functions and lawmaking would undermine the judiciary's capacity to wield properly its function, being therefore inappropriate.[15]

This brings us to another observation that should also be taken into consideration.

An overall structural transformation of the arrangement of powers, setting forth a redistribution of political power and allotting a share of it to the judicial branch, would be inconceivable without the implementation of a new system of checks and balances guaranteeing a new institutional equilibrium and thereby preventing the tyranny of that branch of government. Indeed, a truly and well-functioning democratic political system always matches power with institutionalised counter-power.

[14]See Urbano (2010: 625).

[15]Kumar (2014: 23) believes that judicial encroachment on legislative and executive domain will boomerang in the form of political class stepping to reach the bench. Thus, one may argue that the more politicised constitutional or hight courts are, the more likely it is that a political partisan appointment of constitutional judges will occur.

Institutional counter-powers are the only instruments able to prevent, in the long run, a dangerous and unhealthy concentration of power. Accordingly, if the judiciary is commited with political decision-making, its actions will require the same kind of oversight dedicated to the actions of the governing bodies. Then, a question that may arise is: Which body/entity is supposed to exercise control over the judiciary's performance of its own political functions? *Quis custodiet ipsos custodes*?

Unfortunately, up to now this major question remains unanswered.

11.3.2 Judicial Activism as a Pathological Phenomenon

With the above in mind, we argue that judicial activism is a pathological phenomenon, which immediately and severely challenges the principle of separation of powers, and harms the rule of law and democracy more than it helps.

It is a pathological phenomenon in the sense that it implies an undue intrusion of the judiciary in the legislative and the executive branches, eventually determining a fusion of state functions and inherently a dangerous concentration of all power in one single branch (or, even worst, in the hands of just a single body: a constitutional court or a supreme court). The hypertrophy of the judicial power is strengthened by the aggravating circumstance that this super-power knows no real legal control, neither by other bodies nor by the people through elections. Last but not the least, it can damage its guardianship role.

One may claim that judicial activism constitutes a pathological phenomenon only accordingly to an inadequated and outdated version of the theory of separation of powers, utterly ignorant of today's realities.

This line of reasoning takes for granted that judicial activism doesn't fit the traditional understanding of the judicial power. Furthermore, it seems undeniable that separation of powers is an important principle of liberal constitutionalism. But we have to accept too that the principle of separation of powers identifies with a series of long-standing values that are not innate or exclusive of liberal ideology, but characterize instead any balanced and stable democratic government. These long-standing values are as following: division of functions, checking and counterbalancing. All of them deserve full support, for they both underpin the quintessential idea that no power is superior to another.

11.4 Remedies for Fighting off Judicial Lawmaking

Taking into account the previous sections, we would like to propose now some remedies aimed to prevent judicial lawmaking. It's not too hard to think of some remedies, but undeniably the great majority of them correspond to mere wishful thinking. Besides, beyond that, some of them most possibly are not feasible or are probably unrealistic. And yet, let us come up with some, most certainly naïve, recommendations. We do so at risk of being subject to severe criticism.

(a) Promotion of judicial self-restraining. [16] The meaning of judicial self-restraint was defined by Chief Justice Stone, who supported this judicial attitude in US v. Butler (1936). According to Stone "The power of courts to declare a statute unconstitutional is subject to two guiding principles of decision which ought never to be absent from judicial consciousness. One is that courts are concerned only with the power to enact statutes, not with their wisdom. The other is that while unconstitutional exercise of power by the executive and the legislative branches of the government is subject to judicial review, the only check upon our exercise of power is our own sense of self-constraint".
In this 'structural or separation of powers sense',[17] judicial self-restraint indicates a deferential attitude towards the political branches of government (and therefore towards the Constitution), not to be confused with a passive posture. The judge's role is to interpret and enforce the law, not to make it. In brief, the rule of law cannot and must not be replaced by the law of the judges.
(b) Empowerment of the majoritarian institutions. To some degree, judicial activism is itself the result of problems and failures of regulation. In other words, judicial activism is often seen as a remedial measure for the supposed deficiencies of the ordinary political process, such as ineffective, inadequate and erroneous policies adopted by legislatures and executives; inability to address the problems concerning the population, and therefore to protect their rights, interests and needs; and lack of communication.
If the legislature and the executive wish to remain viable and central policy-making institutions, they ought to perform their constitutional functions effectively; they must be responsive to popular needs and they must foster their representative capacity; and they most certainly should not systematically eschew the highly controversial and sensitive policy issues of the day.[18]
It can be reasonably anticipated that, if parliament and governmental actions meet with popular approval, there will be no much room left for judicial involvement in politics, mainly in the lawmaking function. If the opposite occurs, the willingness to freely accept parliamentary and governmental decisions will decline sharply, with serious consequences for the legitimacy of the entire political system.
(c) Imposition of unanimous or near-unanimous judicial decisions on sensitive, controversial and highly divisive constitutional issues. In order to avoid the political, ideological or personal content of judicial decisions, whether this is the result of a personal and conscious call or the result of the manipulation of

[16] In truth, the term 'judicial self-restraint' is as open to a wide variety of interpretations as the term 'judicial activism'.

[17] See Posner (1999: 332).

[18] As Landfried puts it, "The more political questions are decided by the Constitutional Court, the more political alternatives are reduced". See Landfried (1995: 307).

constitutional control by the opposition parties, we should consider imposing an unanimity or near unanimity rule for deciding upon the constitutionality of acts of the legislative or the executive.
Some clarification is needed here. This unanimous or near-unanimous judicial decisions rule would be valid:

- Only for sensitive, controversial and highly divisive constitutional issues, such as social rights/Welfare State issues, financial and economic issues and major ethical issues, which are more likely to engage judicial activism;
- Only in relation to invalidating decisions, meaning that only the overturning of acts of the legislature or the executive would require unanimity or near-unanimity.

(d) Implementation of systems of case selection. When courts are called upon to determine the validity of legislation whose constitutionality is challenged, what's really is at stake is frequently a political disagreement or a strong dissatisfaction with some political choices taken by the majority. A system of case selection would allow the court not to be left in the uncomfortable position of settling a political dispute.
(e) Reinforcement of the presumption of constitutionality of laws. This particular presumption, established in 1937 (West Coast Hotel Co v. Parrish), constitutes one of the principal limitations to the power of judicial review. Indeed, this presumption imposes judicial deference towards the legislator. According to it, judges should seldom invalidate legislation, as their power to strike down statutes is understood to be exceptional and therefore to be only used when 'unavoidable'. From this perspective, courts should wield their power of judicial review very sparingly, nullifying statutes only upon a plain showing of their unconstitutionality. As said by Alexander Hamilton in The Federalist n. 78, the courts should strike down only those laws "contrary to the manifest tenor of the Constitution".
(f) Reaffirmation of the duty of justification of judicial decisions. The duty upon judges to justify their decisions, providing reasoned arguments, is also important to neutralize judicial activism, as the availability of reasons allows the public at large to realise whether or not judges are deciding cases according to their own personal, political or ideological views.
(g) Avoidance of the mediatization of constitutional justice and of justices in particular. The arcanic justice system is long extinguished and we are obviously not propounding its return. We also have not in mind restrictions to the freedom of the press or to the public's access to court hearings and proceedings, nor some other kind of blackout. We believe, however, that excessive media exposure—as evidenced in TV programs such as Court TV, providing live and daily televised coverage of court proceedings, mainly Supreme Court or Constitutional Courts proceedings—is counterproductive. Indeed, it may encourage people to believe that constitutional judges would take care of them and that courts make right what the political branches have

done wrong. Put in other words, it could induce a veneration of judges and it could foster the judges' personal desire to be prominent national political actors, therefore promoting judicial activism.

11.5 Conclusion

"Government by judiciary, as Boudin once called it, is—and it is most markedly where constitutional questions are concerned—far more a government of men, not laws, than of laws, not men".[19]

With this quotation of Fred Rodell, which concisely and sharply expresses our own (negative) view about judicial activism, we would like to conclude with a few final thoughts.

As observed, in these last decades, judges, mainly constitutional judges (those assigned with constitutional review tasks), were transformed, from mere mouths that pronounce the law into the constitution's mouth, in particular the social rights' mouth. In truth, they are having a quite important role in the enforcement of social rights, mainly in those countries with constitutions that don't provide for social rights or in countries with weak social policy-making capacity (for instance, in South Africa, India, Colombia and Brazil).[20] That explains why so many people believe that judges are using their powers to correct injustices, especially when the political branches do not act to do so.

In reality, however, judicial activism is a very complex and multifaceted phenomenon, influenced by multiple factors (such as social, political, legal, cultural) and expressed in multiple ways.[21] Notwithstanding, at the risk of oversimplification, we should distinguish the activist posture of the 'lower judiciary'—inspired by constitutional humanism—that, mostly in 'weak states', is leading a 'rights revolution'[22] (a social rights revolution), from the activist posture of the 'higher judiciary', basically inspired by judicial populism, sometimes embodied in grand gestures, made primarily (but not exclusively) in the social rights realm.

We may also distinguish judges who use the bench to "give a single remedy to a single plaintiff for provision of a treatment, pension or subsidy",[23] from judges who use the bench to enact social, moral and political changes. In both cases, judges argue that they are merely filling the gaps in the laws, shaping legal solutions (and at times setting legal rules) in light of constitutional meanings. In fact, sometimes they are, and sometimes they are not. Plainly, judicial activism is not a myth and at times it may not even be reprehensible by itself. But in the short run, if not

[19]See Rodell (1962: 700).

[20]See Landau (2012: 403).

[21]See Shapiro (1995: 43).

[22]Using Dobbin and Sutton's terms—'weak states' and 'rights revolution'—on a different context.

[23]See Landau (2012: 404).

refrained, it constitutes a threat to the other branches of government within the system of checks and balances, and therefore to the rule of law and to democracy. This is precisely why a set of remedies should be put forward in order to prevent the erosion of the political branches of government and the concomitant overgrowth of the judiciary. In the past, both the executive and the legislative overstepped their functional limits. Why should we trust a politicised judiciary and accept its candid nature?

References

Boudin, L.B. 1911. Government by judiciary.*Political Science Quaterly* 26. Issue 2 [in www.jstor.org/stable/view/2141031].

Cappelletti, Mauro. 1990. Des juges législateurs?. *Le pouvoir des juges*. Aix-en-Provence/Paris.

Kmiec, Keenan D. October 2004. The origin and current meanings of 'Judicial Activism'. *California Law Review* 92. Issue 5.

Kumar, Vipin. 2014. The Role of Judicial Activism in the Implementation and Promotion of Constitutional Laws and Influence of Judicial Overactivism.*IOSR Journal Of Humanities And Social Sciences* 19, Issue 2.

Landau, David. 2012. The reality of Social Rights Enforcement. *Harvard International Law Review* 53.

Landfried, Christine. 1995. Germany. In *The Global Expansion of Judicial Power* (edited by C. Neal Tate & Torbjörn Vallinder): New York University Press. New York/London.

Posner, Richard A. 1999. *The Federal Courts: challenge and reform*: Harvard University Press.

Rodell, Fred. 1962. Judicial Review: Its Role in Intergovernmental Relations: A Symposium: For Every Justice, Judicial Deference Is a Sometime Thing. *Faculty Scholarship Series*. Paper 2755 [in http://digitalcommons.law.yale.edu/fss_papers].

Shapiro, Martin. 1995. The United States. in *The Global Expansion of Judicial Power* (edited by C. Neal Tate & Torbjörn Vallinder): New York University Press. New York/London.

Sowell, Thomas. 1989. Judicial Activism Reconsidered. In *Essays in Public Policies* 13. Stanford University.

Sunstein, Cass R. 2005. *Radicals in Robes. Why Extreme Right-Wing Courts Are Wrong for America*. New York.

Tate, C. Neal. 1995. Why the Expansion of Judicial Power? in *The Global Expansion of Judicial Power* (edited by C. Neal Tate & Torbjörn Vallinder): New York University Press. New York/London.

Tate, C. Neal and Vallinder, Torbjörn. 1995. The Global Expansion of Judicial Power: The Judicialization of Politics. in *The Global Expansion of Judicial Power* (edited by C. Neal Tate & Torbjörn Vallinder): New York University Press. New York/London.

Urbano, Maria Benedita. 2010.The law of judges: attempting against Montesquieu's legacy or a new configuration for an old principle?. *Boletim da Faculade de Direito da Universidade de Coimbra* LXXXVI.

Young, Ernest A. 2002. Judicial Activism and Conservative Politics. *University of Colorado Law Review* 73. 4.

Chapter 12
The Judicial Activism of the European Court of Justice

Lourenço Vilhena de Freitas

12.1 The Concept of Activism and Its Application by the European Court of Justice

1. The discussion regarding the judicial activism of the European Court of Justice (ECJ) was launched by Hjalte Rasmussen in 1986,[1] who labeled its practice in that way—not without some rebuttal voices provided namely by Joseph Weiler and Mauro Capelletti, who questioned the corresponding assumption.[2] The debate also took place in the field of Political Science with Anne-Marie Burley and Walter Maltti considering that the ECJ has an activist perspective developing beyond the control of EU's member states.

Even if one takes ECJ's activism for granted, two further aspects, regarding its nature, must be analyzed. The strength of such activism is the first aspect to be considered. The second aspect concerns the differences between activism at the level of states, on the one side, and activism at the level of international organizations, on the other, in particular those resulting from integration such as the European Union.

In order to analyze these aspects, one must begin by briefly considering the concept of judicial activism, the situations it entails and the areas in which it has become usual to consider the ECJ's practice to be of an activist nature.

The concept of judicial activism is a fuzzy one, entailing situations such as result oriented judging, invalidation of actions of other branches, failure to adhere to

[1]See Rasmussen (1986) and also De Waele (2010).
[2]See Weiler (1987), Capelletti (1987) and also De Waele (2010).

L.V. de Freitas (✉)
Faculdade de Direito da Universidade de Lisboa, Alameda da Universidade, Lisbon 1649-014, Portugal
e-mail: lourenco.freitas@cuatrecasasgoncalvespereira.com

L.P. Coutinho et al. (eds.), *Judicial Activism*,
Ius Gentium: Comparative Perspectives on Law and Justice 44,
DOI 10.1007/978-3-319-18549-1_12

precedent or judicial legislation and system building.[3] One can also distinguish two levels of intensity of judicial activism based on the degree of intervention of the judicial branch in the legislative and executive areas.

If one used this scale and applied it to the ECJ, its practice could be qualified as strongly activist, since it has actually overstepped into the mentioned areas as it will be elaborated below.

Another way of measuring the real impact of judicial activism, though, is to assess the corresponding inputs into a legal framework, namely the creation of new rules and the definition of positive obligations of citizens.[4] In this sense, strong and weak forms of activism can also be distinguished: whereas a strong activism has a direct impact in material regulation, a weak activism has only an indirect material impact, concerning procedural rules, sources of law and system building principles and concepts.

In a way, one could say that a strong activism is Kelsenian in nature—implying the judge to actually intervene in politics, as Kelsen admitted he would[5]—and a weak activism is of an Hartian[6] nature, interfering only in areas of penumbra.[7]

2. At the procedural and system building levels, one can identify three main areas of intervention of the ECJ: (i) supremacy of the EU Law; (ii) direct effect; (iii) extension of the judicial review powers, implied powers and enhancement of the internal market. At the material level, the protection of human rights, particularly LGBT rights, can be mentioned even if it is sustained that the intervention of the ECJ is mostly aimed, in that case, at enhancing European Union powers and not, primarily, at protecting rights.

Regarding the supremacy of EU Law in face of national legal orders, the well known decisions of *Costa Ennel*[8] *(6/64), Internationales Handelsgesellshaft (111/70)*[9] *and Simmenthal (106/77)*[10] are the best examples of ECJ intervention. As it is known, supremacy has no direct basis on the treaties—that still being the case since the Treaty establishing the EU Constitution was not ratified and the Lisbon Treaty doesn't, expressly, foresee it. Even if one takes into account Declaration 17 annexed to the Final Act of the Intergovernmental Conference—considered by some as an interpretative instrument of the Treaty of Lisbon, in light of article 31 of the Vienna Convention[11]—one must still consider the primacy rule as previously developed by the ECJ, who was thus unquestionably responsible for a major innovation in EU Law.

---

[3]See Zarbiyev (2012) and Harwwod (1996).

[4]See Bossuyt (2014).

[5]For further developments, see the contribution by De Brito in this volume.

[6]See Hart (1957).

[7]See Zarbiyev (2012).

[8]See *Costa v. Ennel* [1964] EUCJR 1141.

[9]See Internationales Handeslgesellshaft [1970], EUCJR 114.

[10]See Amministrazione delle Finanze dello Stato v. Simenthal SpA [1978], 629.

[11]See Quadros (2013).

The innovative role of the ECJ has been recently observed in the *Kadi* decision,[12] which aimed at establishing that EU Law prevails over International Law—at stake were UN Security Council decisions—and not only over national legal orders, thus taking the meaning of "supremacy" to an entire new level.

The direct effect doctrine, connected with the supremacy aspect, but not to be confused with it, was also a construction of the ECJ, developed with no express basis on the Treaties in cases such as *Van Gend & Loos (26/62)*,[13] *Van Duyn (71/74)*,[14] *Grad (9/70)*,[15] *Defrenne (43/75)*,[16] *Les Verts (249/83)*[17] *and Chernobyl.*[18] Moreover, despite rejecting the direct horizontal effect of some EU acts (namely directives and third pillar decisions, now extinguished), some decisions accepted their indirect effect, namely on the cases *Marleasing (C-106/89)*,[19] *CIA (C-194/94)*,[20] *Unilever (443/98)*[21] *Pupino (C-105/03).*[22] The indirect effect was also accepted in the *Chen* case *(C-200/02).*[23] These cases serve as particular examples of the self-image of the ECJ as an adjudicator of competences and even as a constitutional builder.

It should be mentioned that there are different readings regarding the real meaning of the said decisions, some pointing out that the corresponding activism concerns mostly the super-constitutionality of Treaty provisions,[24] or that the Court has used its legal reasoning and interpretative methods as tools for the evolution of European social law.[25]

Either way, the ECJ's innovations have proven to be resilient, namely in face of efforts by member states to resist them. In the case *Metock (127/08)*,[26] the ECJ even required Ireland to grant some rights to third country family members of EU nationals.

The innovative nature of the doctrines of primacy and of direct and indirect effect can be seen, not only as lacking base in the Treaties, but also as challenging the principles of conferral and constitutional pluralism. The position of the ECJ, as established by those doctrines, may even entail a relaxation of the ultra vires

[12]See Yassin Abdullah. Kadi and Al Barakaat International Foundation [2008], EUCJR I-6351.

[13]See Van Gend and Loos [1963] EUCJR 3.

[14]See Van Duyn [1974] EUCJR, 1337.

[15]See Franz Grad [1970] EUCJR 825.

[16]See Defrenne [1976], EUCJR, 455.

[17]See Parti Ecologiste "Les Verts" [1986], EUCJR, 166.

[18]See Parliament v. Council (Chernobyl), [1990] EUCJR, I-204.

[19]See Marleasing [1990], EUCJR, I, 4135.

[20]See CIA Security International SA [1996], EUCJR, I-2201.

[21]See Unilever Italia SpA [2000] I-7535.

[22]See Maria Pupino [2005], EUCJR, I-5285.

[23]See Zhu and Chen [2004], I-9925.

[24]See Oreste Pollicino (2004).

[25]See footnote 25.

[26]See Blaise Maheten Metock and others [2008], ECJUR, I 6241.

doctrine of the EU acting, a doctrine that should only be annulled when there is a manifest violation of competences (case Honeywell, 610/10[27]).

Also in light of the *Mangold decision (C-144/04)*[28] there might be an evolution in the judicial review control since it has suggested that general principles of EU law may now qualify for direct effect.

Regarding the judicial review, some cases are worth mentioning taking into account that the ECJ fostered its jurisdiction to new, and previously unknown, frontiers. Amongst these cases we can mention *Foto-Frost (181/73)*,[29] *Haageman (269/81)*,[30] *SPI (267/81)*[31] *and Busseni (221/88)*,[32] adding to the already mentioned cases *Les Verts, Chernobyl, Pupino e Ecowas (C-91/05)*,[33] which extended judicial review to the then CFSP.

Regarding fundamental rights and the activity of the ECJ in such field, its system building activity is well known (even if some of the liberties contained in the initial treaties can be considered as fundamental rights) and the classic cases *Stauder (29/69)*,[34] *Nold (4/73)*[35] *and Rutili (36/75)*[36] worth mentioning. However, in the first period of its activity, and in the mentioned cases, the ECJ was more concerned in creating a framework for the protection of fundamental rights than in effectively protecting them, since it allowed significant restrictions to their content (Coppel and O' Neil 1992).

There are, however, some exceptions. In some areas the ECJ effectively created certain rules that can be considered as new material law. Regarding LGBT rights, one should mention cases *PU.S (13/94)*,[37] *Richards (C-423/04)* (regarding a British pension fund refusal to grant a male to female transgender an entitlement to an old age pension, which was considered unlawful discrimination), and *Grant, C-421/04*[38] (regarding the granting of benefits to same sex spouses). These cases are the ones most notoriously involving a material activist perspective, with the exception of Grant, were some found a form of "creative "self restraint"" (Oreste Pollicino 2004).

[27]See Solvay SA v. Honeywell Fluorine Products Europe BV, Honeywell Belgium Nv and Honeywell Europe NV [2012], EUCJR 1230.

[28]See Werner Mangold [2005], EUCJR—I 10013.

[29]See Foto-Frost [1987], EUCJR 4179.

[30]See Hageman [1974] EUCJR 449.

[31]See Amministrazione delle Finanze dello Stato v. SPI [1983] EUCJR 801.

[32]See Busseni [1990] EUCJR I-495.

[33]See Comm'n v. Counsil [2008],EUCJR I-3651.

[34]See Stauder [1969], EUCJR, 419.

[35]See Nold [1974] EUCJ, 491.

[36]See Rutili [1975], EUCJR, 1219.

[37]See P v. S. and Cornwall City [1996], EUCJR I-2143.

[38]See Lisa Jacqueline Grant [1998], EUCJR I-621.

One other area of active intervention of the ECJ is the area of residence and social rights. For example, regarding residence and social assistance for students under Directive 93/96, the court created new rights in the *Rudy Grzelezyk case* (at stake was a minimum subsistence allowance to a foreign student in the University of Louvain).

Notwithstanding these later cases, it can still be said that the ECJ developed a more activist oriented jurisprudence in formal terms—engaging in weak activism, in the aforementioned sense—than in material terms. This is not meant at denying the vast effects of the ECJ's system building activity, which exceeded by far the wording of the Treaties. However, one can argue that the inner nature of international organizations fosters the possibility of more activist jurisprudence.

In fact, one could argue that the ECJ's activism would be a strong one if the degree of innovation were taken into consideration. In light of the distinction made, it is a weak activism, though: the ECJ has been mostly focused in system building principles rather than in intervention in the social arena, protecting human rights. The main concern of the ECJ was strengthening the constitutional edifice[39] or acting as a constitutional adjudicator between powers and limitations of powers.[40]

12.2 Judicial Activism and International Organizations

Several aspects determine that an international organization is different from a State in what concerns the main features of the judicial function, that having consequences when conceptualizing and assessing judicial activism. Some of these aspects are also present in EU Law.

Indeed, the concept of the judicial function as applied to international organizations and in EU Law differs from the corresponding concept as applied to states. In the first case, courts may emerge as true political actors of organizations, transcending the position of passive dispute settlers that is traditionally reserved to states's courts.

Aware of the possible scope of their activity, some international bodies consciously establish limits to it. The rejection by the WTO Appellate Body of a law making power is worth mentioning.[41,42] Differently, the International Court of

---

[39]Waele de (2010). The expression is from Henri de Waele.

[40]Pollicino (Oreste). The expression is from Oreste Pollicino.

[41]In the case *United States Measure Affecting Impacts of Woven Wool and Blouses from India* (of 25 April of 1997), the WTO Appelate Body stated that it does "*not consider that Article 3.2. of the DSU is meant to encourage either panels of the Appellate Body to "make law" by clarifying the exiting provisions of the WTO Agreement outside the context of resolving a particular dispute.*", see DSR, 697.

[42]On this, see Zarbiyed (2012).

Justice for former Yugoslavia and the European Court of Human Rights have both considered that their judgments may have an impact in society.[43]

Several aspects determine a more activist perspective from the international courts.

Firstly, one must admit that international courts in general the ECJ in particular, in absence of a clear system of separation of powers setting limits to judicial practice, tend to have more leeway to engage in law making and to assume a policy guiding role. That is reinforced by the normal existence of advisory functions held by the judicial bodies and by the absence of a clearly organized judicial system. To these aspects, one should add the existing limited control—the political control being almost nonexistent and the specialized control incipient, given the undeveloped character of corresponding legal literature. The vertical separation of powers inherent to regional integration organizations, and to the EU in particular, also enhances the said leeway: the areas of intervention are large and the actions taken can cause preemption of member states competences, with the latter having difficulty in controlling such actions (in the EU, for example, the member states parliaments' control over the subsidiarity principle is limited to legislative acts and does not entail judicial acts).[44]

These aspects inevitably result in judicial activism. In the case of the ECJ, the institutional balance principle does not compensate for the lack of a clear separation of powers. The absence of a defined legislative power worsens the situation: the definition of legislative acts proposed at the Project of the Treaty Establishing a Constitution for Europe was never ratified and only after the Lisbon Treaty did it become possible to speak about a proper a legislative procedure.

The vertical division of powers is also not very clear within the EU, with some scholars believing the ECJ to be obliged to correct the treaties in that regard, promoting further integration, that resulting in further activism. And one must acknowledge that the indeterminacy and generality of the corresponding principles called for an active role of the ECJ.

One other aspect to consider is the lack of control over the ECJ's extended powers. Its rulings were reversed in very few situations. Two cases of reversion can be mentioned though. One is the Grogan Protocol at Maastricht, approved in order to accommodate the fears of the Irish Government arising from the ECJ ruling Case 159/90, Grogan.[45] Another example can be found in the Barber Protocol, intended to limit the effect of the Case C-262/82, Barber.[46]

In most cases, then, the ECJ could count on the cumbersome nature of the Treaties amendment regime to secure its rulings: unanimity as a revision process is

[43]See Ireland versus United States ECHR, Judgment of 18 January of 1978, series A 25, par. 154, Guzzardi v. Italy, Judgment of 6 November 1980, series A, n. 39, par. 86, and Karmer v. Austria, Judgment of 24 July 2003, par. 26. See also Zarbiyed, Fuad (2012).

[44]Zarbiyed (2012).

[45]See SPUC v. Grogan [1991] EUCJR 4685. Waele de (2010).

[46]See D. Harvey Barber v. Guardian Royal Exchange Assurance Europe [1990] EUCJR 1889.

required to reverse them, with amendment initiatives being frequently held back given the uncertainty of results.

Thirdly, the nature of the law applied by the courts and the balance of power framework in which the courts are inserted in—aspects that are present in EU Law—may determine a need for more intervention by the Court.

In fact, some argue that the nature of the treaties, and their indeterminacy regarding central aspects, encourages law creation and law making and demands a teleological method of interpretation (case CILFIT of 1982, process 283/81).[47] In fact, the treaties are Framework treaties that regulate few topics in exhaustive detail.[48]

The enumerated reasons explain why the international courts, and the ECJ in particular, are left free to develop an activist posture without facing the same kinds of reaction state courts face before other state agencies. It is clear that they are subject to less stringent regulations and checks and balances.

The same reasons justify why the jurisprudence of the ECJ regarding the nature of EU Law, and its primacy over national law and International Law (according to the aforementioned Kadi case), has not been challenged (apart from the temporary reaction of the German and Italian constitutional courts in the cases Solange Bechluss[49] and Fratelli Costanzo (103/88)[50] and recently by eastern European constitutional courts, such as the Czech Republic or the Polish Constitutional Courts).

12.3 The Costs of Judicial Activism

There is of course a price to be paid for the achievements of the ECJ. Traditionally, some arguments are used against judicial activism, such as the drawbacks in terms of coherence and clarity inherent to Judge-Made Law. The democratic argument (or the lack of democratic legitimacy of the judges) must be considered as well. Costs may be felt also at the level of judicial authority, which may result weakened (even if some believe that judicial activism can have the opposite effect, creating a culture of obedience).[51]

There are however some compensating aspects that deserve attention.

The coherence arguments, regarding the ECJ, may fail taking into account that the bulk of its activity is to create principles of law for the functioning of the system and not to produce material law and positive obligations, with the corresponding activism not disturbing legal coherence but enhancing it instead.

---

[47]See CILFIT and Lanificio di Gavardo SpA [1982], EUCJR 3415.

[48]Pollicino (2004).

[49]See BverfGE, 37, 271.

[50]See Fratelli Costanzo [1989], EUCJR 1839.

[51]De Waele (2010).

A weakening of judicial authority is also something that (at least until now) has not reached the ECJ, also taking into account that the sanction systems within the EU are enough to avoid non-compliances.

The democratic argument persists however, being repeatedly used against the EU in general and the ECJ in particular. And at this level it is indeed hard to escape the fact that the ECJ activism raises delicate questions, as complex as they may interfere with the legitimacy of the whole integration process.

References

Bossuyt. 2014. Prof. Dr. Baron Marc, Judicial activism in Europe: the case of the European Court of Human Rights.

Cappelletti, Mauro. 1987. The European Court of Justice "Running Wild", European Law Review: 4.

Coppel and O' Neil. 1992. The European Court of Justice: Taking Rights Seriously? *C.M.L. Review* 29: 699.

Hart, HLA. 1957. Positivism and the Separation of Law and Morals. *Harvard Law Review* 71: 593.

Harwood, Sterling. 1996. *Judicial Activism: A Restrained Defense*, Austin & Winfield Pub.

Pollicino, Oreste. 2004. Legal Reasoning of the Court of Justice in the Context of the Principle of Equality Between Judicial Activism and Self-restraint, *German Law Journal* 3: 293.

Rasmussen, Hjalte. 1986. *On Law and Policy in the European Court of Justice. A Comparative Study in Judicial Policy-Making*, Dordrecht: Martinus Nijhoff Publishers.

Waele, Henri de. 2010. The Role of the European Court of Justice in the Integration Process: A Contemporary and Normative Assessment. *European Law/Europarecht* 1: 3.

Weiler, J.H.H. 1987. The Court of Justice on Trial, *C.M.L. Review* 24: 555.

Zarbiyev, Fuad. 2012 Judicial Activism in International Law – A Conceptual Framework for Analysis, *Journal of International Dispute Settlement* 2: 247.

Chapter 13
Courts and European Integration

Francisco Pereira Coutinho

In 1963, the European Court of Justice (ECJ) proclaimed in *van Gend & Loos* that the European Economic Community (EEC) constitutes a new legal order for the benefit of which the States limited their sovereign rights.[1] This decision was sharply compared to a "declaration of independence" of European Union (EU) law *vis-à-vis* the authority of the Member States (Maduro 2003: 504). It began a praetorian process of transformation of international law treaties into an autonomous constitutional legal order, which gradually was incorporated into the domestic legal orders of the Member States. Since this process of legal integration had the epicenter in the ECJ, the Luxembourg court is commonly identified as its "lonely hero" (Conant 2002: xiii).

Legal integration, however, does not rest solely on the isolated efforts of a court located in a remote European capital. It develops through a complex cooperative process that includes several others national and supranational actors. Among them, the role of national courts is decisive. The EU legal order has been, to a large extent, a byproduct of a judicial dialogue between national and European judges that revolves essentially on an ongoing "negotiation" over the interpretation of legal norms (Alter 2001: 38).

This article explores how the relation between national courts and the ECJ explains legal integration in the EU. The institutional framework of the Communities foresaw judicial enforcement mechanisms similar to other international organizations (Sect. 13.1). A procedural mechanism that allowed national judges to communicate directly with the ECJ opened the path for the constitutionalisation of EU law. Through this mechanism national judges started "internalizing" European Union law (Sect. 13.2). The causes for this behavior are discussed in a multidisciplinary debate on the causes that led national courts to foster legal integration by gradually incorporating into the domestic legal realm the fundamental constitutional principles of EU law developed by the ECJ (Sect. 13.3).

[1]ECJ, 26/62, *van Gend & Loos*, ECR [1963] 1 at 12.

F.P. Coutinho (✉)
Universidade Nova de Lisboa, Rua dos Lusíadas, 118, 4 D, 1300-376 Lisbon, Portugal
e-mail: fpcoutinho@hotmail.com

L.P. Coutinho et al. (eds.), *Judicial Activism*,
Ius Gentium: Comparative Perspectives on Law and Justice 44,
DOI 10.1007/978-3-319-18549-1_13

13.1 Law Enforcement Mechanisms in the European Communities Treaties

I. The EU legal order was able to elude the coercive debilities of public international law by progressively imposing compliance on Member States. The evolution to a supranational model was not likely to occur within the conventional framework adopted in the 50s.

The ECJ was created in 1952 within the European Coal and Steel Community (ECSC) as an appeal chamber for the decisions of the High Authority—the predecessor of the European Commission (art. 33 ECSC Treaty). With the EEC Treaty, the ECJ was given the task of ensuring that in the interpretation and application of the Treaties the law is observed (art. 164 EEC Treaty). The mission to monitor institutions remained untouched: the court had to review the validity of legislative acts of the institutions of the Community (arts. 173 and 177 (1) b) EEC Treaty), as well as its omissions (art. 175 EEC Treaty).

In the ECSC, the High Authority had the power to sanction, namely through fines, Member States that breached the Treaty or its decisions and recommendations (art. 8 ECSC Treaty). The mission of being the "keeper of the Treaties" was afterwards given to the Commission (art. 155 EEC Treaty).

Either the Commission and/or the Member States could bring an action before the ECJ based on a Member State failure to fulfill an obligation under the Treaty (art. 169 and 170 EEC Treaty). This soon revealed to be a fragile mechanism of enforcement of EU law. On the one hand, although recognizing the ECJ's mandatory jurisdiction, Member States avoided instituting proceedings against each other. On the other hand, the Commission had its wings clipped by an incipient political autonomy from the Member States and an insufficient human and financial infrastructure (Stein 1981: 6). The ECJ's decisions had, moreover, no teeth. Member States were not liable to fines if they failed to abide to a decision of the ECJ.[2] A declarative condemnation from an obscure court in Luxembourg was usually not enough to force compliance. Most infractions went under the radar and/or had to be tackled through political compromise (Alter 2001: 16). The numbers are overwhelming. Until 1970 the Commission started 27 proceedings. The Member States none.

II. The "declaration of independence" of the EU legal order was made by the ECJ in the context of a preliminary reference. The procedure is quite simple and develops in three phases: (1) the national judge refers a question to the ECJ whenever it has doubts on the interpretation or the validity of the applicable EU law provision, (2) the ECJ answers through a preliminary ruling and (3) the national judge applies the ECJ's preliminary ruling to the pending case. Art. 267 of the Treaty on the Functioning of the European Union (TFEU) foresee a procedural

[2]The possibility to sanction monetarily Member States was introduced later in the Maastricht Treaty (1993).

mechanism aimed at enabling communication between national courts and the ECJ. In other words, it works as a "legal bridge" between EU and national law.

The preliminary rulings procedure was originally created within the ECSC Treaty to review the legality of High Authority acts (art. 41 ECSC Treaty). It was not aimed at monitoring the application of ECSC law by the Member States because it did not allowed for preliminary references directed at the interpretation of ECSC provisions. The inclusion of this possibility in the Treaties of Rome was the trigger for the transformation of the EU legal order.

13.2 The Constitutionalisation of European Union Law

I. The ECJ emerged as one of the most powerful institutions in the EU after answering a set of explosive interpretative preliminary references sent by national judges (Scheingold 1971: 22). In the 60s, the Court proclaimed the doctrines of direct effect and supremacy based on the argument that the Treaties could not be interpreted merely as an agreement between States but as having been created for the "peoples of Europe" (Maduro 1997: 9). Direct effect determines that EU law creates rights that can be enforced by individuals in the courts of the Member States.[3] Supremacy states that EU law should always prevail over national law.[4] The two doctrines introduced a "genetic mutation" that prevented the EU to remain "an abstract skeleton" (Stein 1981: 6) "barely distinguishable from so many other international organizations whose existence passes unnoticed by ordinary citizens" (Mancini and Keeling 1994: 183).

The proclamation of direct effect and supremacy of EU law founded a praetorian process of constitutionalisation of the Treaties (Weiler 1991, Timmermans 2001–2002). The ECJ declared the Treaties a "basic constitutional charter" of a "Community based on the rule of law" supported in an autonomous and self-sufficient legal order.[5] National courts were given the mission of incorporating EU

[3]ECJ, 26/62, *van Gend & Loos*, ECR [1963] 1. The EEC treaty stated that regulations were binding in every respect and directly applicable in each Member State [art. 189 (2)]. The recognition of direct effect to other primary and secondary EU law provisions depends on an analysis by the ECJ of the fulfilment of certain conditions, such as clarity and unconditionality. The proclamation of direct effect was not in itself original. In 1932, the Permanent Court of International Justice referred that *exceptionally* an international agreement could, if that was the *intent* of the parties, adopt rules creating individual rights and obligations directly enforceable in national courts (*Treatment of Polish Nationals and Other Persons of Polish Origin or Speech in the Danzig Territory*, Advisory Opinion, (1932) PCIJ Series B 44, at 24 and 25).

[4]ECJ, 6/64, *Costa* [1964] ECR 585.

[5]ECJ 294/83, *Les Verts* [1986] ECR 1365, at 23.

law into the domestic legal realm and protect the rights derived from it for individuals.[6] They have become "EU courts of ordinary jurisdiction".[7]

II. The announcement of the birth of a new legal order was extremely controversial (Alter 2009: 95). The ECJ was accused of "hallucinating" and of judicial activism "running wild" (Rasmussen 1986: 14). The declaration that the Community was a new legal order (*van Gend & Loos*) and that the law stemming from the Treaty ("an independent source of law") had a "special and original nature" (*Costa*) was qualified as an unacceptable interpretation of the Treaties *vis-à-vis* the 1969 Vienna Convention on the Law of the Treaties (Schilling 1996).

Within national legal orders with dualistic and/or with strong parliamentary traditions the ECJ requested nothing short of a legal revolution. National courts were mandated to participate in a monist legal system in which the Luxembourg court would have always the last word (Kumm 1999: 354). As "EU courts of ordinary jurisdiction" national courts were told to directly apply EU law and trump conflicting national law, even of constitutional rank.[8] The reaction of national constitutional and supreme courts, the ultimate gatekeepers of national law, was understandably not enthusiastic.

III. The transformation of the EU legal order was possible thanks to some provocative questions sent to Luxembourg by national judges. Those references allowed the ECJ to develop its case law within a decentralized jurisdictional system, in which national courts act as European courts whenever they deal with the application of EU law.

An activist ECJ fueled by national courts has been driving legal integration in Europe. The "constitutional cases" (*van Gend & Loos*, *Costa* and others) materialized through windows of opportunity opened by questions sent by national judges. Those cases would, however, remain *wishful thinking* if not applied internally by the same judges. ECJ's case law evolution and enforceability is thus totally dependent on national courts cooperation. This boosts the latter's capacity of influence in the definition of the ECJ's jurisprudence. The incorporation by the case law of the ECJ of fundamental principles of the national legal systems, such as the protection of fundamental rights,[9] came as no surprise. The outcome of this process of "cross-fertilization" was the creation of community of legal actors committed to the development of a "quasi-federal" legal order (Chalmers 1997: 164).

[6]Individuals usually lack direct access to Luxembourg. Natural or legal persons may only institute proceedings against an act addressed to that persons or which is of direct and individual concern to them, and against a regulatory act which is of direct concern to them and does not entail implementing measures [art. 263 (4) TFEU].

[7]ECJ, opinion of Advocate-General Léger. C-224/01, *Köbler*, [2003] ECR I-10239, at 66.

[8]ECJ, 11/70, *Internationale Handelsgesellschaft*, [1970] ECR 1125, at 3.

[9]ECJ, 11/70, *Internationale Handelsgesellschaft*, [1970] ECR 1125, at 4.

13.3 Factors that Promote Legal Integration in the European Union

National judges are decisive actors in the dynamic that fosters legal integration in the EU. But why did they accept this role? What incentives did they have to make preliminary references, bypass domestic judicial hierarchies and obey the ECJ? Why did they start trumping national law that conflicted with EU law? Why did they forego their "veto power" (Chalmers 1997: 180) towards the domestic implementation of EU law?

This section presents several possible answers to these questions that propose different causes to explain the judicial reception of the EU legal order in the Member States.

13.3.1 The Legal Answer

13.3.1.1 Law and Legal Reasoning as Factors of Legal Integration

I. Among EU lawyers, the prevailing explanation for legal integration is found in the EU legal order itself, which genetically has a federalist *ethos*. In the words of Robert Lecourt (1976: 305):

> (EU law) is at the service of an objective. The objective is also here the driving force of the law (…) and an instrument of legal integration.

This *ethos* was incorporated by the judicial institution specifically created to interpret the Treaties, which assumed a catalyst stance towards the expansion of the reach of EU law, usually with the functionalist argument that it had to safeguard its *effect utile*. This explains the use by the ECJ of interpretative methods that went beyond the letter of the Treaties and secondary law and tried to capture its spirit though a lenses that refracted a "certain idea of Europe"—to use a famous expression of a former ECJ's judge (Pescatore 1983: 157).[10]

This *modus operandi* of the ECJ is a consequence of the declaration of autonomy of EU law regarding international law and diverts the criticism that the court was "running wild". International courts cannot intervene without being accused of

[10]This functionalist methodology is well documented in the constitutional cases. In *van Gend & Loos*, the Court declared that Treaty law could have direct effect, although the advocate-general Roemer said the Court could not say that without dealing first with the question of supremacy (ECJ, 26/62, *van Gend & Loos*, ECR [1963] 1: 23 and 24). One year afterwards, in *Costa*, the Court proceeded to state that supremacy is a necessary condition of direct effect (ECJ, 6/64, *Costa* [1964] ECR 585, at 3).

judicial activism and of encroaching on States competences whenever they rule on questions not explicitly mentioned in treaty provisions. However, this critic is not directly extensible to the ECJ. The latter acts like a constitutional jurisdiction and simply has made the most of framework treaties, which are materially a "Constitutional Charter" and, therefore, regulate few topics in exhaustive detail (Tridimas 1996: 205). At least among the core issues of European integration (the constitutional principles of direct effect, supremacy, state responsibility and the fundamental freedoms), there is a large consensus among legal authors that the ECJ "has been faithfully interpreting the rules, legitimately filled some gaps, and rarely engaged in excessive activism. Rather, it has acted in an overall manner that has genuinely corresponded with the tasks entrusted to it under the treaties, and it continues to do so" (Waele and Vleuten 2011: 651).[11]

II. Legal integration is assumed to develop smoothly in a non-political and self-sufficient judicial environment: (i) litigants present claims based on EU law; (ii) national courts refer questions and obediently follow the case law of the ECJ; (iii) the Court adopts preliminary rulings that foster European integration. This narrative explicitly downplays national courts' importance by identifying the ECJ as the only relevant actor in the process. This idea is implicit in Stein's (1981: 1) famous quote:

> Tucked away in the fairyland Duchy of Luxembourg and blessed with benign neglect by the powers that be and the masse media, the Court of Justice created a new legal order with a federal architecture.

National courts' acceptance of the new legal order is explained with the strength of the arguments used by the ECJ in the hermeneutic mission of revealing EU law. It was either the brilliancy of the ECJ's decisions (Kakouris 1994: 37) or, in a more modest tone, a persuasive dialogue in "legalese" that convinced eminent judges in the Member States (Volcansek 1986: 18, Weiler 1982: 39, Claes 2006: 247). Cases of disobedience are observed as pathologies that result from lack of preparation. Informed national judges apply EU law in accordance with the ECJ guidelines and refer questions whenever doubts arise on the interpretation or validity of EU law (Alter 1998: 230).

III. The use of legal hermeneutics methodologies certainly gave the ECJ an authority and legitimacy that could not be ignored. By presenting its decisions as the only possible legal outcome, the ECJ made it hard for the development of a critic discourse due to the auto-referential nature of the normative discourse (Maduro 2006: 77). Since law and legal reasoning are the pillars of the judiciary, many national judges observed the ECJ decisions as the law of the land they had a duty to follow.

[11]On this topic, see the chapter on this book of Lourenço Vilhena de Freitas that qualifies case law of the ECJ as an example of "weak activism".

13.3.2 Critic

I. Not all national judges were convinced by the arguments used by the ECJ to justify supremacy and direct effect. In the words of a prominent Portuguese constitutional law scholar:

> (Constitutional Courts) never surrendered, at least explicitly, to a radical or pure and simple supremacy of EU law, nor did they waived to the defense, as a last resource, to the rights and basic vectors of their Constitutions (Miranda 2002–2003: 12–13).

Some Supreme and Constitutional courts argued that the constitutional provisions that regulate the domestic incorporation of international law act as intermediary in the relation between EU law and national law of ordinary rank. These courts accepted only a limited supremacy of EU law that stemmed from the national constitutions. They never waived the authority to determine if a EU law act is *ultra vires.*[12] The question of the *kompetenz-kompetenz,* that is to say who holds the competence to define in last instance the allocation of competences between the Member States and the European Union, remains unanswered.

A refusal to apply EU law is not an outcome of sheer ignorance of national judges whenever it results from an antinomy with constitutional law. Challenges to the ECJ constitutional case law may be based in a different perspective on the hierarchical position of EU law inside the domestic sources of law.

II. The argument that national judges were convinced by the constitutional rhetoric of the ECJ implies that the judicial reception of EU law was expected to be relatively uniform throughout the Member States. But that did not happened even inside some Member States. In France, for instance, the swift recognition of supremacy and direct effect by the *Cour de Cassation* (Civil Supreme Court)[13] contrasts with the hesitations and even denials of those doctrines in the *Conseil d'État* (Administrative Supreme Cour).[14]

Different patterns in the judicial reception of EU law may be explained with the diversity of legal cultures (Maher 1994: 238, Mare 1999: 233, Claes 2006: 261), with legal pluralism, namely the influence of dualism (Bebr 1981: 682) or the

---

[12]This was path followed, amongst others, by the German Constitutional Court (case 2 BvR 2134/92 and 2 BvR, 2159/9212.10.1993, "Maastricht", *Entscheidungen des Bundesverfassungsgerichtes*, 89, 155, at 188 or case 2 BvE 2/08, 30.06.2009, "Lisbon", *Entscheidungen des Bundesverfassungsgerichtes*, 123: 267, at 240 and 241), the Italian Constitutional Court (case 232/1989, 21 May 1989, "Fragd", available at www.giurcost.org), the Danish Supreme Court (case I-361/1997, 6 April 1998, "Carlssen", translation available at *Common Market Law Reports* 3 1999: 854), the Polish Constitutional Court (case K 18/04, 11 May 2005, translation available at www.trybunal.gov.pl/, at 13) or the Czech Constitutional Court (case P1.ÚS 19/08, 26 November 2008, "Lisbon", translation available at http://www.usoud.cz/en/decisions/?tx_ttnews%5Btt_news%5D=484&cHash=621d8068f5e20ecadd84e0bae0527552, n.º 120).

[13]"Vabre", 24 May 1975, available at www.lexinter.net.

[14]"Cohn Bendit", 22 November 1978, available at www.lexinter.net.

existence of a Constitutional Court and/or constitutional review mechanisms. However, Members States with dualistic traditions, such as Germany of Belgium, did not had a harder reception of the principles of direct effect or supremacy when compared with Member States with monist systems, like France (Alter 1998: 231, 232). Moreover, the existence of a Constitutional Court was also not decisive. The Italian Constitutional Court struggled for many years to accept lower courts' competence to trump national law that conflicted with EU law.[15] The German Constitutional Court recognized this competence in 1971.[16]

III. A purely normative analysis of legal integration is unable to explain the different patterns in the reception of EU law observed in the Member States. It fails because it ignores the importance of extralegal factors in the dynamics that foster legal integration. It is like "constitutional law without politics", in which the EU is considered:

> (…) as a juristic idea; the written constitution as a sacred text; the professional commentary as a legal truth; the case law as the inevitable working out of the correct implications of the constitutional text; and the constitutional court as the disembodied voice of right reason and constitution teleology (Shapiro 1980: 538).

But judges are not robots. Judicial neutrality associated to syllogistic answers in the application of the law is a myth (Maduro 1997: 20). In many cases, judges have some discretion when adjudicating because several interpretative paths are viable. The example of the different perspectives on supremacy reveals that is not always possible to find in legal instruments univocal interpretations of the law.

13.4 The Neo-realist Answer

13.4.1 National Interest as the Factor for Legal Integration

I. Political scientists identified Member States governmental preferences as the key factor for explaining legal integration in the EU. Mary Volcansek (1986: 252–264) argued that domestic judicial shifts favoring the reception of supremacy and direct effect were directly connected to pro-European positions developed by governments in the Member States. More radically, Geoffrey Garrett (1992: 557–559) contended that ECJ case law mirrors the interests of the stronger Member States. The latter were identified with the adoption of a cheap system of enforcement of EU law that reduced information and transaction costs in a supranational environment.

[15]Case 232/1975, 30 October 1975, "Ministero del commercio con l'estero", and case 170/1984, 5 June 1985, "Granital", both available at www.giurcost.org.

[16]Case 2 BvR 225/699.06.1971, "Lütticke", *Entscheidungen des Bundesverfassungsgerichtes*, 31: 145, n.º 3, a).

Neo-realists believe that judicial discretion is always politically conditioned due to the effectiveness of instruments that governments have to influence judicial behavior, namely by influencing the nomination of judges or by ignoring judicial decisions. When adjudicating, judges take into consideration the possible reaction of the executive and adopt the decisions that will not jeopardize their independence and authority (Garrett and Weingast 1993: 200, Garrett 1993: 173).

In the EU, national and European judges simply followed the interests of the Member States governments because they were afraid of the consequences (Garrett and Weingast 1993: 201 and 202).

13.4.2 Critic

The argument that any ECJ decision could be interpreted as mirroring the interests of the Member States does not survive an empirical check. Member States governments often participate in the preliminary rulings procedure by presenting observations, which are frequently not followed by the Luxembourg Court.

Judicial discretion is much wider than what neo-realist imagine. On a supranational level, although Member States are the masters of the Treaties and may reverse the effects of an ECJ decision, a Treaty amendment procedure is a "nuclear option" that requires unanimity. It does not represent an effective and credible method of monitoring the ECJ (Pollack 1997: 188 and 189). On a domestic level, Member States government's hands are tied by the fact that national courts are the sole responsible for the implementation of EU law. The executive branch cannot prohibit direct communicating with the ECJ and the domestic application of the latter's decisions (Chalmers 1997: 172).

13.4.3 The Neo-functionalist Answer

13.4.3.1 Self-interest as the Factor for Legal Integration

Neo-functionalists metaphorically compare the evolution of legal integration to a machine nurtured by the interest of actors that have seized the opportunities presented by EU law (Stone Sweet 1998: 310–311).

Litigants invoke rights based on EU law (Stone Sweet and Sandholtz 1998: 4–5). A community of specialists in EU law made up of lawyers and law professors continuously promotes these efforts. Both form a "neo-functionalist interest group *par excellence*" (Burley and Mattli 1993: 65) because their careers benefit immensely from the domestic growth and expansion of EU law.

The ECJ empowered lower court national judges with the competence to trump national law that conflicted with EU law even if that meant defying the case law of higher courts.[17] It also refused any attempts to curb their competence to use the preliminary reference procedure.[18] Not surprisingly, national judges were pleased. Not only did they got external help in solving cases more quickly and without having to compromise directly (Sweet and Brunnel 1998: 73), but, more importantly, they felt empower:

> Lower courts and their judges were given the facility to engage with the highest jurisdiction in the Community and, even more remarkable, to gain the power of judicial review over the executive and legislative branches, even in those jurisdictions where such judicial power was weak or nonexistent. Has not power been the most intoxicating potion in human affairs. (Weiler 1994 :523).

The ECJ created communities made up of national judges and litigants directly interested in fostering the domestic application of EU law. The court triggered what neo-functionalist called a "spill-over" or "snowball" effect. After rendering a couple of initial decisions (on direct effect and supremacy) that breakes the *status quo*, litigants press for further jurisprudential developments that are met by the ECJ in a spiraling process that leads to an ever-deeper level of legal integration in the EU.

Member States were unable to reverse the trend because the process developed in a hermetic and apolitical judicial environment. Legal discourse, due to its technical nature, worked as "mask" for the political questions at stake and, due to its normative nature, acted as a "shield" that protected judges from political pressure (Burley and Mattli 1993). EU law acted as a link between litigants, judges and lawyers in the Member States. Governments simply did not understood what was going on until it was too late. In other words, until the costs to reverse the constitutional case law of ECJ were just too high. The EU's legal system will thus develop as long as it stays away from politics and maintains the myth of legal objectivism.

Disparities in the internal incorporation of EU law are explained with the different dimension of GDP and commercial transactions between Member States. The number of preliminary references and the patterns in judicial reception of EU law are said to be directly connected with the level of economic integration of each Member State (Sweet and Brunell 1998, Sweet and Caporaso 1998).

13.4.3.2 Critic

Neo-functionalists argue that litigants invoke rights that derive from EU law and that judges base their decisions in the EU legal order in order to skip the constraints of national law and judicial hierarchies. Both have allowed the ECJ to initiate a

---

[17]ECJ, 106/77, *Simmenthal II* [1978] ECR 629; Case C-105/03, *Pupino* [2005] ECR I-5285.

[18]ECJ, 166/83, *Rheinmuhlen* [1974] ECR 33, at 4; ECJ, 126/80, *Salonia* [1981] ECR 1563; Case C-2/06, *Kempter* [2008] ECR I-411, at 42.

constitutionalisation process that entails an ever-increasing expansion of EU law into the domestic legal orders.

However, neo-functionalist arguments ignore that litigants that benefited from national law, and, specially, supreme and constitutional courts, which saw their traditional influence and authority in the judicial hierarchy menaced by legal integration, favored the *status quo* and had powerful disincentives to oppose the expansion of EU law. There are thus no reasons to believe that legal integration has a predictable and unidirectional dynamics towards a further continuous penetration of EU law into the national legal orders (Alter 2001: 42).

13.4.4 The Historic-Institutionalist Answer

13.4.4.1 A Competition Between Courts as the Factor for Legal Integration

I. If legal integration provokes conflicting interests in national and supranational actors, its evolution cannot be harmonic, but instead it has to be modulated by a continuous set of episodes. Historic-institutionalist authors reject the argument that legal integration has a predictable and unidirectional path, in which sovereign competences and powers are continuously transferred to supranational institutions. They argue that the ECJ is an institution located outside the domestic legal realm that can be used either by national or supranational actors to contest both national and EU law.

II. Karen Alter (2001: 47) identifies a competition between national courts as the key factor for explaining legal integration. She argues that judges have a specific set of interests and form a community in which EU law is used as a tool in their internal conflicts in order to obtain increased domestic authority and independence.

National judicial reactions to the constitutional case law of the ECJ can be traced to the different judicial identities that stem from the institutional position of each judge in the domestic judicial hierarchy.

Supreme and constitutional courts judges see themselves as the natural guardians of national law and, for that reason, do not accept the "subversive nature" of the principles of direct effect and supremacy of EU law to the traditional national judicial hierarchies (Alter 2001: 48).[19]

Lower courts judges are only concerned with the resolution of the case at hand. They are like a child and the ECJ works as one of the parents in a conflict in which a parental permission avoids a potential sanction for bad behavior. If a lower court does not like what one parent says (the supreme court) then she may ask the other

[19]According to Karen Alter (1999: 243) this behavior of supreme courts is merely a tendency. Supreme courts may favor the reception of the case law of the ECJ. That happens when they challenge the validity of EU law. In that case, a supranational decision increases their domestic influence *vis-à-vis* the national governments and the European institutions.

(the ECJ) to get the answer she wants. Having the approval of one parent will increase the chances of the action not being contested by the other (Alter1998: 242).

Karen Alter (2009: 98–100) argues that if they had the chance, national supreme courts would not have made preliminary references that implied a directly defiance to their internal authority. This explains the absence of preliminary references made by constitutional courts and the fact that supreme courts usually refer technical issues. It also explains the decisions that curbed lowers courts′ discretion to refer questions to the ECJ[20] and the challenges episodically made to the constitutional case law of the Luxembourg court.[21] These preferences, however, did not survive the possibility granted to lower courts to freely decide to refer a question to the ECJ. Supreme courts were suddenly confronted with the domestic application of the ECJ's preliminary rulings. This forced them to inflect their case law in order to avoid an open conflict with the Luxembourg court. They end up recognizing the fundamental tenets of the constitutional case law of the ECJ. But the surrender was not unconditional. Constitutional and supreme courts continued to qualify supremacy as a constitutional issue under their control thereby rejecting the argument that the Treaties created a new legal order. This compromise creates tensions that one day may imply ruptures in the complex relation between the national and European legal orders:

> The very same cases that have advanced European integration have contributed to the perception that European integration, and the European Court, unduly compromise national sovereignty and threaten the national constitutional order. As it expanded the reach of European law, the ECJ also increased the number of national actors on which it and European authority encroached. And the success of the European Court in creating influence for itself in national and European policy debates has led it to become a target of Euro-skeptics and sovereignty jealous actors, and or national supreme courts (Alter 2001: 54).

13.4.4.2 Critic

The argument that lower courts were the crucial "integration engines" through a utilitarian use of EU law to challenge the authority of supreme courts also faces substantial empirical hurdles.

[20] *House of Lords*, 22 May 1974 ("Bulmer"), at 9, available at http://links.laws.londoninternational.ac.uk/bookmarkpress/hp-bulmer-ltd-anor-v-j-bollinger-sa-ors-1974-ewca-civ-14-22-may-1974/.

[21] The French *Conseil d'État*, in a decision of 22 November 1978 ("Cohn Bendit"), available at www.lexinter.net, and the German *Bundesfinanzhof*, in a decision of 25 April 1985 (case VR 123/84, "Kloppenburg", *Entscheidungen des Bundesfinanzhof*, 143, at 383), rejected the direct effect of directives. The Italian Constitutional Court in a decision from 30 October 1975 (case 232/1975, "Ministero del commercio con l'estero"), available at www.giurcost.org, declared that ordinary courts did not had the power trump Italian law that conflicted with EU law.

Karen Alter considers that the preliminary reference procedure subtracts lower courts of any control exercised by supreme courts. This ignores that the decision to refer questions to the ECJ may in some national legal orders be appealed.[22] Moreover, even if that appeal is not possible, an indirect control may still be exercised. This will certainly be the case in the Member States where career progression is organized in a system of cooptation by older judges.

Karen Alter also assumes that supreme courts, had they had the chance, would have refused the submission of relevant preliminary questions. This explains the technical nature of the questions actually posed by supreme courts and the attitude of defiance towards the ECJ revealed by constitutional courts. Although it is impossible to find a precise definition on what could be a technical question, several cases that, at a first glance, seemed rather technical had a large impact on the development of EU law.[23] Moreover, in last decade we can find several preliminary references made by constitutional courts made in a "spirit of dialogue" with the ECJ.[24] This spirit is

[22]This possibility is available in the Netherlands (ECJ, 13/61, *Bosch*, [1962] ECR 45, at 11), in Spain (Cienfuegos Mateo 2008: 68), in the United Kingdom (*Court of Appeal*, 16 October 1992, "International Stock Exchange", *Common Market Law Reports* 2 1993, at 715–716) and in Hungary (ECJ, Advocate-General Poiares Maduro, opinion of 22 May 2008, C-210/06, *Cartesio*, ECR [2008] ECR I-9641, at 11).

[23]Amongst others, see the ECJ case C-213/89, *Factortame*, [1990] ECR I-2433, in which the Court recognized a duty on national courts to secure the full effectiveness of EU law, even when it is necessary to create a national remedy where none had previously existed.

[24]This was the case of the preliminary references made by the constitutional courts of Austria (*v. g.* ECJ, C-143/99, Adrian-Wien Pipeline, [2001] I-8365), Belgium (*v. g.* ECJ, C-93/97, *Fédération Belge des Chambres Syndicales de Médecins, ASBL*, [1997] ECR I-4837), Italy (ECJ, C-169/08, *Presidente del Consiglio dei Ministri* [2009] ECR I-10821), Lithuania (ECJ, C-239/07, *Sabatauskas*, [2008] ECR I-07523) and Spain (ECJ, C-399/11 Melloni [2013] ECR). The same, however, cannot be said of the preliminary reference made by the German Constitutional Court in February 2014 concerning the decision of the European Central Bank (ECB) to implement the Outright Monetary Transaction (OMT) Program. The German court considers the program unlawful both under national constitutional law and EU law and asked the ECJ to declare it *ultra vires* and in violation of the Treaty no-bailout provision (art. 123 TFEU). On 14 January 2015, the Spanish Advocate General Cruz Vilallón upheld the general compatibility of the OMT program with the European Treaties (C-62/74, *Gauweiler*). However, the German Constitutional Court hinted that it would declare the OMT decision to be *ultra vires*, unless the Court of justice restricts the current scope of the program. Contrary to what happened, for instance, in the "bananas saga" in the mid 90s, where the German Constitutional Court established an indirect dialogue with the ECJ on the level of protection of fundamental rights through the intermediation of lower courts (Claes 2006: 445), in this case the Karlsruhe court assumed the possibility of a direct confrontation with the Luxembourg court using the preliminary reference procedure. We have then a constitutional crisis in the making that could still be avoided if the ECJ incorporates some of the concerns of the German Constitutional court and restrains the current scope of the OMT program. Such a decision would be most to the prejudice of Member States like Portugal that have benefited greatly from a more un-orthodox approach to its monetary competences by the ECB and could be interpret as vindicating Garrett's (1992: 557–559) argument that the ECJ is a faithful agent of the most powerful Member States interests.

also found in decisions of constitutional courts that recognized that a breach in an obligation to refer from an ordinary court of last instance in accordance with article 267 (3) TFEU is also a violation of the constitutional principles of the right to the judicial body laid down by law and to effective judicial remedies.[25]

13.5 Conclusions

Proposals on the causes that explain judicial reception of EU law in the Member States share an intrinsic heuristic value that helps capturing the dynamics of legal integration in the EU.

The use by the ECJ of legal hermeneutics methodologies certainly gave its decisions an authority and legitimacy that could not be ignored by national courts and probably explains why most of them peacefully incorporated the constitutional case law of the Luxembourg court.

Other accounts on legal integration transpose the limits of legal discourse by observing courts as part of the "political process, rather than a unique body of impervious legal technicians above and beyond the political struggle" (Shapiro 1964: 15). Political factors are intrinsic to judicial adjudication and, therefore, national courts incorporation of EU law is necessarily filtered by their perception of their political role. The identification of judges as agents in the political process may sound at odds with the guaranties of independence and impartiality that surround the judiciary. However, although the "judicial system may be autonomous, it is not autarkic. It will often be used instrumentally by political actors. Indeed, a feature of the legal system is that it is particularly vulnerable to these outside pressures" (Chalmers 2000: 1).

The study of legal integration should not be made exclusively through legal lenses, but it should also not be made only through political lenses. The latter identify the application of EU law by national courts as a mere expression of interests and fail to understand the constraints that legal reasoning imposes on courts due to its capacity to reach forms of knowledge that transcend external interests (Joerges 1996: 118–121, Chalmers 2005: 155, Maduro 2006: 66–69).

[25]German Constitutional Court, 22 October 1986 ("Solange II") 2 BvR 197/83, Entscheidungen des Bundesverfassungsgerichtes, 73: 339, 1, a) and aa); Austrian Constitutional Court, 11 November 1995, B2300/95-18, available at www.ris.bka.gv.at/vfgh/, 4, b)); Spanish Constitutional Court, Case 58/2004, 19 April 2004, available at www.tribunalconstitucional.es.

References

Alter, Karen. 1998. Explaining National Court Acceptance of European Court Jurisprudence: a Critical Evaluation of Theories of Integration. In *The European Court of Justice and National Courts. Doctrine and Jurisprudence*, Anne-Marie Slaughter, Alec Stone Sweet and Joseph Weiler (eds.). Oxford: Hart.

Alter, Karen. 2001. *Establishing the Supremacy of European Law – The Making of an International Rule of Law in Europe*. Oxford: Oxford University Press.

Alter, Karen. 2009. The European Court's Political Power: the Emergence of an Authoritative International Court in the European Union. *The European Court's Political Power: Selected Essay*. 92. Oxford: Oxford University Press.

Bebr, Gerhard. 1981. *Development of Judicial Control of the European Communities*. The Hague: Martinus Nijhoff.

Burley (now Slaughter), Anne-Marie, and Mattli, Walter. 1993. Europe Before the Court: A Political Theory of Legal Integration. *International Organization*. 47: 41.

Cienfuegos Mateo, Manuel. 2008. El planteamento de cuestiones prejudiciales por los órganos jurisdicionales españoles: teoria e práctica. In Santiago Ripol Carulla (dir.) e Juan Ignacio Ugartemendia Eceizabarrena (coord.), *España ante los tribunales internacionales europeos. Cuestiones de politica judicial*. 47. Oñati: IVAP.

Chalmers, Damien. 1997. Judicial Preferences and the Community Legal Order. *Modern Law Review*. 60: 164.

Chalmers, Damien. 2000. The Much Ado about Judicial Politics in the United Kingdom: a Statistical Analysis of Reported Decisions of United Kingdom Courts Invoking EU Law 1993–1998. *Jean Monnet Working Paper*. 1/00.

Chalmers, Damien. 2005. Judicial Understandings of the Authority of EC Law in the United Kingdom. In Bedanna Bapuly, Sonja Puntscher Riekmann e Peter Slominski (coord.). *Europäiserung durch Recht: zwischen Anspruch und Wirklichkeit*. 151. Baden-Baden: Nomos.

Claes, Monica. 2006. *The National Courts Mandate in the European Constitution*. Oxford: Hart.

Conant, Lisa. 2002. *Justice Contained – Law and Politics in the European Union*. Ithaca: Cornell University Press.

Garrett, Geoffrey. 1992. International Cooperation and Institutional Choice: the European Community's Internal Market. *International Organization*. 46: 533.

Garrett. Geoffrey. 1993. The Politics of Legal Integration in the European Union (response to Anne-Marie Burley and Walter Mattli, *Internatinal Organization*, 47, 1993, p. 41). *International Organization*. 47: 171.

Garrett, Geoffrey, and Weingast, Barry R.. 1993. Ideas, Interests and Institutions: Constructing the European Community's Internal Market. In Judith Goldsmith and Robert E. Keohane (coord.). 173. New York: Cornell University Press.

Joerges, Christian. 1996. Taking the Law Seriously: on Political Science and the Role of Law in the Process of European Integration. *European Law Journal*. 2: 105.

Kakouris, C. N.. 1994. La mission de la Cour de Justice des Communautés européennes et l'"ethos" du juge. *Revue des Affairs Européennes*. 4: 35.

Kumm, Mattias. 1999. Who is the Final Arbiter of Constitutionality in Europe? – Three Conceptions of the Relationship between the German Federal Constitutional Court and the European Court of Justice and the Fate of the European Market Order for Bananas. *Common Market Law Review*. 36: 351.

Lecourt, Robert. 1976. *L'Europe des Juges*. Bruxelles: Bruyllant.

Maduro, Miguel Poiares. 1997. *We the Court*. Oxford: Hart.

Maduro, Miguel Poiares. 2003. Contrapunctual Law: Europe's Constitutional Pluralism in Action. In *Sovereignty in Transition*, ed. Neil Walker. 501. Oxford: Hart.

Maduro, Miguel Poiares. 2006. *A Constituição plural*. Cascais: Principia.

Maher, Imelda. 1994. National Courts as European Community Courts. *Legal Studies*. 14: 226.

Mancini, G. F. and Keeling, David T. 1994. Democracy and the European Court of Justice. *Modern Law Review*. 57: 175.

Mare, Thomas de la. 1999. Article 177.º in Social and Political Context", The Evolution of EU Law. In Paul Craig and Gráinne de Búrca (coord.). 214. Oxford: Oxford University Press.

Miranda, Jorge. 2002–2003. A "Constituição Europeia" e a ordem juridical portuguesa. *O Direito*. 134–135: 9.

Pescatore, Pierre. 1983. The Doctrine of Direct Effect: an Infant Disease of Community Law. *Europe Law Review*. 3: 155.

Pollack, Mark. 1997. Delegation, Agency, and Agenda Setting in the European Community. *International Organization*. 51: 99.

Rasmussen, Hjalte. 1986. *On Law and Policy in the European Court of Justice. A Comparative Study in Judicial Policy-Making*, Dordrecht: Martinus Nijhoff Publishers.

Scheingold, Stuart. 1971. The Law in Political Integration. The Evolution and Integrative Implications of Regional Legal Processes in the European Union. *Occasional Papers in International Affairs*. 27: 1.

Shapiro, Martin. 1964. *Law and Politics in the Supreme Court*. New York: Free Press.

Shapiro, Martin. 1980. Comparative Law and Comparative Politics". *Southern California Law Review*. 53: 537.

Schilling, Theodor. 1996. The Autonomy of the Community Legal Order: An Analysis of Possible Foundations". *Harvard Internacional Law Journal*. 37: 389.

Stein, Eric. 1981. Lawyers, Judges, and the Making of a Transnational Constitution. *American Journal of International Law* 71: 1.

Stone Sweet, Alec. 1998. Constitutional Dialogues in the European Union. In Anne-Marie Slaughter, Alec Stone Sweet and Joseph Weiler, *The European Court of Justice and National Courts – Doctrine and Jurisprudence*. 305. Oxford: Hart.

Stone Sweet, Alec, and Brunnel, Thomas. 1998. Constructing a Supranational Constitution: Dispute Resolution and Governance in the European Community. *American Political Science Review*. 92: 63.

Stone Sweet, Alec, and Caporaso, James. 1998. La Cour Européenne et l'intégration. *Revue Française de Droit Politique*. 48: 195.

Stone Sweet, Alec and Sandholtz, Wayne. 1998. Integration, Supranational Governance, and the Institutionalization of the European Polity. In Alec Stone Sweet and Wayne Sandholtz, *European Integration and Supranational Governance*. 1. New York: Oxford University Press.

Timmermans, Christiaan. 2001–2002. The Constitutionalisation of the European Union. *Yearbook of European Law*. 21: 1.

Tridimas, Takis. 1996. The Court of Justice and Judicial Activism. *European Law Review*. 21: 199.

Volcansek, Mary. 1986. *Judicial Politics in Europe*. New York: Peter Lang.

Waele, Henri de, and Vleuten, Anna van der. 2011. Judicial Activism in the European Court of Justice – The case of LBGT rigths. *Michigan State Journal of International Law*. 19: 639.

Weiler, Joseph. 1982. Community, Member State and European Integration: Is the Law Relevant?. *Journal of Common Market Studies*. 21: 39.

Weiler, Joseph. 1991. The Transformation of Europe. *Yale Law Journal*. 108: 2403.

Weiler, Joseph. 1994. A Quiet Revolution: The European Court of Justice and its Interlocutors. *Comparative Political Studies*. 26: 510.

Chapter 14
Judicial Activism, Judicial Independence and Judicial Hubris: The Case of International Courts

Maimon Schwarzschild

14.1 Judicial Activism and Judicial Independence

What are the implications of judicial activism for the ideal of judicial independence, and contrariwise, what does the ideal of judicial independence imply about the proper scope and the proper limits of judicial activism?

Judicial activism is notoriously something of an epithet rather than a well-defined concept. In a fairly narrow sense, judicial activism is perhaps a way of characterising (or a dysphemism for) judicial review—especially judicial review in the American sense: judicial power to nullify enacted laws as unconstitutional. (Such judicial review can mean the constitutional nullification of executive acts or policies, and administrative policies or rules, as well as legislatively enacted statutes.) Judicial activism, one might say, is the aggressive use of this power, or what a critic considers an aggressive or over-aggressive use of it. Judicial review is most apt to be called judicial activism when judicial findings of unconstitutionality are based on uncertain or controvertible interpretations of the constitution, not when whatever is nullified is really unconstitutional "beyond a reasonable doubt". A cognate kind of judicial review, now more common in European countries although not in the United States, is judicial nullification based not on unconstitutionality but on inconsistency, or alleged inconsistency, with international treaties: in particular, although not exclusively, with "human rights" treaties.

In a broader sense, judicial activism implies the making or imposition of social policy by judicial decree, whether through constitutional judicial review, or through statutory interpretation ("creative" or otherwise), or through common law adjudication. The more transformative the judge-made social policy, and the more it

M. Schwarzschild (✉)
University of San Diego School of Law, 5998 Alcala Park,
San Diego, CA 92110, USA
e-mail: maimons@sandiego.edu

L.P. Coutinho et al. (eds.), *Judicial Activism*,
Ius Gentium: Comparative Perspectives on Law and Justice 44,
DOI 10.1007/978-3-319-18549-1_14

contradicts the letter and spirit of existing laws and perhaps the sentiments of democratic majorities, the more it appears as an exercise in judicial activism.

There may be times, and cases, where judicial activism is warranted, and even essential to the rule of law or to a decent public order. There may also be times, and cases, where it is unwarranted, and an abuse of judicial power.

Judicial activism has implications for the ideal of judicial independence, both because judicial independence is, in a sense, a pre-condition or prerequisite for judicial activism (including for judicial activism that is warranted or even essential), and because judicial activism can threaten judicial independence or transmute it into an indefensible kind of judicial irresponsibility.

Judicial independence is widely, and rightly, said to be a cornerstone of liberal government, of good government, and of the rule of law. For the courts of law to be a check and balance upon the other forces of government, judicial independence would seem to be essential: one cannot be a counterweight against powers of whom one is not independent. It might seem perverse, therefore, to suggest that judicial independence is not unequivocally a good thing. But good ideas, like the phrases or catchwords that describe them, are often bent or distorted in behalf dubious interests. Judicial independence in some senses of the phrase is surely good and even crucial to what Lon Fuller called the (internal) morality of law.[1] But judicial independence in another sense can imply judicial over-reaching and abuse of authority: an indefensible sort of independence. Predictably enough, that sort of independence is liable in the long run to undermine or to destroy judicial independence in the good sense.

It is not merely in theory that judicial independence is equivocal. There are growing tendencies in many developed countries towards a dubious sort of judicial independence. These tendencies are associated, at least in part, with judicial activism, and especially with excesses or abuses of judicial activism. Moreover, international legal institutions, and enthusiasm for international norms, may be especially susceptible to fostering the bad sort of judicial independence.

14.2 Judicial Independence and the Changing Ambitions of the Courts

Judicial independence in the good sense implies that judges should be free from improper interference by political authorities; that they should be free from improper pressure by powerful private forces as well, or from mob pressure; and at a bare minimum, that judges should not yield to corruption or bribery or to personal conflicts of interest. Perhaps a little more broadly, judicial independence implies that a judge should be intellectually independent: a judge should not be a slave, at least, to intellectual or social conformity.

[1]Fuller (1965).

Some aspects of judicial independence might coincide with the sort of independence generally expected from executive and legislative officials as well as from judges—or that might be expected from any honest human being. Bribery and corruption, for example, are not evil only when they involve judges.

Yet insofar as adjudication is distinct from politics, judges ought to be independent in some ways that are distinctive. Examples or symbols of such independence include lengthy and secure tenure in office (such as is enjoyed by federal judges in the United States who have life tenure),[2] and judges being given elaborate deference in the courtroom and often outside the courtroom.[3] When judges fulfil their proper role—interpreting and applying the law in accordance with the letter and the spirit of the law, faithful to text and precedent as the morality of law requires—then we might want judges to be independent of public or private pressures, to be above the fray, in ways that we don't necessarily want elected officials to be "independent" of the people who elect them.[4] Judges are expected to be impartial. Officials elected on a partisan basis cannot be non-partisan or in that sense impartial.

But this implies that there can be judicial independence in a bad sense:

- Independence from democratically enacted laws;
- Independence from democratic responsibility: from reasonable public expectations as to the values and the spirit that will inform adjudication, both judicial interpretation of the positive law and "interstitial" judicial lawmaking;
- Independence, in short, from an obligation to interpret and enforce the law rather than the judge's own will, or the will of unrepresentative interests or elites with whom the judge might identify;
- Independence, more briefly still, from the rule of law itself.

There is no clear or uncontroversial boundary, to be sure, between legitimately interpreting the law, which is a judge's proper function, and substituting the judge's own will for the law. In a constitutional system like the United States, the idea of judicial review—the power of the courts to strike down legislation held to violate the Constitution—is long established in principle.[5] The idea that judges should do

---

[2]U.S. Const. art. III, § 1 ("The Judges, both of the supreme and inferior Courts, shall hold their Offices during good Behaviour …").

[3]But cf., Posner (2005) ("Cocooned in their marble palace, attended by sycophantic staff, and treated with extreme deference wherever they go, Supreme Court Justices are at risk of acquiring exaggerated opinions of their ability and character").

[4]Edmund Burke's classic defence of a representative's independence was that "[y]our representative owes you, not his industry only, but his judgment; and he betrays, instead of serving you, if he sacrifices it to your opinion." But Burke does not suggest that a representative ought to be immune from lobbying by his constituents, whose "wishes ought to have great weight with him; their opinion, high respect". Burke (1992: 50).

[5]The power of judicial review is not explicit in the US Constitution, but it was proclaimed by the decision in *Marbury v. Madison*, 5 US (1 Cranch) 137 (1803), and has been traced to earlier currents in American legal thinking. See Hamburger (2008). But after *Marbury*, the US courts very rarely struck down Acts of Congress as unconstitutional during the nineteenth century; judicial review in that era was directed almost exclusively against the states. See Thayer (1893).

justice under natural law has still older roots. More than a century and a half before American independence, an English court suggested that "when an Act of Parliament is against common right and reason, or repugnant… the common law will control it, and adjudge such Act to be void".[6] The risk, of course, is that natural law, or the meaning of the Constitution, will be too much in the eye of the judicial beholder. Much of modern constitutional theory in the United States, and increasingly elsewhere in the world, is devoted to the question of judicial review, its proper scope, its proper limits, and its legitimacy. Yet it is widely agreed that however narrow or broad the boundaries of legitimate judicial authority, those boundaries can be exceeded: and that when they are, judges abuse their authority. Criticism of judicial decisions as reflecting the judges' will, not the law, can—and at various times often has—come from any point on the political spectrum. In the United States, during the first third of the twentieth century, such criticism generally came from the political left; since the mid-twentieth century, it has mostly come from the political right.[7]

There are a variety of reasons why judges might push the limits of their authority and presume to act as unelected legislators. There is always a human impulse to maximise one's own power. But there are also ideals—sometimes legitimate, sometimes perverse, likely in many cases a mixture of the two—that may underlie a judicial reach, or over-reach, for power.

One ideal, both in the United States and around the world, has undoubtedly been the role of the United States Supreme Court in the latter half of the twentieth century, which issued far-reaching decisions against racial discrimination in the mid-twentieth century, and then went on—inspired or misled by the model of those decisions—to hand down decisions on a wide array of public policy questions: police procedure, electoral constituencies, abortion, sexuality, the death penalty, and much more.[8]

There is virtual unanimity today—although there was controversy at the time—that the mid-century Supreme Court acted properly and admirably in striking down racially discriminatory laws as unconstitutional. Racial discrimination, unjust and evil, was pervasive in much of America and almost monolithic in the South. It

[6]Dr. Bonham's Case, (1610) 77 Eng. Rep. 646 (K.B.).

[7]See Bernstein (2006) for an account of the vehement Progressive opposition to the conservative pre-New Deal Supreme Court's laissez-faire jurisprudence. In recent decades, American academic commentary was overwhelmingly enthusiastic about ambitious judicial review, whereas criticism of US Supreme Court decisions as legally ill-grounded impositions of judicial preference tended to come from right-of-centre critics, few of whom hold academic posts. But see e.g. Epstein (1973). More recently still, with the appointment of more conservative Justices by Republican Presidents, the academic pendulum began to swing against judicial activism. See e.g. Sunstein (2001), Tushnet (1999), Kennedy (1998).

[8]The paradigmatic racial desegregation decision was *Brown v Board of Education* (1954) 347 US 483. Leading decisions on other matters in the years following *Brown* include *Miranda v Arizona*, 384 US 436 (1966) (police procedure); *Baker v Carr*, 369 US 186 (1962) (electoral constituencies); *Roe v Wade*, 410 US 113 (1973) (abortion); *Romer v Evans*, 517 US 620 (1996) (sexuality); *Furman v Georgia*, 408 US 238 (1972) (death penalty).

seemed practically impervious to extra-judicial challenge, despite America's having fought a Civil War to abolish slavery nearly a century earlier. And after all, the post-Civil War constitutional amendments, by their intent and in their language and spirit, were surely at odds with discriminatory government.

Inspired by decisions like Brown v Board of Education, and eager to maintain or increase the prestige and the influence that these decisions won for the courts, it is perhaps understandable that the American judiciary—cheered on by much of the legal profession and the legal academy—should have begun to adjudicate many other controversial questions of public policy. Yet these new questions did not necessarily present so clear a right and a wrong as "Jim Crow" segregation had done. It was less clear in these cases that representative democracy could not cope: that if the courts did not intervene, then nothing would change for the better. And the legal basis for the courts' rulings, in the language, intent, and spirit of the Constitution or of the laws, was often less persuasive than it had been in the decisions striking down racial discrimination.[9]

It is evident that in at least some areas of public policy, the American Supreme Court has become a kind of super-legislature in recent decades, pre-empting the representative branches. As such, the Court's rulings invite comparison with federal court decisions in the early decades of the twentieth century, now widely discredited, in which the judges would read or misread their preference for laissez faire into the Constitution.[10] But whereas the pre-New Deal laissez faire decisions aroused growing opposition among opinion leaders and in the American legal academy, and attracted no admiration or emulation in foreign countries, the more recent transformation of the Court into an oracle of (generally "progressive") policy has been warmly welcomed by influential sympathisers, especially in the legal academy. As such, the role of the court as super-legislature has become increasingly institutionalised.[11]

Partly as a result of the Supreme Court taking on the role of super-legislature, and partly further promoting this tendency, there is the noteworthy fact that the American federal courts do less ordinary judicial work than they used to do. The Supreme Court now hears only cases that it chooses to hear, through purely discretionary writs of certiorari—unlike in the past, when there were categories of cases on appeal that the Court was legally obliged to hear.[12] In fact, the Court hears and decides fewer cases altogether than it did in the past.[13] There is considerable evidence that the Justices choose their cases with a strategic eye toward advancing

[9]John Hart Ely, for example, an eminently mainstream scholar, wrote of *Roe v Wade* that "it is not constitutional law and gives almost no sense of an obligation to try to be." Ely (1973: 926).

[10]The paradigm laissez faire "substantive due process" decision *was Lochner v New York*, 198 US 45 (1905).

[11]See Carrington and Cramton (2009) documenting the evolution of American courts into superlegislatures and makers of controvertible public policy, and urging that the trend is incompatible with traditional claims for judicial independence.

[12]Carrington and Cramton (2009: 590, n. 17).

[13]See Starr (2006: 1369).

their ideological or policy goals, although the process itself by which the Court chooses its cases is notably non-transparent.[14] The implication is that deciding ordinary lawsuits, cases that are of primary interest only to the parties, is beneath the dignity of today's Justices in their role as lawgivers, if not as social prophets.

Lower courts in the United States, and not only in the United States, tend to follow, as much as they can, the model and spirit of the US Supreme Court. Hence, just as the Supreme Court hears and decides fewer cases, so federal circuit and district judges increasingly offload their ordinary adjudicative tasks to law clerks, magistrates, special masters, administrative law judges, arbitrators, mediators, and the like; not to speak of their encouragement of prosecutorial plea bargaining, which radically reduces their dockets of criminal trials.[15]

There are parallel tendencies in other developed countries. In England, for example, High Court judges hear fewer cases as ordinary litigation is increasingly channelled to lower courts or to bureaucratic agencies.[16] Appeals in England are increasingly limited, and there has been extensive promotion of "alternate dispute resolution", pre-empting adjudication altogether. A somewhat similar abdication of judicial obligation is discernible in the practice of the European Court of Justice, which issues its decisions *ex cathedra*: the European Court's procedure forbids individual opinions or dissents, so the ordinary judicial responsibility of an individual judge to state his or her reasoning is thwarted.[17]

14.3 The International Dimension

International norms, international legal institutions, and activist organisations promoting an international legal agenda have all gained strength and influence in recent decades. As such, international influence might in principle encourage judicial independence in the good sense around the world. This is especially urgent in countries where the rule of law has traditionally been weak or nonexistent. At a minimum, one might wish that international influence would discourage "telephone

[14]See Cordray and Cordray (2004).

[15]"Thus, at all levels, the Justices and judges "holding office" under the Constitution are increasingly preoccupied with making political decisions and are diminishingly concerned with the humdrum task of enforcing the preexisting applicable law to disputed facts or with assuring litigants that their interests have been seriously considered by members of an independent judiciary." Carrington and Cramton (2009: 629).

[16]See Kritzer (2004). In the early 1990s, before the "Woolf Reforms" took effect, there were some 350,000 civil cases launched each year in the High Court in England. This fell to some 20,000 such cases in the mid-2000s. See Dowell (2009).

[17]Some, but by no means all, domestic courts in civil law countries in Europe also dispense with individually signed judicial opinions and dissents. There, the implicit idea is that the court is straightforwardly applying the civil code, not exercising discretion. This fiction seems considerably less plausible for the European Court of Justice, which is adjudicating a body of law less well-codified than the developed civil codes of Europe's Napoleonic or quasi-Napoleonic legal systems.

justice", as it used to be called in Soviet Russia, and which evidently persists in Russia and undoubtedly in many other countries as well: that is, judges taking instructions (over the telephone or otherwise) from government or police authorities about how to decide politically sensitive cases.[18] One may hope—whether or not one can realistically expect—that international promotion of judicial independence does actually strengthen the rule of law in this way.

But there is at least the danger, if not the reality, of a growing international legal culture promoting a more dubious sort of judicial independence and judicial activism of an indefensible kind.

One troubling model is the growing power of judges in European Union countries to make public policy under the banner of European norms and treaties which are often vague and open-ended, and which therefore seem to invite judicial over-reaching. A euphemism for this is "teleological" adjudication, which can mean interpreting or pushing, not to say twisting, the law in a particular direction or towards a particular goal. Often, the goal in question is more power for the European Union and its institutions—"deeper union"—at the expense of the democratic institutions of the constituent nation states.[19] This is a goal, in many cases at least, that the public in European countries would not vote for: a goal that the electorates would reject, not merely in the heat of passion, but upon sober reflection. It may be especially troubling for the broader judicial culture that this power to use or abuse European norms is not restricted to a handful of specifically European tribunals, but is devolved—in the name of subsidiarity—to ordinary national judges as well. This tends to enlist the judges in the teleological project and vests them with new, broad, and nebulously accountable powers.[20]

The citation of foreign law by American courts, at least in some contexts, is open to similar criticism. If judicial interpretation of the Constitution or of domestic law is guided by the law of other countries, that tends to circumvent domestic democratic processes. Moreover, on many debatable questions, foreign law is liable to differ from country to country. This creates an obvious risk of arbitrary selectivity about which foreign law to cite, or rather, of tendentious selectivity: that the judge will "pick and choose" whichever bits of foreign law suit the result the judge favours, especially where the result might not be straightforwardly justified under duly enacted domestic law.[21]

---

[18]See Bowring (2009).

[19]"The central organ of the EU legal system is the European Court of Justice… Almost from the outset of the Common Market, the ECJ took an extremely activist approach to the Treaty of Rome, interpreting it as a proto-constitution." Rabkin (2005: 131).

[20]"National judges were systematically wooed by judges of the European Court at conferences and professional gatherings. And national judges learned to appreciate the extra power and status they would gain as enforcers of European law against their own governments." Rabkin (2005: 141).

[21]There is a running debate between Justices Breyer and Scalia about the citation of foreign law in American courts, in particular in cases involving constitutional interpretation. See Breyer (2003); *Lawrence v Texas*, 539 US 558, 598 (2003) (Scalia, J., dissenting); *Atkins v Virginia*, 536 US 304, 347–48 (2002) (Scalia, J., dissenting). See also Ramsey (2004).

More broadly, international legal institutions sometimes seem to promote, and even to embody, judicial independence in a dubious rather than in a desirable or defensible sense. Judges appointed to international tribunals from countries ruled by dictatorships, for example, are unlikely to enjoy much judicial independence in the positive sense. Coming from countries with little or no tradition of the rule of law, where the judge has family members who can be implicitly or explicitly threatened, where the judge himself or herself might hope to retire or to pursue a later career, where an independent-minded person is in any event unlikely to have reached a professional position from which appointment to an international tribunal would be plausible, the foundations for judicial independence are scarcely promising.

For international jurists, however, there is often a kind of judicial independence in the dubious sense of being unmoored from a developed legal system, and unaccountable to a democratic citizenry. The body of international law, to put it charitably, is less than fully evolved: it embraces uncertain "custom", treaties sometimes drafted broadly, highly arguable "general principles", and so forth. Members of international tribunals are often appointed in a none-too-transparent process of horse trading among governments, international organisations, and sometimes activist pressure groups.[22] There is no global hierarchy of international courts or a responsible body of supervising jurists. Few if any international jurists are known to the public, much less are they politically removable or otherwise answerable to democratic scrutiny.

There are surely examples of international adjudication which might be charged with unwarranted judicial activism: decisions that appear to be more political than legal. Thus, the International Court of Justice (the "World Court") issued an advisory opinion condemning Israel's security barrier and demanding that it should be dismantled, a judgment that has been criticised for bias both in its procedure and in outcome[23]; in another advisory opinion, the World Court came close to declaring nuclear deterrence illegal, although such deterrence is a basic and long-standing element in the defence strategy of the major powers[24]; in yet another controversial ruling, the World Court held that United States actions concerning Sandinista Nicaragua were illegal, prompting the United States to withdraw from the "compulsory jurisdiction" of the Court.[25] International law has also been invoked to

[22]"In practice, the nomination and election of judges to international courts and tribunals are politicized processes, subject to little transparency, and to widely varying… nomination mechanisms at the national level." Mackenzie and Sands (2003: 278).

[23]Legal Consequences of the Construction of a Wall in the Occupied Palestinian Territory, Advisory Opinion, 2004 I.C.J. 136 (July 9). For a detailed account and criticism of the decision, see Wedgwood (2005).

[24]Legality of the Threat of Use of Nuclear Weapons, Advisory Opinion, 1996 I.C.J. 226 (July 8).

[25]Case Concerning the Military and Paramilitary Activities in and Against Nicaragua (Nicar. V. U.S.), 1986 I.C.J. 14 (June 27). The United States took the position that the Court had no jurisdiction in the case and did not participate in the proceedings on the merits. For the United States withdrawal from the Court's "compulsory" jurisdiction, see Department Statement, Jan. 18, 1985, DEP'T ST. BULL., No. 2096, March 1985, at 64, reprinted in 24 ILM 246 (1985).

justify "universal jurisdiction" over a variety of international crimes, evoking criticism that this has great potential for selective enforcement and for politicised show trials. A common thread in all these controversies, and in others, is the suggestion that there are growing tendencies towards bias and politicised adjudication under international law, and that there are too few safeguards against these tendencies.

14.4 Conclusion: Judicial Hubris Versus Judicial Independence

When adjudication intrudes, perhaps even when it appears to intrude, excessively on the prerogatives of representative democracy, legitimate judicial independence is liable to suffer. Judicial independence sits uneasily with the idea of judges as "teleological" lawgivers or arbiters. After all, the democratic impulse is anti-deferential: it rightly holds lawmakers accountable, sometimes none too respectfully, to the will of the people. Judges are entitled to a unique kind of independence and to special immunities that others do not enjoy, only so long as they act as judges: that is, only so long as they interpret and apply the law in a way that conforms, within somewhat ill-defined limits, to the morality of law.

When judges follow a model of judging which too often exceeds those limits, the claim for judicial independence and deference is less and less plausible. This can be seen, in practical terms, in the greatly increased bitterness and polarisation, and corresponding decrease in deference, in the judicial appointments and confirmation process in the United States in recent decades.[26] There are implications for a wide variety of issues that touch on the judiciary. For example, the proposal that judges in England should be exempt from compulsory retirement at a given age is less plausible if the judges are active in taking public policy decisions and are increasingly seen as political or ideological partisans.[27] Such a proposal would have to reckon with the example of American Supreme Court Justices, who enjoy life tenure, and who are widely seen as timing or manipulating their retirements for political reasons to ensure that their successors will be nominated by an ideologically sympathetic President.

If judges around the world are encouraged—by academic opinion, by the Zeitgeist among political elites, by international lawyers and pressure groups—to overstep their authority, and especially if an "activist" judiciary is seen to be a partisan force in the great political and cultural disputes of the era, then democratic public opinion is liable, sooner or later, to ensure that there will be less judicial independence, not more. That, sadly, will be as it ought to be.

---

[26] Wittes (2006).

[27] Cf., Blom-Cooper (2012: 339–348).

References

Bernstein, David. 2006. Lochner v. New York: A Centennial Retrospective. *Washington University Law Quarterly* 85: 1469.

Blom-Cooper, Sir Louis. 2012. The Age of Judicial Responsibility: The Retirement and Resignation of Appellate Court Judges. In *The Culture of Judicial Independence*, eds. Shetreet, Shimon and Fosythe, Christopher. Leiden: Martinus Nijhoff Publishers.

Bowring, Bill. 2009. Legal Nihilism in Russia. Open Democracy Russia. https://www.opendemocracy.net/article/email/legal-nihilism-in-russia. Accessed 3 September 2010.

Burke, Edmund. 1992. Speech to the Electors of Bristol. In *The Democracy Reader*, eds. Diane Ravitch and Abigail Thernstrom. New York: Harper Collins.

Carrington, Paul and Cramton, Roger. 2009. Judicial Independence in Excess: Reviving the Judicial Duty of the Supreme Court. *Cornell Law Review* 94: 587.

Cordray, Margaret and Cordray, Richard. 2004. The Philosophy of Certiorari: Jurisprudential Considerations in Supreme Court Case Selection. *Washington University Law Quarterly* 82: 389.

Dowell, Katy. 2009. Woolf reforms: lawyers continue to wrangle over merits a decade on. The Lawyer. http://www.thelawyer.com/analysis/opinion/practice-areas/city-analysis/woolf-reforms-lawyers-continue-to-wrangle-over-merits-a-decade-on/1000991.article. Accessed 25 October 2014.

Ely, John Hart. 1973. The Wages of Crying Wolf: A Comment on Roe v Wade. *Yale Law Journal* 82: 920.

Epstein, Richard. 1973. Substantive Due Process By Any Other Name: The Abortion Cases. *Supreme Court Review* 1973: 159.

Fuller, Lon. 1965. *The Morality of Law*. Rev'd Ed. New Haven: Yale University Press.

Hamburger, Philip. 2008. *Law and Judicial Duty*. Cambridge: Harvard University Press.

Kennedy, Duncan. 1998. *A Critique of Adjudication: Fin de Siecle*. Cambridge: Harvard University Press.

Kritzer, Herbert. 2004. Disappearing Trials? A Comparative Perspective. *Journal of Empirical Legal Studies* 1: 735.

Mackenzie, Ruth and Sands, Philippe. 2003. International Courts and Tribunals and the Independence of the International Judge. *Harvard International Law Journal* 44: 271.

Posner, Richard. 2005. The Supreme Court 2004 Term–Foreword: A Political Court. *Harvard Law Review* 119: 31.

Rabkin, Jeremy. 2005. *Law Without Nations?* Princeton: Princeton University Press.

Ramsey, Michael. 2004. International Materials and Domestic Rights: Reflections on Atkins and Lawrence. *American Journal of International Law* 98: 69.

Starr, Kenneth. 2006. The Supreme Court and Its Shrinking Docket: The Ghost of William Howard Taft. *Minnesota Law Review* 90: 1363.

Sunstein, Cass. 2001. *One Case at a Time: Judicial Minimalism on the Supreme Court*. Cambridge: Harvard University Press.

Thayer, James. 1893. The Origin and Scope of the American Doctrine of Constitutional Law. *Harvard Law Review* 7: 129.

Tushnet, Mark. 1999. *Taking the Constitution Away from the Courts*. Princeton: Princeton University Press.

Wedgwood, Ruth. 2005. The ICJ Advisory Opinion on the Israeli Security Fence and the Limits of Self-Defense. *American Journal of International Law* 99: 52.

Wittes, Benjamin. 2006. *Confirmation Wars: Preserving Independent Courts in Angry Times*. Stanford: Hoover Institution.

CPSIA information can be obtained at www.ICGtesting.com
Printed in the USA
BVOW04*0205110615

404211BV00003B/7/P

9 783319 185484